IMAGES
of America

LIVINGSTON COUNTY

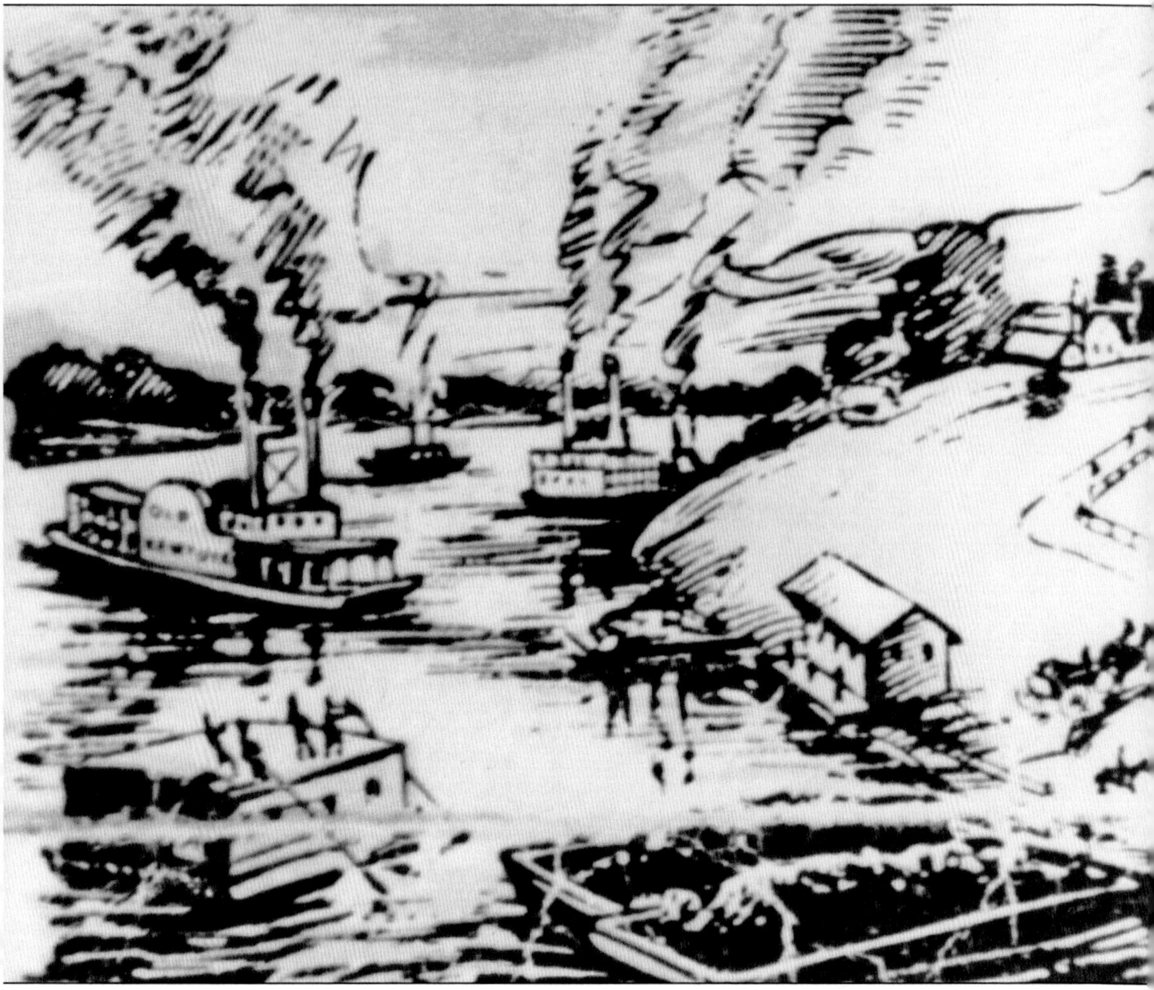

This is a sketch of the Smithland riverfront in the early 1850s. Smithland was considered the best port on the Ohio River between Louisville and Memphis. All steamboats and packets called at her wharf. Smithland had elaborate inns, hotels, and taverns, including the Waverly House with a marble floor and the Clark House with a popular ballroom for dancing. Smithland boasted a population of nearly 3,000 during the Civil War. (Courtesy of Livingston County Historical Society.)

On the Cover: Taken in 1901 of the courthouse in Smithland, this image shows the scene of a big political rally. Notice these candidates for office are all men, as women were not allowed to vote until 1920. The Livingston County Courthouse was completed in 1845 at a cost of $6,800. It houses many official record books and papers dating from 1799. (Courtesy of Livingston County Historical Society.)

IMAGES
of America

LIVINGSTON COUNTY

Faye Tramble Teitloff

ARCADIA
PUBLISHING

ISBN 978-0-7385-6702-0

Published by Arcadia Publishing
Charleston SC, Chicago IL, Portsmouth NH, San Francisco CA

Printed in the United States of America

Library of Congress Catalog Card Number: 2008930682

For all general information contact Arcadia Publishing at:
Telephone 843-853-2070
Fax 843-853-0044
E-mail sales@arcadiapublishing.com
For customer service and orders:
Toll-Free 1-888-313-2665

Visit us on the Internet at www.arcadiapublishing.com

I dedicate my first book to my parents,
James Normie and Fannie Tramble.
They were both born and raised in Livingston County
and taught me to be strong and independent.

Contents

ACKNOWLEDGMENTS

This book would not have been possible without the assistance of Hazel Robertson. She invited me to her home, entrusted me to use her photographs for as long as I needed, and told me stories to go with them. I hope I have used her materials to preserve the history of Livingston County as she would want it done. Unless otherwise noted, all images appearing in this book were graciously provided by Hazel Robertson.

I want to thank Todd Hansen, editor at the *Livingston Ledger*, who has published my history article "Pathways to the Past" for the last few years. This and my inspiration from God have paved the way for my research and love of history, and ultimately led to this book.

I also wish to thank the Livingston County Historical Society for allowing me free access to their photographs, especially secretary Mary Lou Smith. I am proud to be a member of this group of volunteers who have collected and maintained a vast collection of history for our region.

Thanks to my editor, Luke Cunningham, for his guidance when I needed it and to Arcadia Publishing for allowing me to share the history of our county with the whole world.

I need to thank my husband, Charles, and sons Kevin and Kendall for forgiving me for the many hours I hid out in the computer room. A special thanks to my son "Dr. Tim" for proofreading my book and encouraging my progress all the way from South Carolina. Also, I appreciate my grandchildren, Jonathan, Eric, and Laura, and daughter-in-law Jana for sharing my love of history and reading my collection. Lastly, I wish to thank my aunt Callie Jones for being the storyteller of the family.

INTRODUCTION

On December 13, 1798, the Kentucky General Assembly enacted legislation authorizing the formation of Livingston County. The county seat was first at Eddyville and was later moved to Centerville in 1804. When Caldwell County was formed from Livingston County in 1809, the county seat was moved to Salem. It remained there until 1842, when Crittenden County was formed from Livingston. Since Salem was so near the county line, the county seat was moved to Smithland to be more centrally located. The new courthouse was completed in 1845 at a cost of $6,800. In the years it took to complete the courthouse, the citizens held court in houses, under trees, and in other various places. One of the last legal hangings in Kentucky was here in 1935, with several thousand people coming to witness it. The sheriff swore in more than 100 deputies to assist state police in keeping order.

Before Kentucky became a state in 1792, all of the state was a part of Virginia. The state of Virginia had little money to pay the veterans who had served in the Revolutionary War but had plenty of land in the Kentucky wilderness. In Livingston County, records show that William Brown received 1,200 acres at the fork of the Ohio and Cumberland Rivers on December 18, 1784. A Revolutionary grant was also given to Peter Larue and a Mr. Croghan. The son of Croghan gave the land for the town of Smithland.

Livingston County has an amazing number of waterways. There are three rivers with three dams located on them: Kentucky Dam on the Tennessee River, Barkley Dam on the Cumberland River, and Smithland Dam on the Ohio River. The waterways provide recreation and tourism, and many citizens are employed on the boats that travel them. There are disadvantages also, especially floods. There have been many through the years, with 1937 being the worst.

River ferries were a necessity. There were many operating until bridges were built in the 1930s. The rivers provided transportation to haul livestock to the market and to passengers to buy necessities that could not be bought locally. Packet boats were built in Smithland in the 1800s. Steamboats, sometimes called floating palaces, brought an air of prosperity to Livingston County. Some had a band and dancing, many with a calliope playing upon arrival at the dock.

The boats brought to Livingston County during the Civil War were not the kind people were accustomed to seeing. Smithland was an especially strategic place to build two forts, because it overlooked the Ohio and Cumberland Rivers. This allowed troops to keep control of the rivers and roadways.

Towns have come and gone in Livingston County. The ones that are still around are Bayou, Birdsville, Burna, Carrsville, Grand Rivers, Hampton, Iuka, Joy, Lake City, Ledbetter, Pinckneyville, Salem, Smithland, and Tiline. Each town has its own story, and there are many worth telling. After the Civil War, Hampton was named for Gen. Wade Hampton, a noted officer of the Confederate army who was stationed in the small settlement. Burna and Lola were both named when the Post Office Department asked the people to submit names. Burna was submitted for Burna Phillips, daughter of Grant and Fannie Nelson Phillips. Lola was submitted for Lola Mitchell, daughter of the postmaster, Matthew Mitchell. Iuka is an Indian name meaning "welcome." Joy was first called

Crossroads because the roads forked toward Carrsville, Salem, Hampton, and the Golconda ferry landing. In 1898, the community was named Joy by the postmaster, Lawrence Bishop.

Livingston County schools have changed through the years, considering there were more than 50 in the early 1900s but only 11 in the 1950s. As transportation improved, the one-room schools disappeared. By 2008, there were only two elementary schools, one middle school, and one high school in the county.

The Trail of Tears began in October 1838 when the Cherokees gathered to begin a 1,200-mile trek from Charleston, Tennessee, to Tanlequam, Oklahoma. When they traveled through Kentucky, they crossed into Livingston County via Salem and took the Berry's Ferry Road to the Ohio River. A Mr. Berry had contracted the government to ferry the Cherokees across the river, but it was filled with ice and was too dangerous to cross. Hundreds died at Mantle Rock, near Joy, while waiting to cross. Mantle Rock has a natural bridge 40 feet high and about 180 feet long. Over the years, Cherokees have visited many times because it is customary for Native Americans to show reverence to their ancestors' graves. There is a Kentucky historical marker there. Mandy Falls is a beautiful waterfall nearby where the Native Americans got fresh water.

There are several heritage homes still standing in Smithland. The most famous is the Gower House, once known as Bell Tavern. It was one of the greatest luxury inns on the Ohio River between Louisville and New Orleans. The Gower House has played host to many famous people, including U.S. presidents James K. Polk, Zachary Taylor, and Andrew Jackson. Other noted visitors were Henry Clay, Charles Dickens, Clara Barton, Aaron Burr, James Audubon, and the Marquis de Lafayette. E. Z. C. Judson, who wrote under the pen name of Ned Buntline, lived at the Gower House in the 1840s. Buntline became famous for his stories of Buffalo Bill and famous lawmen such as Bat Masterson and Wyatt Earp. He wrote more than 400 novels, serials, and plays.

There are many minerals found in Livingston County, but all the fluorspar mines are now closed. The county does have four limestone quarries that employ many people and contribute to many organizations within the county.

Henry Hathaway, director of the movie *How the West Was Won*, decided Smithland was the ideal place to film the first part of the movie, so in 1961, Smithland became Albany, New York, as it was in the 1830s. Many local people were used as extras, and 26 were used as the stars' stand-ins. Among the cast of stars were James Stewart, Debbie Reynolds, Carl Malden, Agnes Morehead, Carol Baker, Lee J. Cobb, John Wayne, Andy Devine, Walter Brennan, and Henry Fonda. This movie is still shown often, and we must keep our history alive by telling the younger generations about the summer Hollywood visited Livingston County.

Whether you stand on a hill in Carrsville and view the Ohio River, watch a sunset on Kentucky Lake, walk in the serenity of the woods near Joy, dine at the famous Patti's 1880s Restaurant in Grand Rivers, hunt fossils or fish at Birdsville, walk on the garden tours at Salem, or go on the walking tours of heritage homes in Smithland, you will know that you are in Livingston County, and you will see the unique history it holds. It is my desire for the images and stories in this book to present you with a glimpse of the history of our county and to preserve it for future generations.

One

WATERWAYS

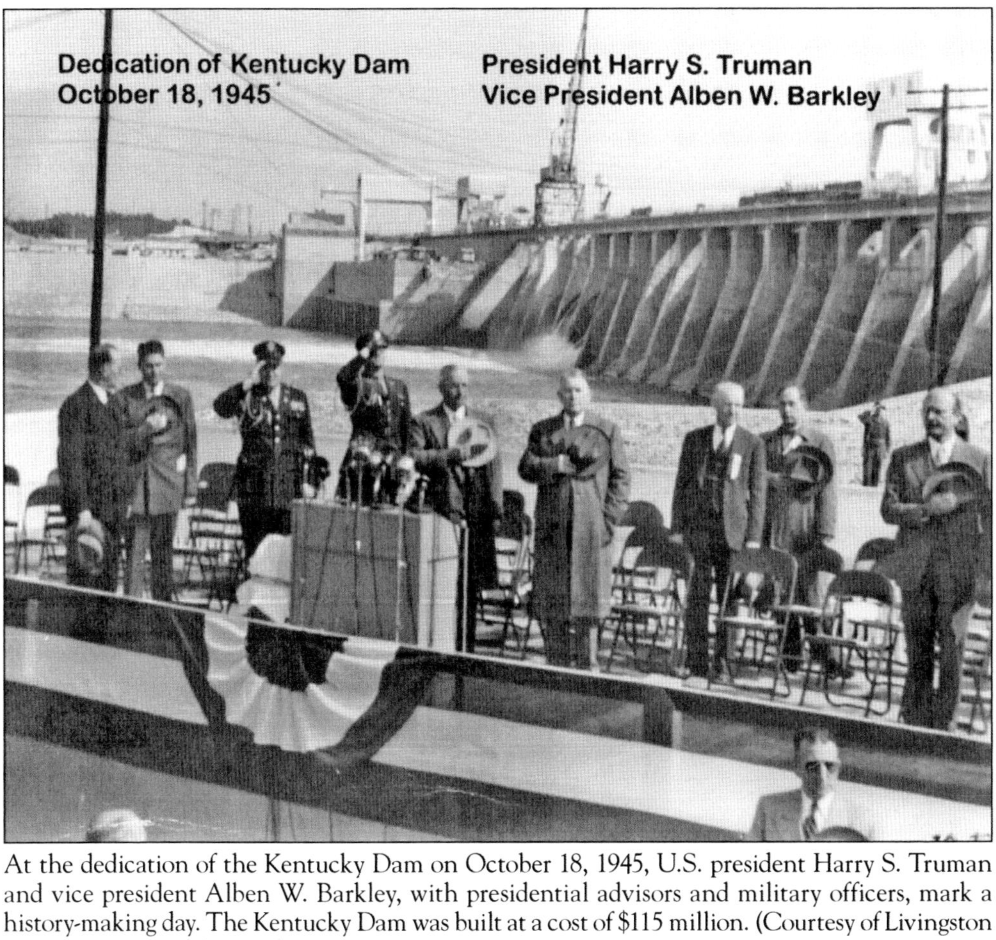

At the dedication of the Kentucky Dam on October 18, 1945, U.S. president Harry S. Truman and vice president Alben W. Barkley, with presidential advisors and military officers, mark a history-making day. The Kentucky Dam was built at a cost of $115 million. (Courtesy of Livingston County Historical Society.)

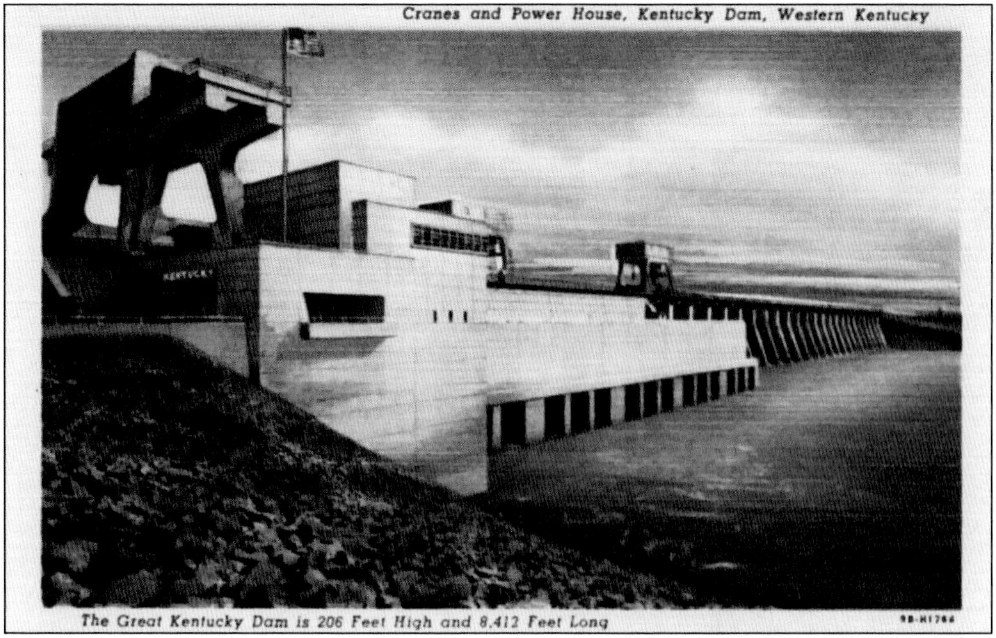

The Tennessee Valley Authority's Great Kentucky Dam, across the Tennessee River in Western Kentucky, attracts many tourists to Livingston County and the surrounding counties. The dam created the Kentucky Lake, which is the largest man-made lake in the eastern United States.

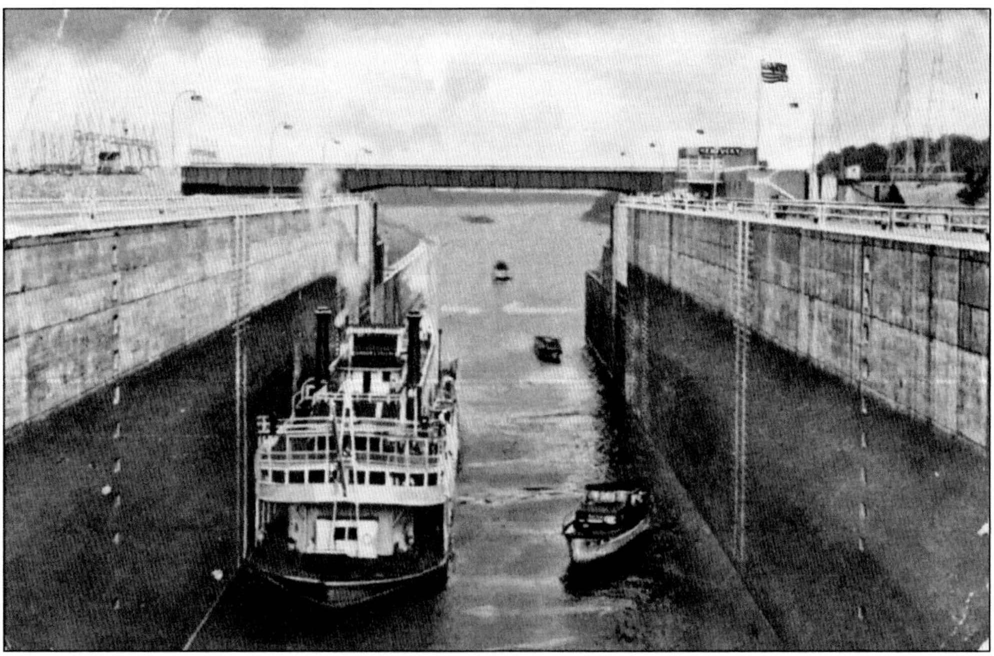

This postcard shows a river packet in the lock at the Kentucky Dam. Packet boats were built at a boatyard in Smithland from 1818 through 1855. In 1834, the Smithland Dock Company was formed.

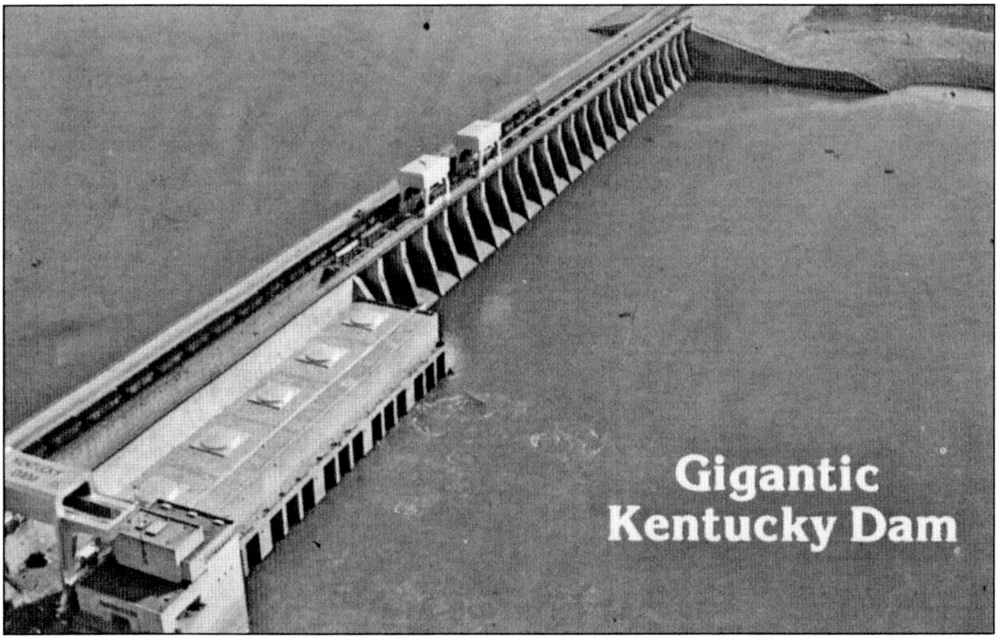

The gigantic Kentucky Dam is used by the Tennessee Valley Authority (TVA) to help control floodwaters and is a major generating plant in the TVA power system. The placement of the Kentucky Dam on the Tennessee River and the Barkley Dam on the Cumberland River directly led to the creation of Land Between the Lakes. A navigation canal located at Grand Rivers links the two lakes.

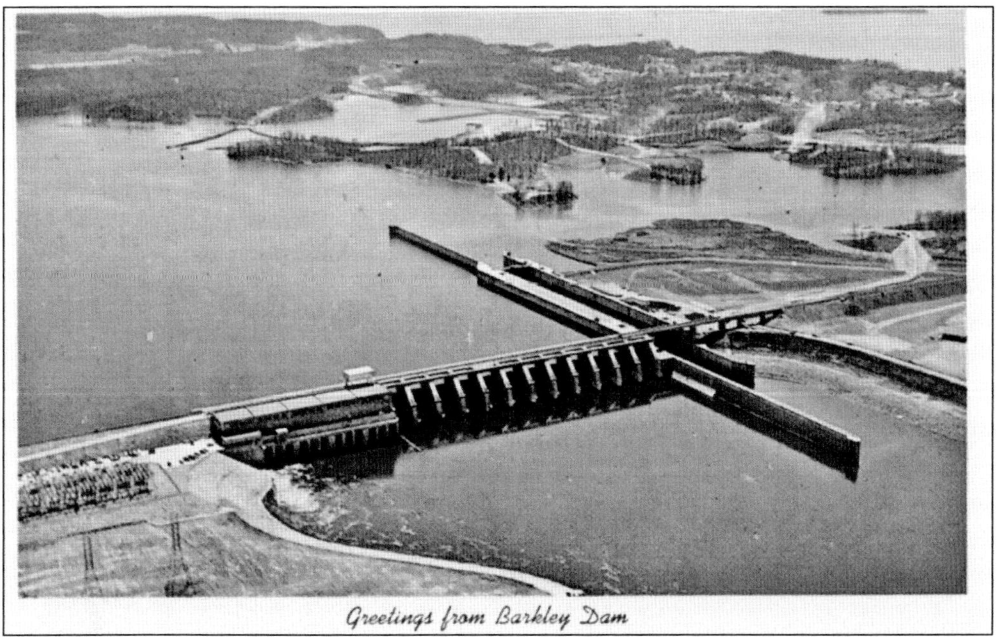

This aerial view of the Barkley Dam on the Cumberland River shows the completed project in the 1960s. It was named in honor of the late Alben W. Barkley, vice president and longtime senator from McCracken County. The impounding of Lake Barkley forced thousands of residents of river communities to relocate.

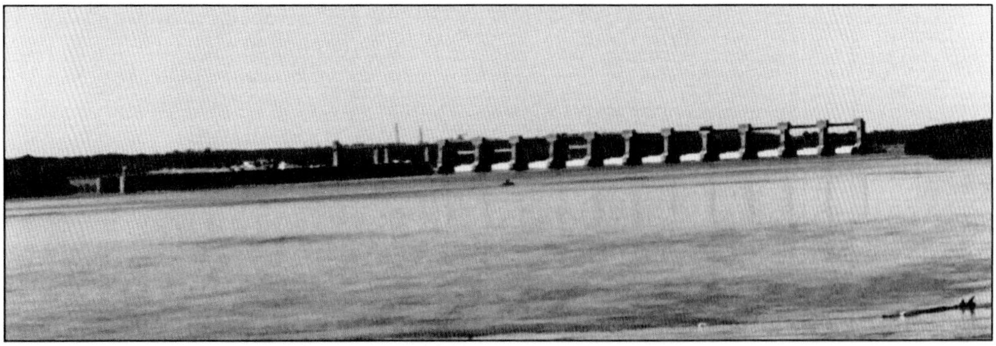

The Smithland Lock and Dam were completed in the late 1970s. It is situated on the Ohio River and can be seen from the Smithland Historic Riverfront, where the Ohio River meets the Cumberland River. Livingston County enjoys the history of having three rivers and three dams located in its boundaries.

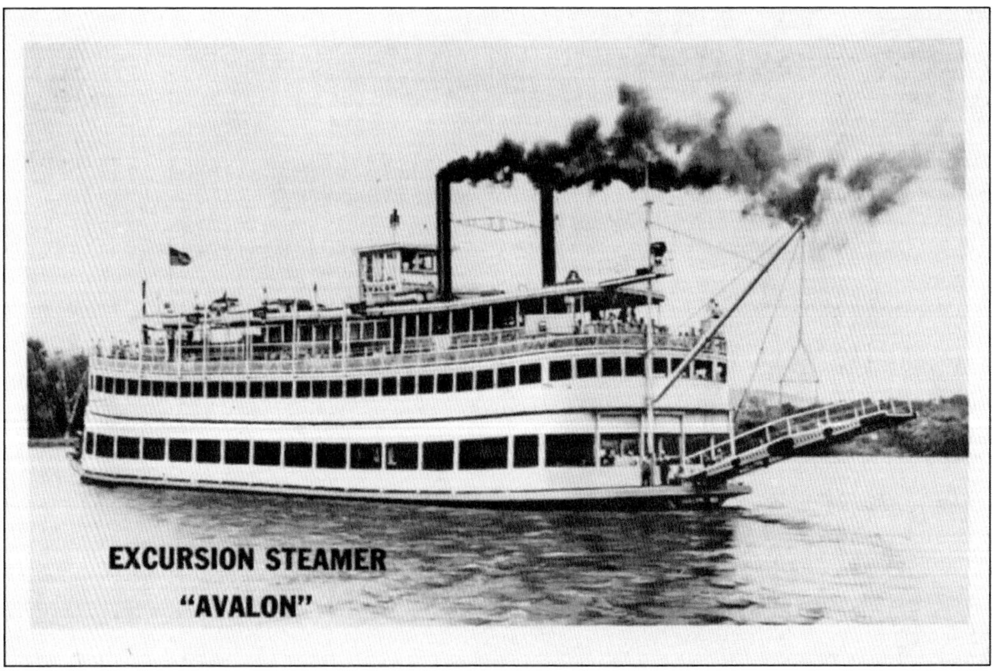

This postcard is of the excursion steamer *Avalon*, which operated on the Ohio and Mississippi Rivers and their tributaries. The *Avalon* was sold in 1962 and became the *Belle of Louisville*. In 1963, it raced for the first time with the *Delta Queen*. They were featured each spring as part of the Kentucky Derby festivities.

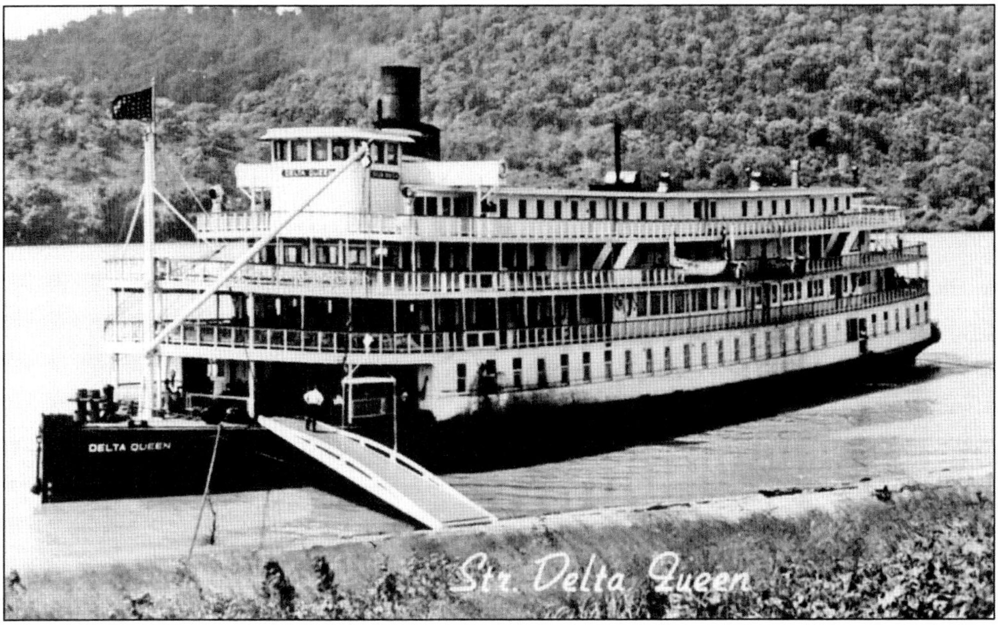

In 1941, the *Delta Queen* was converted into a military transport carrying soldiers through San Francisco Harbor to troop ships bound for war in the Pacific. The *Delta Queen* was later remodeled and then embarked on many years of vacation voyages. It was designated a National Historic Landmark in 1989. The *Delta Queen* has stopped at the riverfront in Smithland many times and has been made available for historic tours.

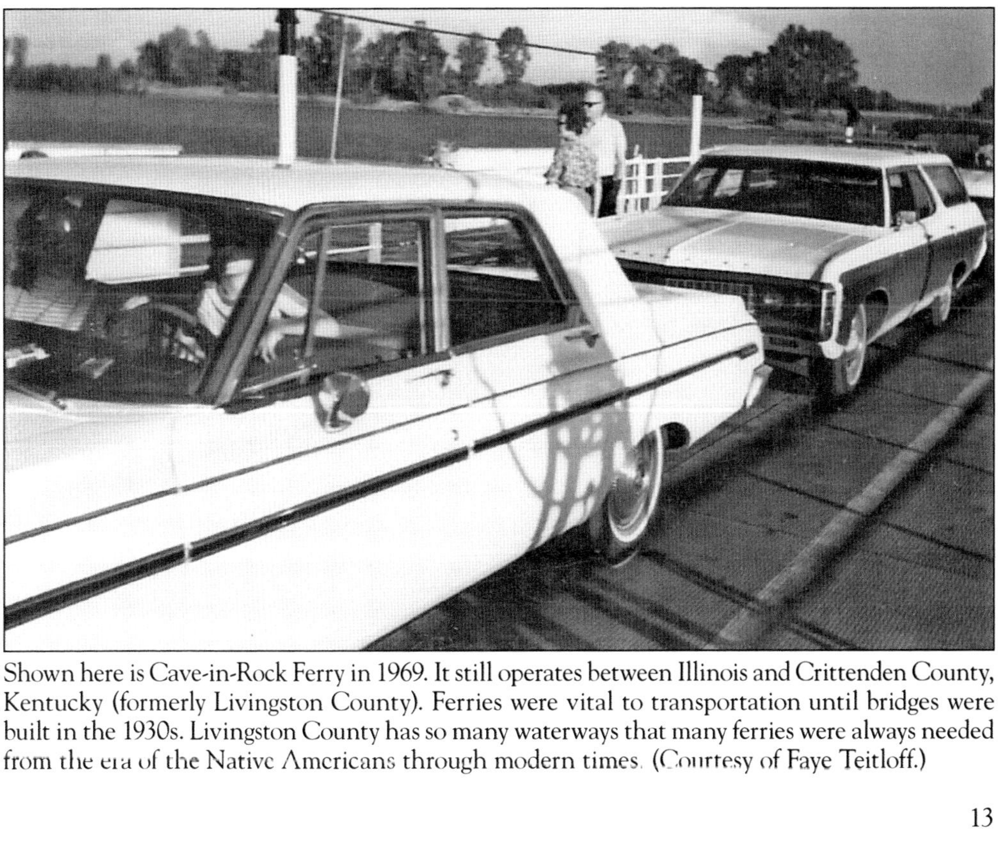

Shown here is Cave-in-Rock Ferry in 1969. It still operates between Illinois and Crittenden County, Kentucky (formerly Livingston County). Ferries were vital to transportation until bridges were built in the 1930s. Livingston County has so many waterways that many ferries were always needed from the era of the Native Americans through modern times. (Courtesy of Faye Teitloff.)

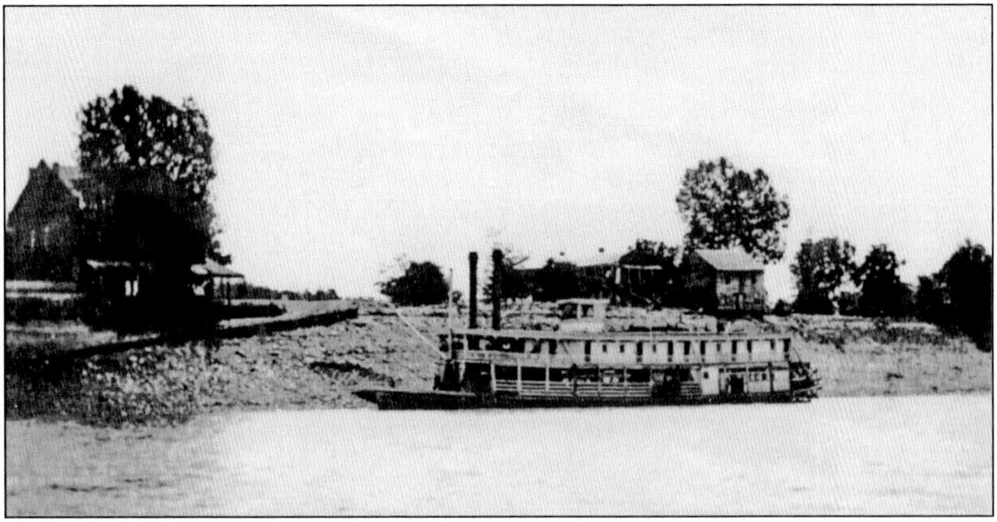

A steamboat cruises by Smithland in the mid-1870s. Since there were no docks, a plank off the long bow gave passengers access to the steamboat. Some of the larger steamboats were called floating palaces and brought a welcome air of luxury for passengers. The showboats caused much excitement when a calliope was heard playing upon their arrival in the river towns. (Courtesy of Livingston County Historical Society.)

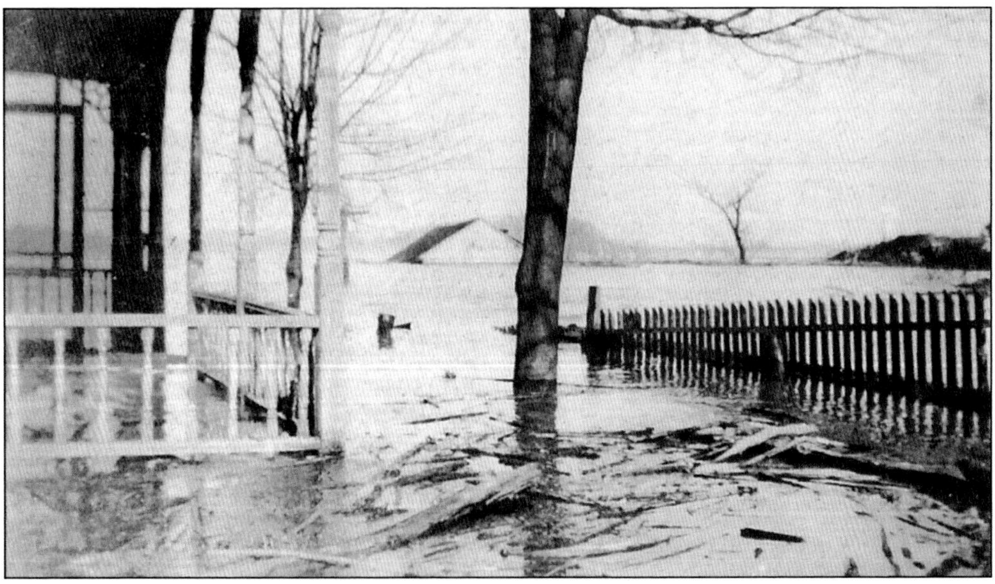

In 1937, the worst flood in the region's history was recorded. This photograph in Carrsville shows the Witherspoon Hotel on Main Street. There was also a terrible flood in 1884, with houses and businesses on Front Street in Smithland taken away by the raging floodwaters. In 1937, sidewalks and porches started disappearing over the riverbank. (Courtesy of Livingston County Historical Society.)

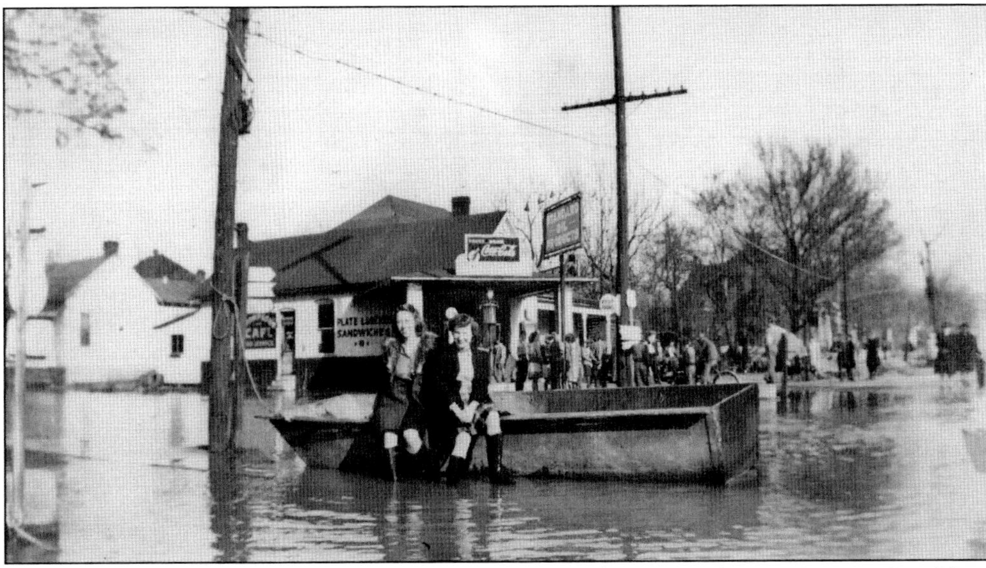

This is the old Standard service station on the corner of Highway 60 and Court Street in Smithland during the 1945 flood. Vera Martin (left) and Virginia Hale are in the boat tied to the utility post. In the background, many people are seen gathered to discuss the happenings. This was a common scene for a river town during flooding.

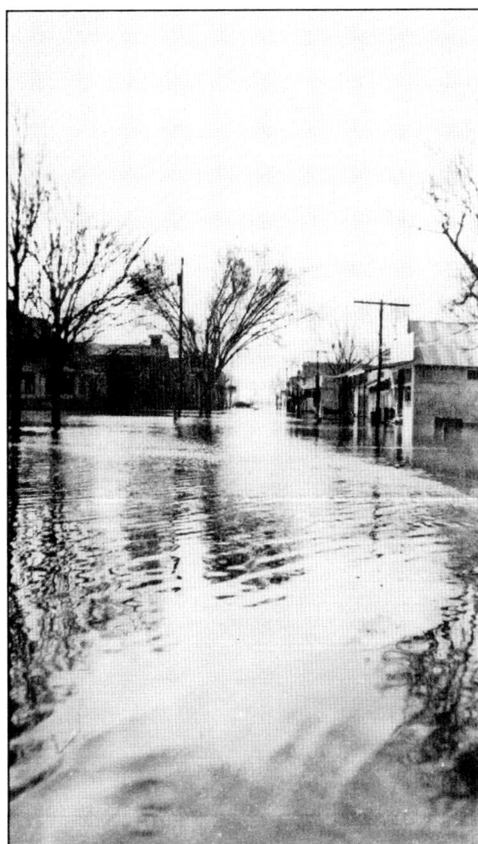

This is the 1950 flood as seen in Smithland while looking down Court Street toward the river. The people living in the hills were kind to all the refugees who were disturbed by the floodwaters. The Red Cross always came to help make arrangements for food and other necessities.

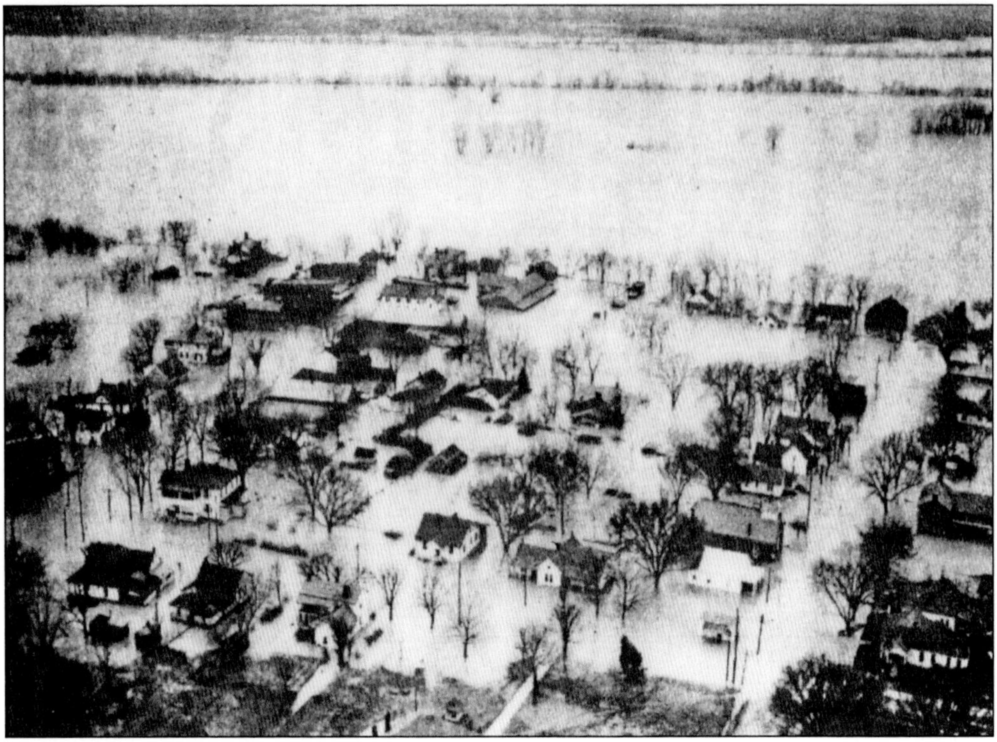

Obviously taken by a government helicopter or by someone with more means than an average citizen of that time, this aerial view of flooding in 1950 shows Smithland. Although there are still many floods, the dams have lessened the dangers and loss of property. (Courtesy of Ruth Powell.)

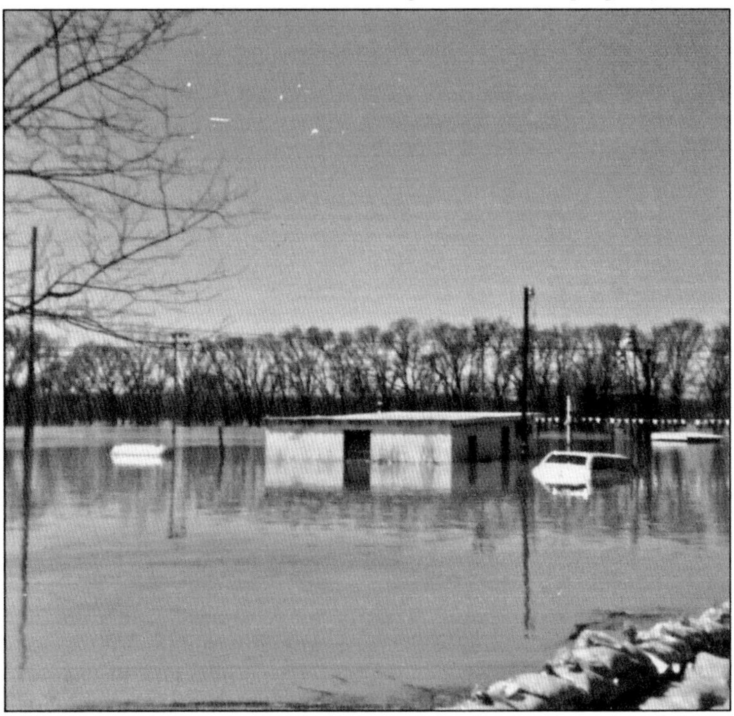

This photograph shows the 1975 flood in Smithland in the area of Gathiel Teitloff's Used Cars. Teitloff's office was the gathering place for checker players to show their skills. Of course, more than a few tall tales were told and problems of the community were solved under this roof. A flood wall was built in 2007 to help protect this area of town.

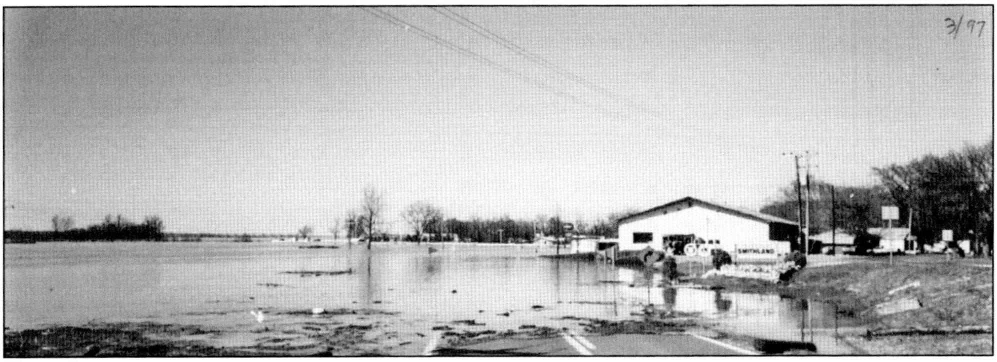

The most recent flood, in 1997, was the highest since 1937, measuring 60 feet on the gauge. Smithland was protected with more than 200,000 sandbags, which required efforts of many volunteers from everywhere. This photograph is on the west end of Smithland.

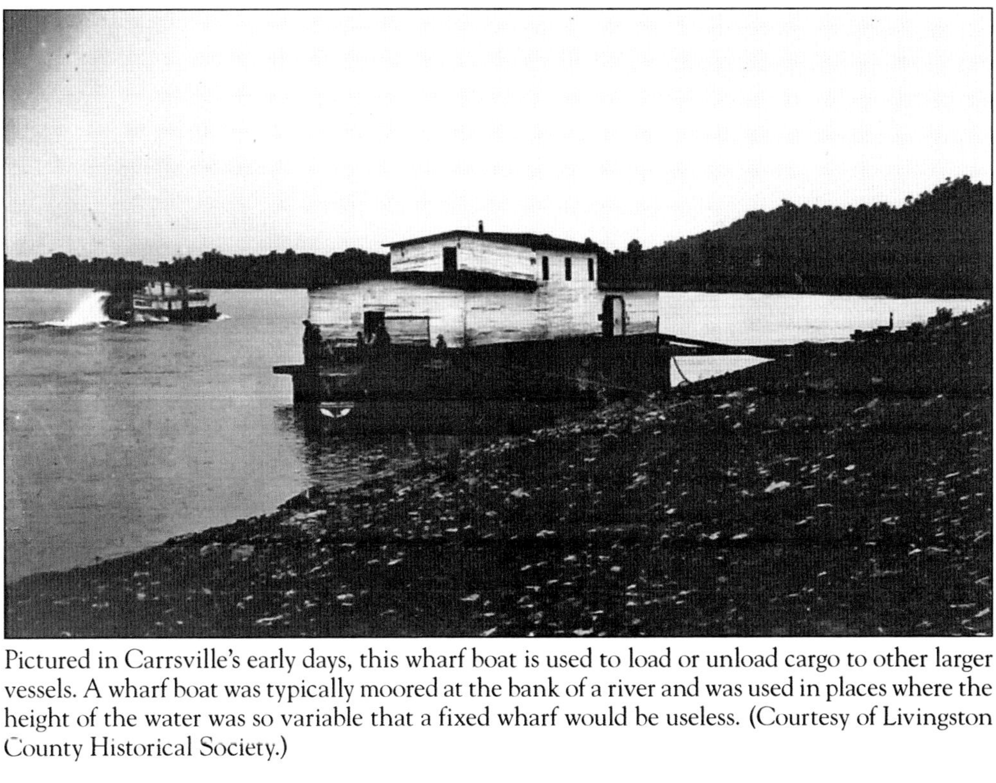

Pictured in Carrsville's early days, this wharf boat is used to load or unload cargo to other larger vessels. A wharf boat was typically moored at the bank of a river and was used in places where the height of the water was so variable that a fixed wharf would be useless. (Courtesy of Livingston County Historical Society.)

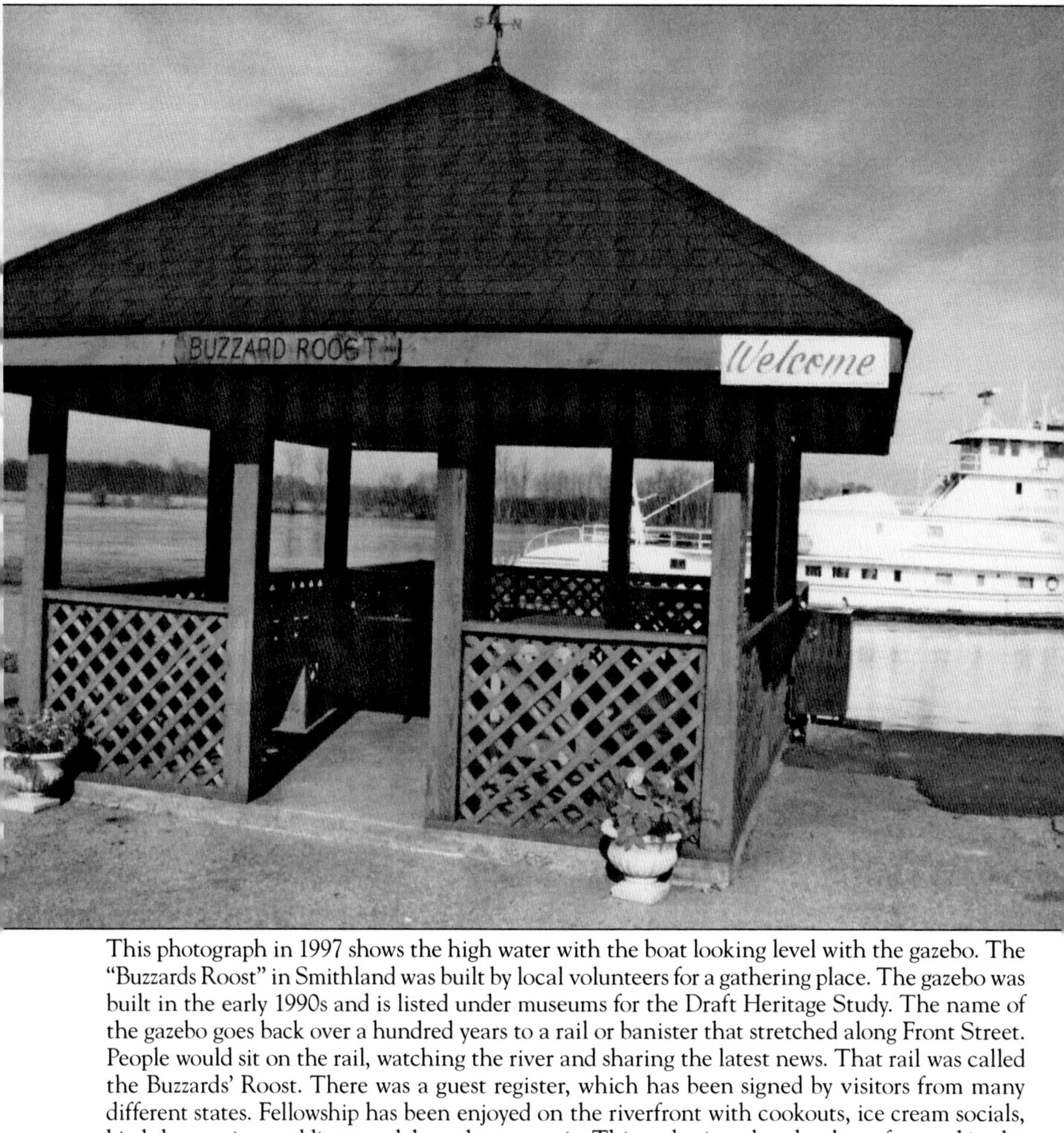

This photograph in 1997 shows the high water with the boat looking level with the gazebo. The "Buzzards Roost" in Smithland was built by local volunteers for a gathering place. The gazebo was built in the early 1990s and is listed under museums for the Draft Heritage Study. The name of the gazebo goes back over a hundred years to a rail or banister that stretched along Front Street. People would sit on the rail, watching the river and sharing the latest news. That rail was called the Buzzards' Roost. There was a guest register, which has been signed by visitors from many different states. Fellowship has been enjoyed on the riverfront with cookouts, ice cream socials, birthday parties, weddings, and down-home music. This gathering place has been featured in the *Baltimore Sun* as a site of local color. (Courtesy of Ruth Powell.)

Two

COUNTY SEAT
SMITHLAND

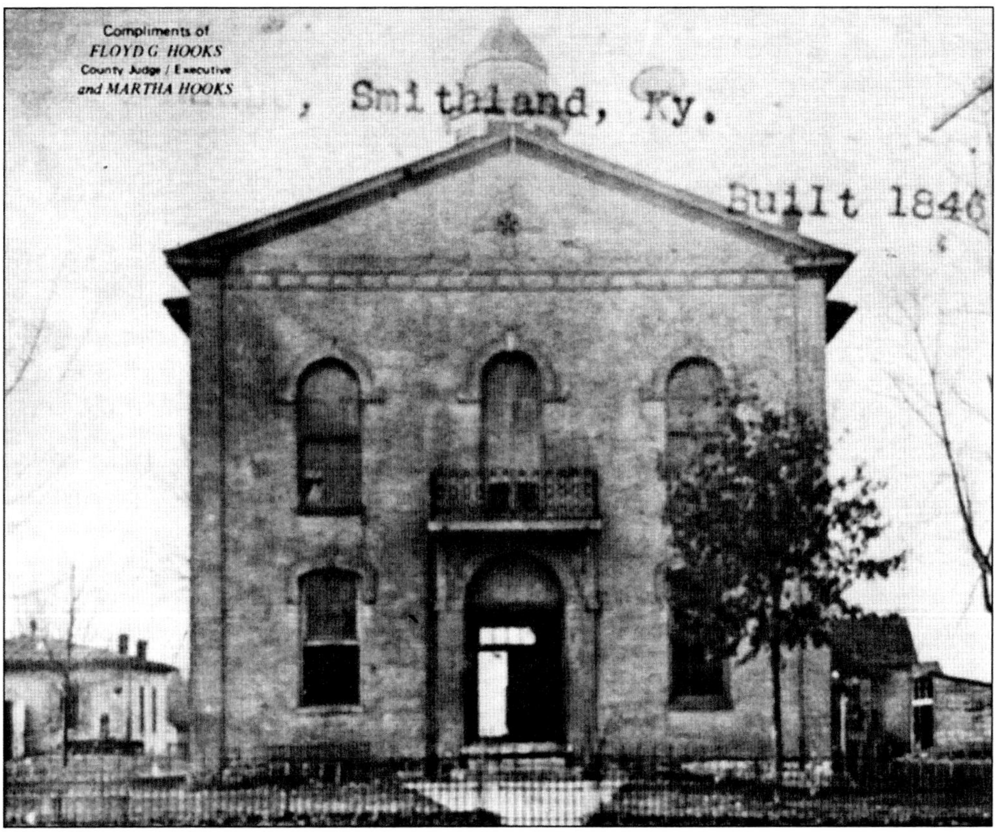

This picture was taken off a penny postcard, mailed in 1910, of the Livingston County Courthouse at Smithland. The county contracted Preston Grace of Princeton, Kentucky, for construction of the courthouse for $6,800. It was completed in 1845 and has stood protectively over its people through heartbreaking trials and difficult decisions. In 1935, it witnessed one of the last legal hangings in Kentucky.

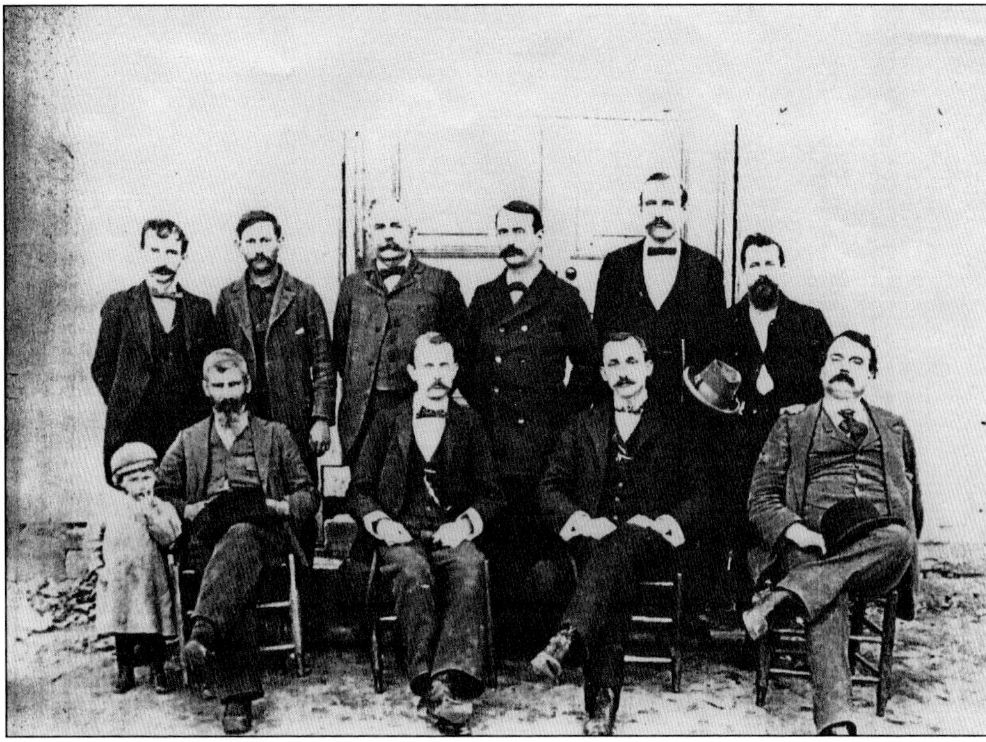

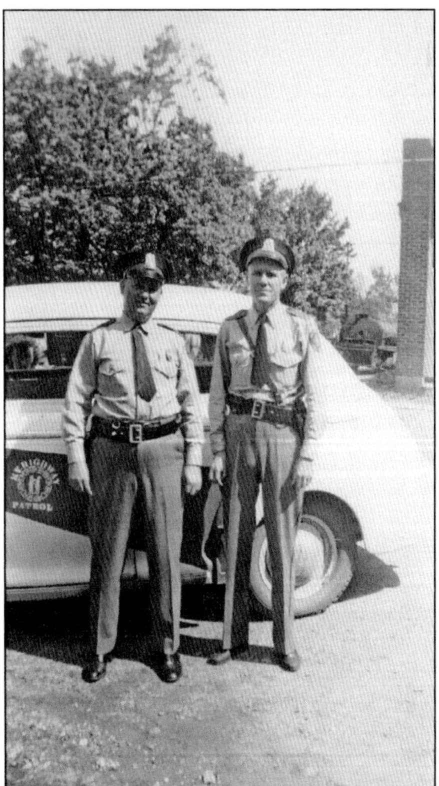

Livingston County officials shown on January 3, 1898, are, from left to right, (first row) jailer W. J. Threlkeld, circuit clerk J. C. Parson, county attorney C. H. Wilson, and county court clerk G. W. Landran; (second row) deputy court clerk D. S. Webb, assessor Charles Vick, sheriff R. B. Cowper, county judge Thomas Evans, superintendent of schools H. V. McChesney, and surveyor W. H. Eaton. (Courtesy of Livingston County Historical Society.)

In about 1942, Roy Vaughn (left) of Tiline and Herve McCaslin (right) worked for the Kentucky Highway Patrol. In 1948, Gov. Earl Clements signed the bill that created the Kentucky State Police. The new department inherited the men and equipment of its predecessor agency, the highway patrol, which 12 years earlier was formed with just 40 officers. Today the number of troopers has reached 1,000.

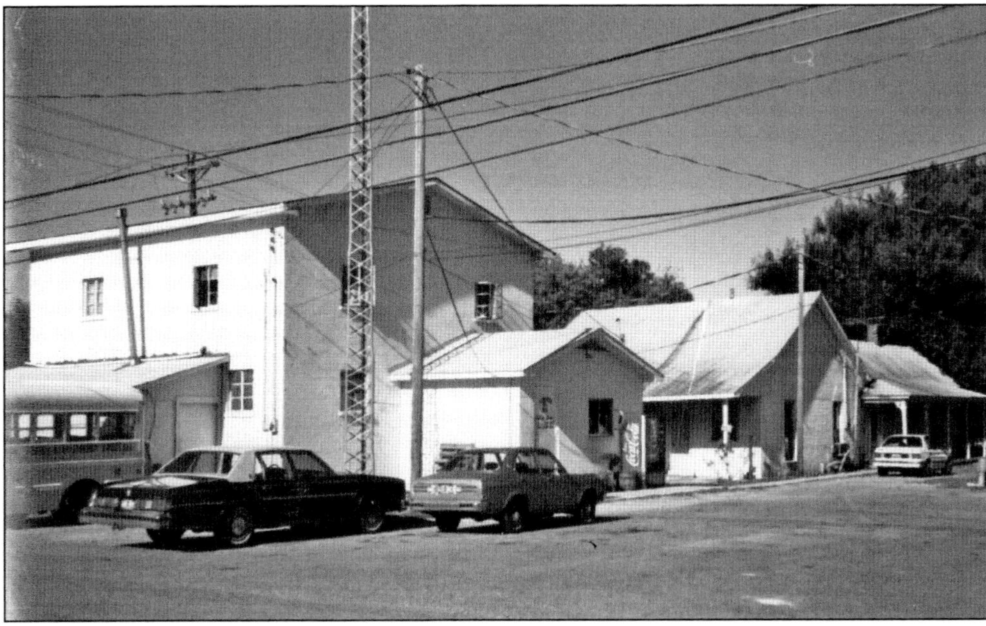

Shown are the Livingston County Jail and the jailer's quarters in 1987. They have been razed to make way for a parking area for the new judicial center, now under construction, behind the old courthouse. There is no jail in Livingston County, so when arrests are made, detainees are housed in adjoining counties.

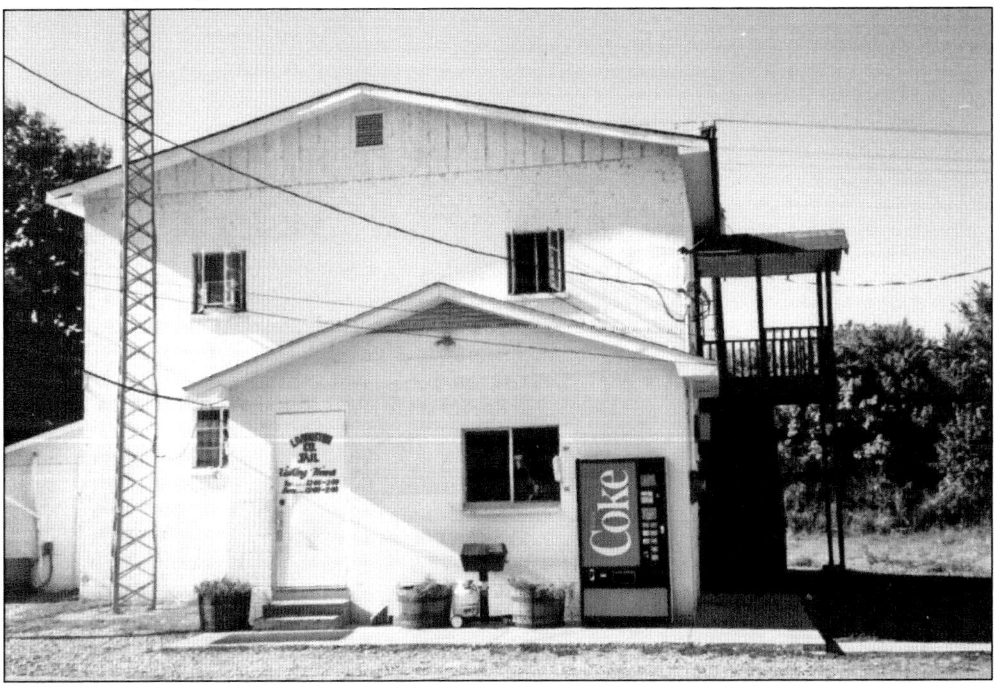

The Livingston County Jail had offices upstairs in earlier years. Everyone called it the Welfare Office. The offices were later moved to the basement of the Hale's Hotel and were called the Bureau for Social Insurance. The hotel building was razed in 1989, and the new Smith Building houses the state offices at the corner of Highways 60 and 453 in Smithland.

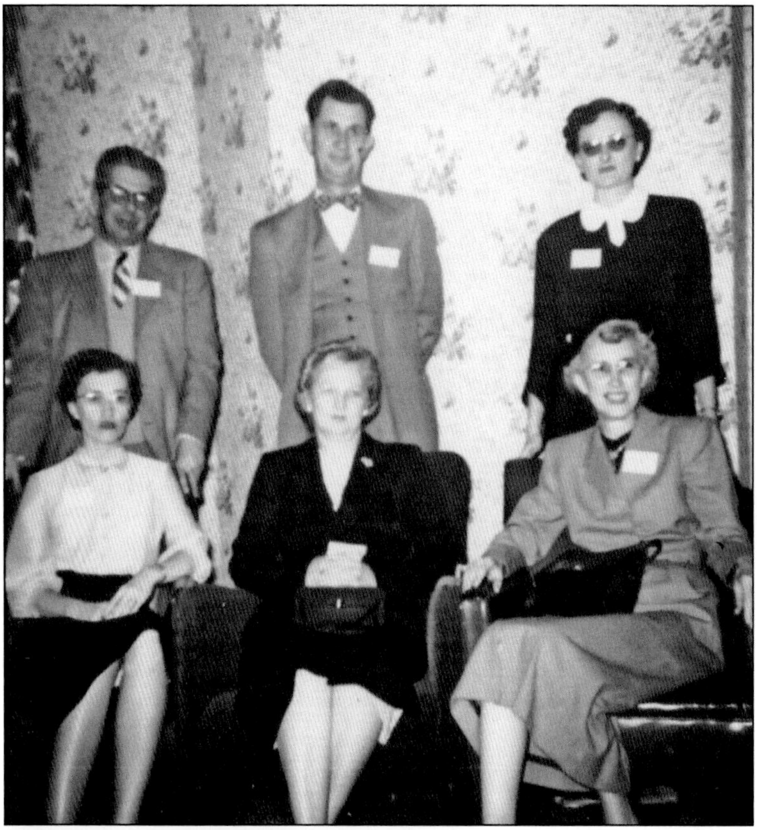

From left to right, (first row) Geneva Woodson, ? Hodges, and Reba Smith; (second row) Rod Keeney, Elmo Hodges, and Hazel Alley are Livingston County officials attending an office convention in Louisville, Kentucky.

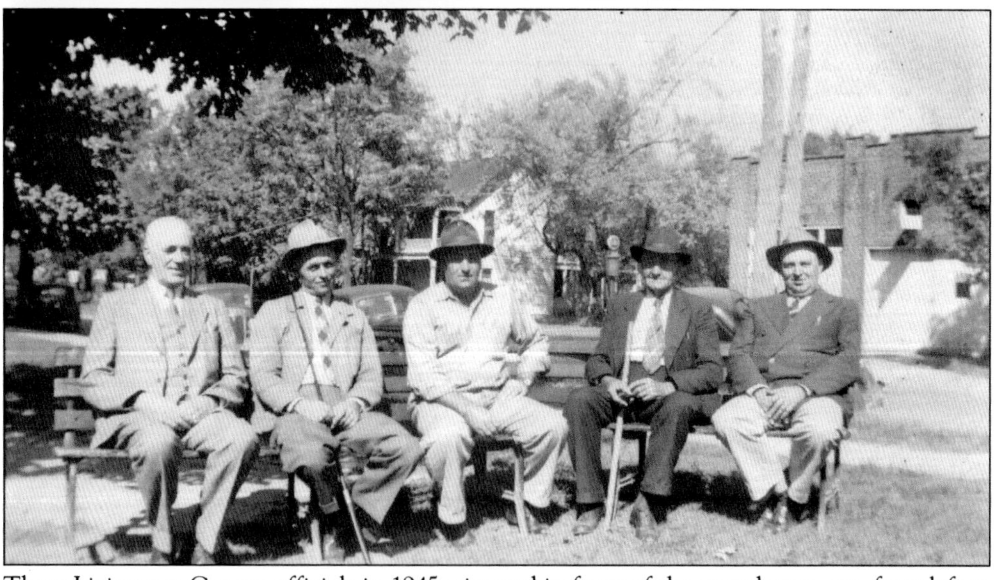

These Livingston County officials in 1945, pictured in front of the courthouse, are, from left to right, county attorney Harry F. Green, Sheriff Eulen Ramage, jailer Ira Driskill, county judge Ed Hughes, and deputy sheriff Truman Baxter. Eulen Ramage was elected sheriff in 1925 and was successful in five more campaigns for either sheriff or county judge. The last 15 of his political years were spent as master commissioner.

Blanch Brown was a public health nurse in Livingston County for almost 24 years. In 1945, Harold and Blanche Brown moved here from Union County. Blanche was born in 1895 and was quite active in her golden years, as was shown when she was campaign chairman of Livingston County for Gov. John Y. Brown. In 1981, she was coordinator of Kentucky delegates to the White House Conference in Washington, D.C.

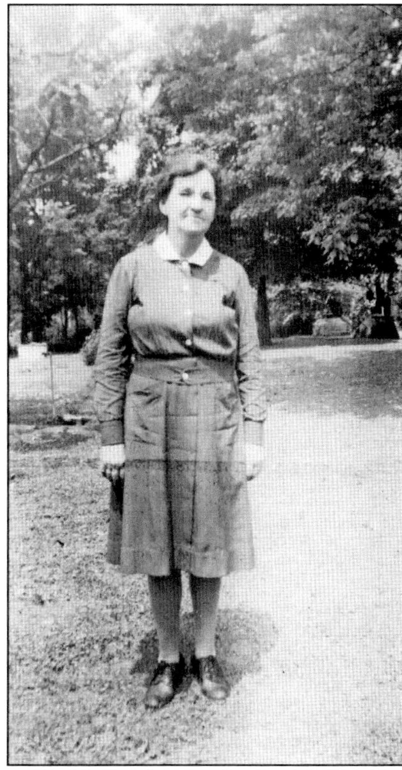

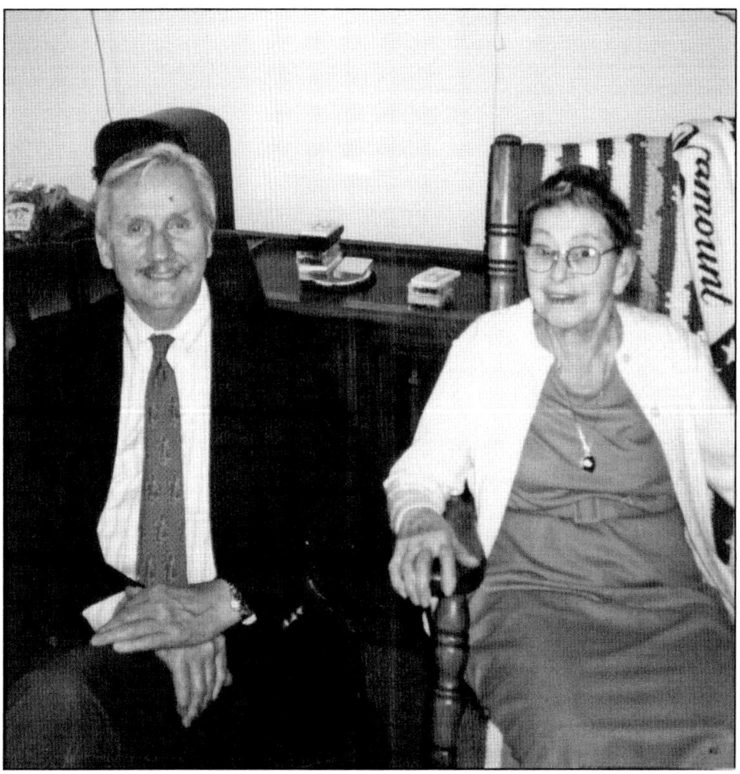

Clara Tapp was the first public health nurse in Livingston County. She started work when the County Health Department opened in 1937 and retired when she started her family. In this photograph, taken in 1994 in Louisville, Tapp is joined by her friend, Wilson Tully (grandson of Judge Charles Wilson). On the back of the photograph is written, "the ole rocking chairs has done and got us."

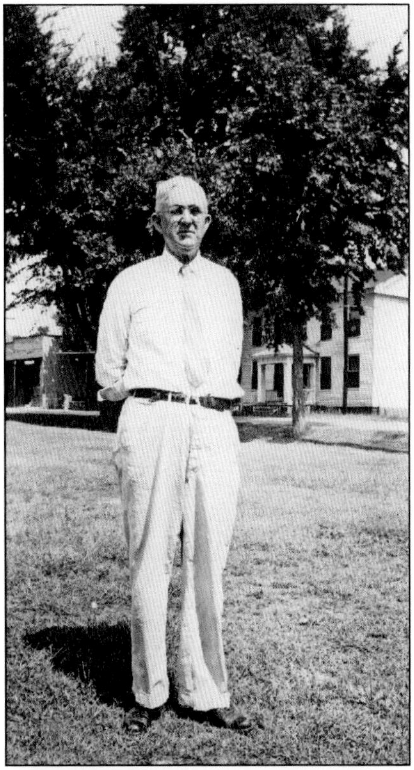

Judge Charles H. Wilson served one term as circuit judge in the early 1940s. Judge Wilson married Sarah Polk on August 26, 1896, and they had three sons and two daughters. He was an attorney in Smithland for many years. His office was in the old Tipton Building on the riverfront.

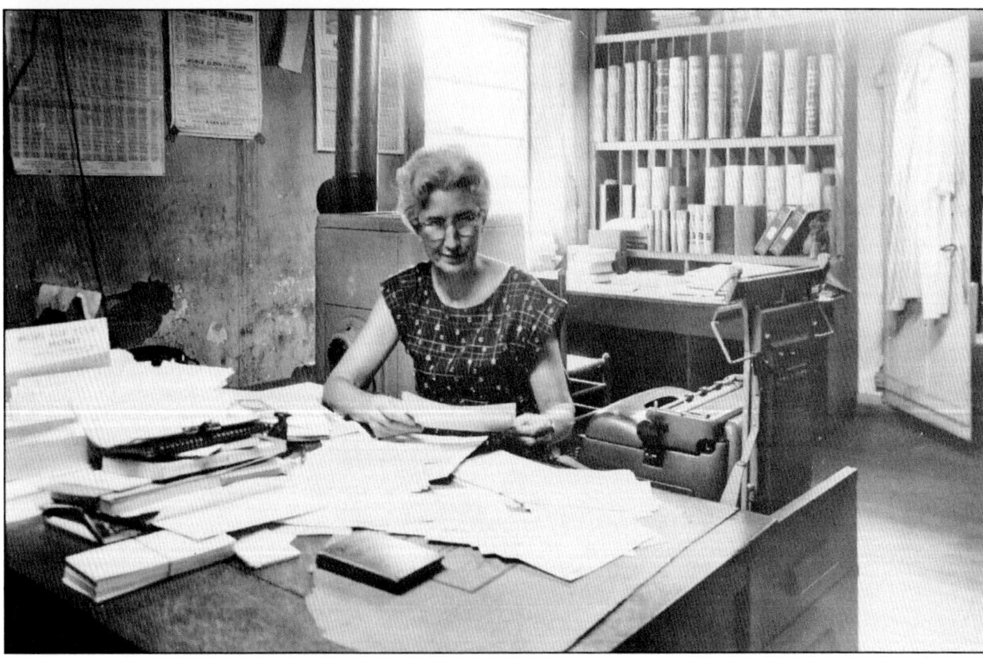

Reba Smith is shown in her courthouse office where she served as circuit court clerk for 29 years. She was appointed to fill out Orman Stegall's term of office, and then was elected until her retirement in 1974. Prior to that, she was a legal secretary to attorney Charles Wilson, and she later served as assistant draft board clerk during World War II.

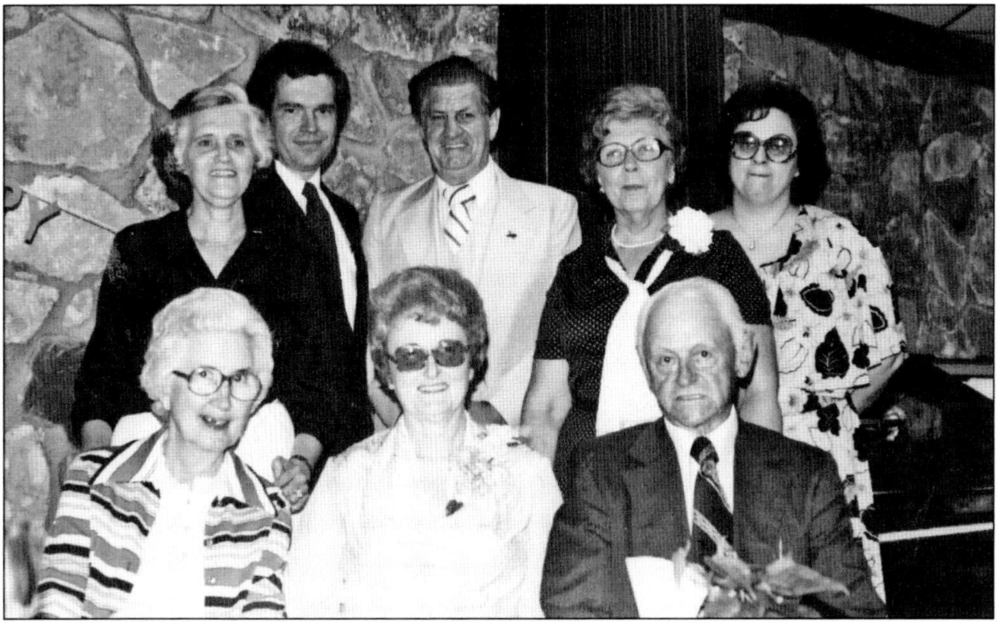

This group was seen quite often around the courthouse, as the photograph in 1981 implies. From left to right are (first row) Reba Smith, Hazel Robertson, and Eulen Ramage; (second row) Martha Hooks, William F. McGee, Floyd Hooks, Emma Lucas, and Mildred King. Floyd Hooks served as the last Livingston County judge for two terms (1970–1978). He was the first judge executive (1978–1982).

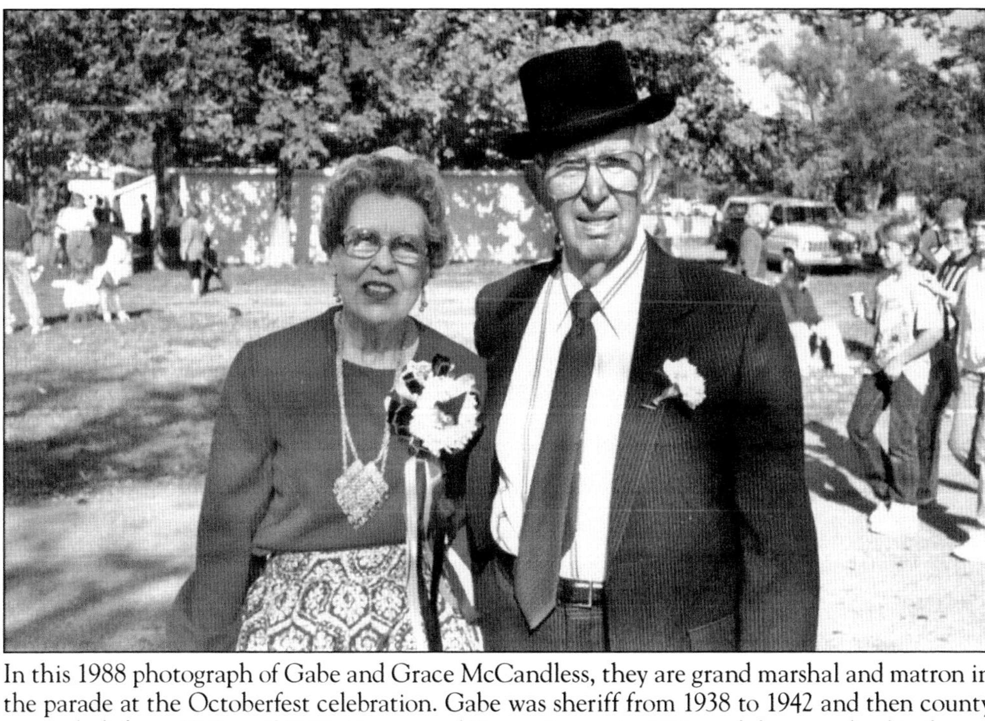

In this 1988 photograph of Gabe and Grace McCandless, they are grand marshal and matron in the parade at the Octoberfest celebration. Gabe was sheriff from 1938 to 1942 and then county court clerk from 1942 until 1974. He married Grace Strong in 1941, and she served as his deputy until their retirement.

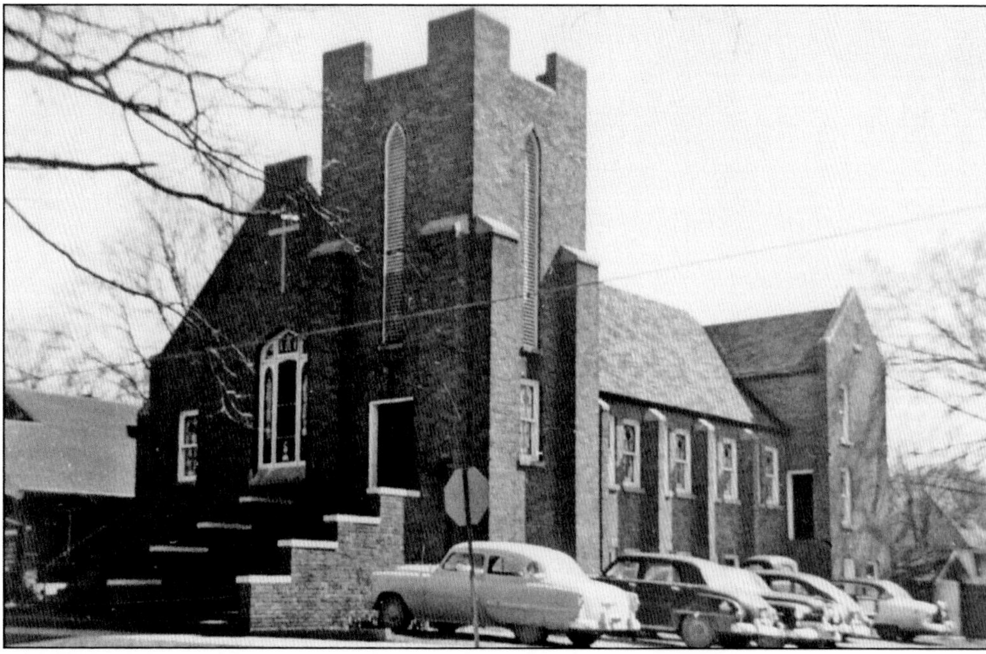

Adjacent to the courthouse is the historic Smithland United Methodist Church, which was completed in 1941. The 1937 flood almost reached the roof and destroyed most of the interior of the old church on Mill Street. Bricks from the historic old Clark Hotel were used for the new church on Court Street. Beautiful stained-glass windows were donated by various members.

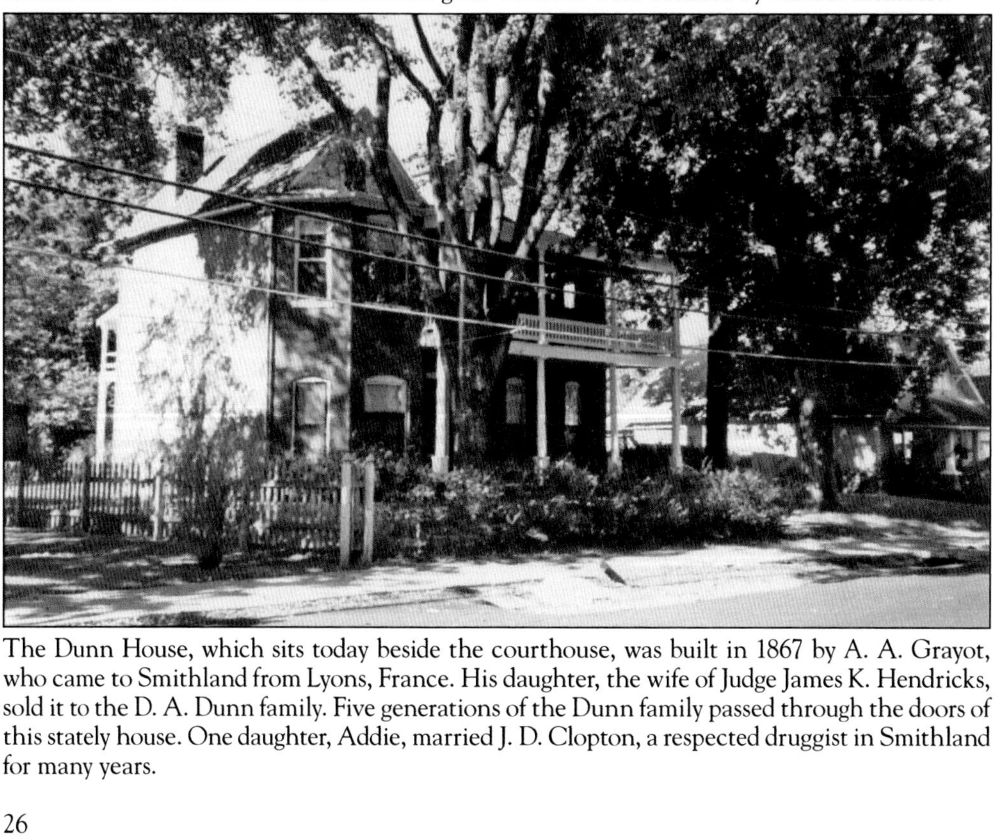

The Dunn House, which sits today beside the courthouse, was built in 1867 by A. A. Grayot, who came to Smithland from Lyons, France. His daughter, the wife of Judge James K. Hendricks, sold it to the D. A. Dunn family. Five generations of the Dunn family passed through the doors of this stately house. One daughter, Addie, married J. D. Clopton, a respected druggist in Smithland for many years.

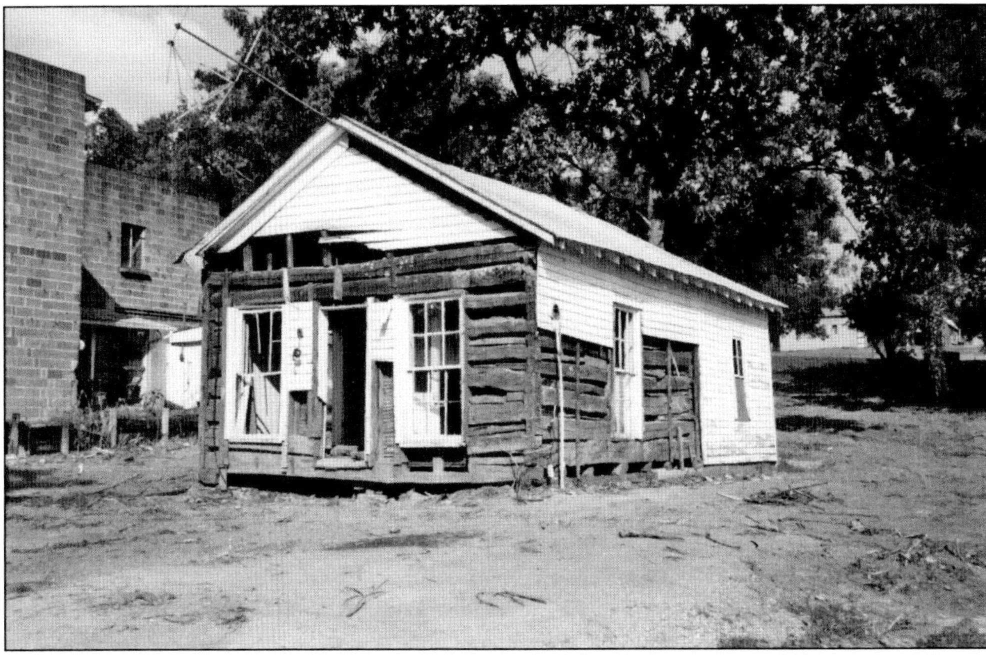

This log cabin was found when Jim and Joyce Woodard decided to raze an old house next door to their drugstore in 1991. After some research, Joyce determined the log cabin was built between 1836 and 1843 by Elisha Heater. Demolition of the house was halted as the bulldozer pulled off the front porch, and a log with wooden pegs fell out. The cabin was moved across from the courthouse.

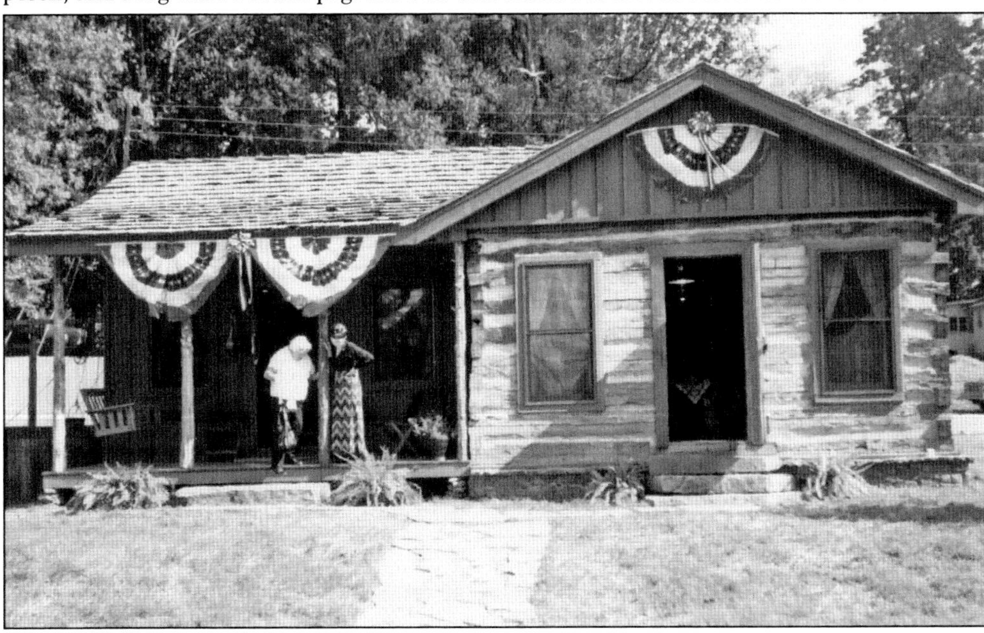

Restored with a grant from the Kentucky Bicentennial Commission and volunteer labor and donations, the log cabin now serves the public as a welcome center and museum on State Street in Smithland. It is operated and maintained by the Livingston County Historical and Genealogy Society and contains artifacts and historical documents relating to the county and surrounding areas. The cabin is open from 1:00 to 4:00 p.m. on weekdays.

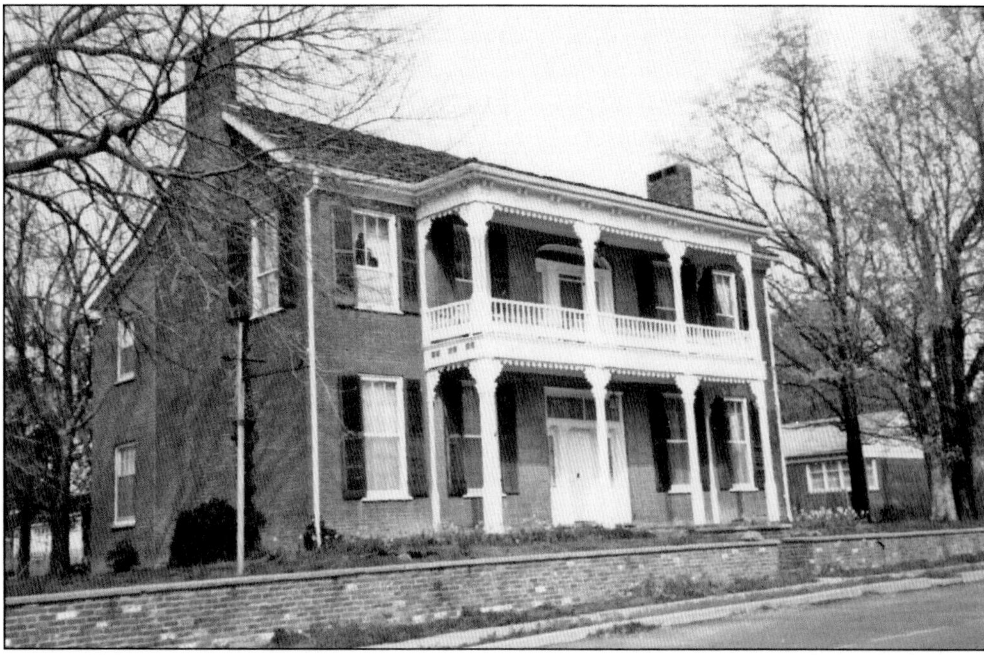

The Rudd House, across from the courthouse in Smithland, was listed on the National Register of Historic Places in 1982. Willie T. Rudd purchased the house in 1970 from the C. B. Davis family. It is believed to have been built in the 1840s. One unique feature of the home is the safe room, which had only one entrance from the parents' bedroom to the daughter's bedroom.

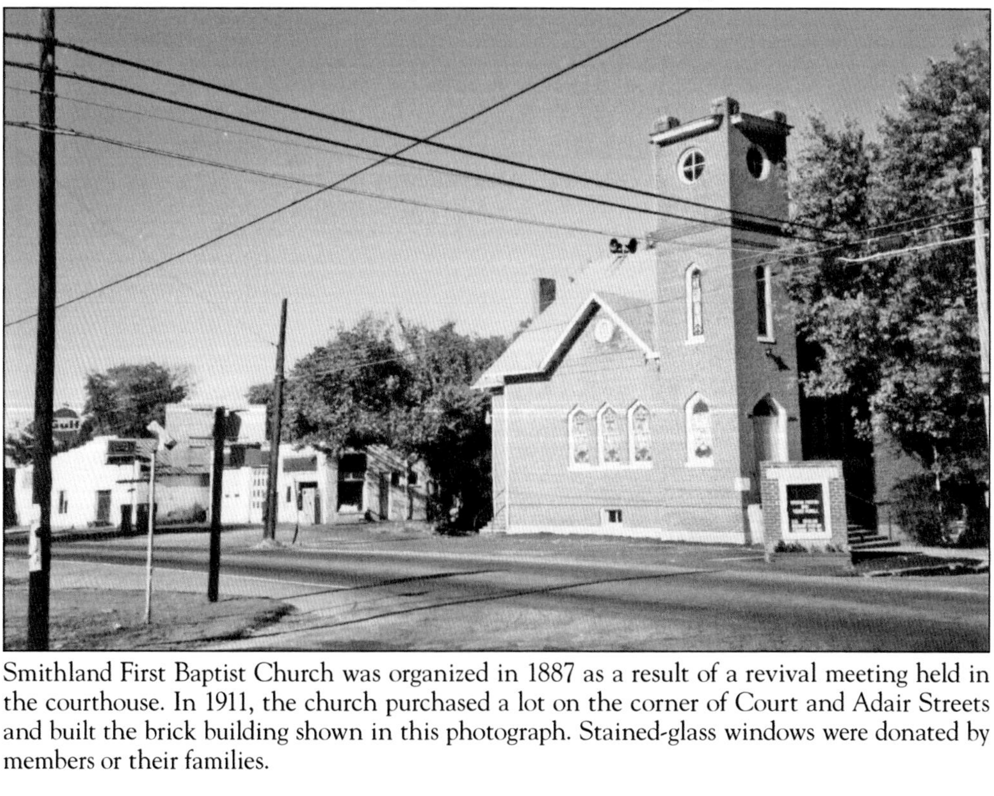

Smithland First Baptist Church was organized in 1887 as a result of a revival meeting held in the courthouse. In 1911, the church purchased a lot on the corner of Court and Adair Streets and built the brick building shown in this photograph. Stained-glass windows were donated by members or their families.

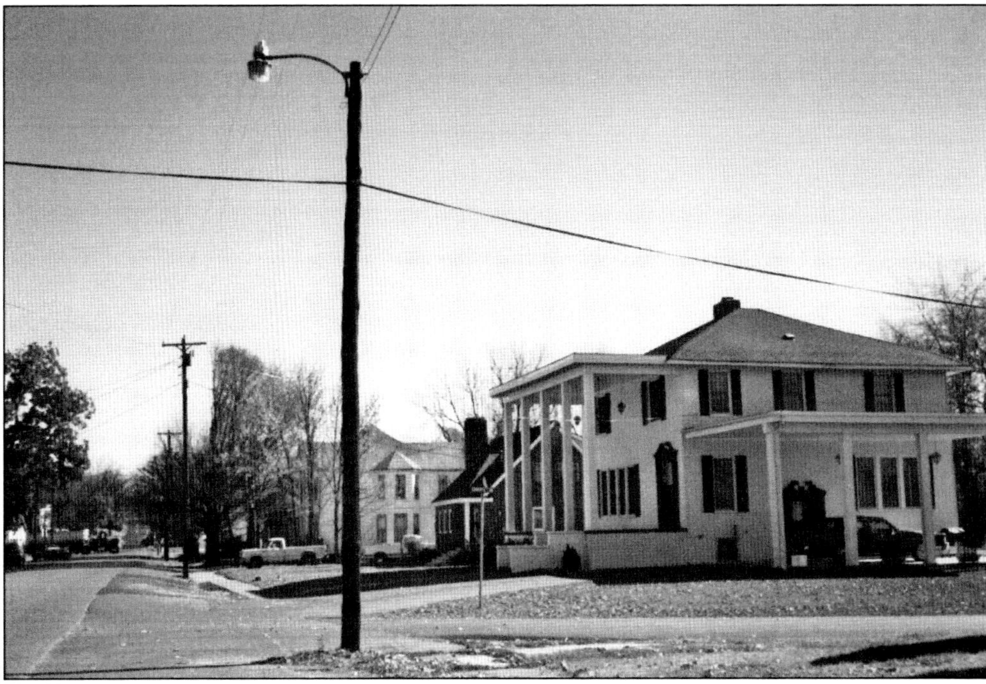

Dr. Lynn Adams built this beautiful home on Court Street in 1912 or 1913. Hiram and Ann Smith renovated it in 1975 to look like this photograph. The Smiths have since sold the house and built a new home on the high hill in Smithland off Mills Street.

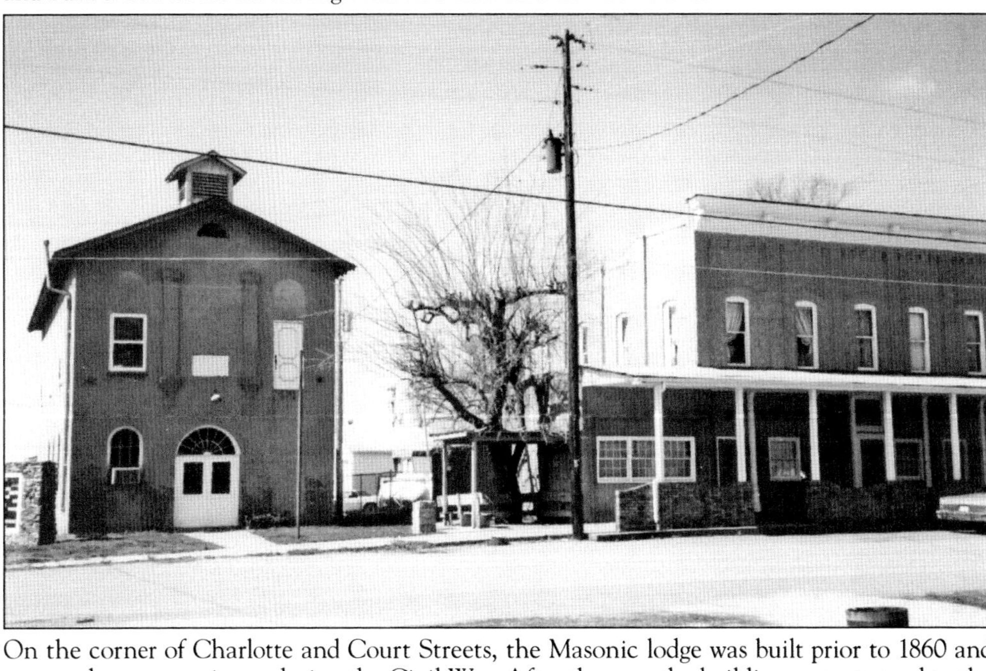

On the corner of Charlotte and Court Streets, the Masonic lodge was built prior to 1860 and was used as a commissary during the Civil War. After the war, the building was returned to the Masons. It has been used for church buildings and restaurants through the years. The building on the right of the photograph is where the post office and old draft board were housed, but it now serves as an apartment building.

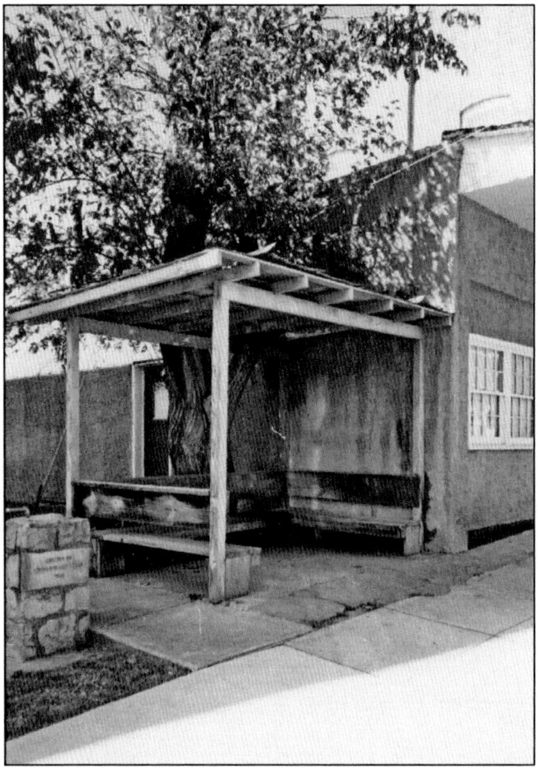

"The Tree of Knowledge" is located between the old lodge and apartment buildings. Under a hedge apple tree, this local hangout has been the place for the finest tale tellers, political debaters, knife swappers, whittlers, and problem solvers. In 1949, the Lions Club added a water fountain, and much later, the Smithland Second Baptist Church paid for the area to be restored. This historic spot still invites people to stop, rest, and chat.

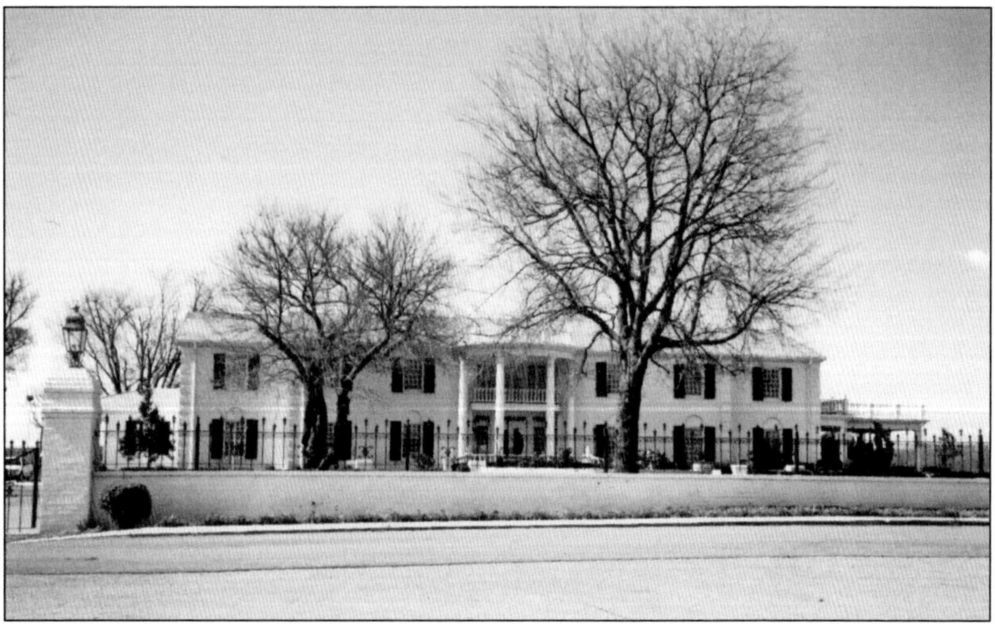

This beautiful home on the riverfront in Smithland was built by J. R. Smith in 1983. It was designed to look like Southfork, the home of the Ewings on the television show *Dallas*. This house replaced a building that in the beginning was an enormous warehouse and later became the St. Felix Hotel. In 1890, it became the Clopton Drug Store; then it was a home for several residents before Smith razed it.

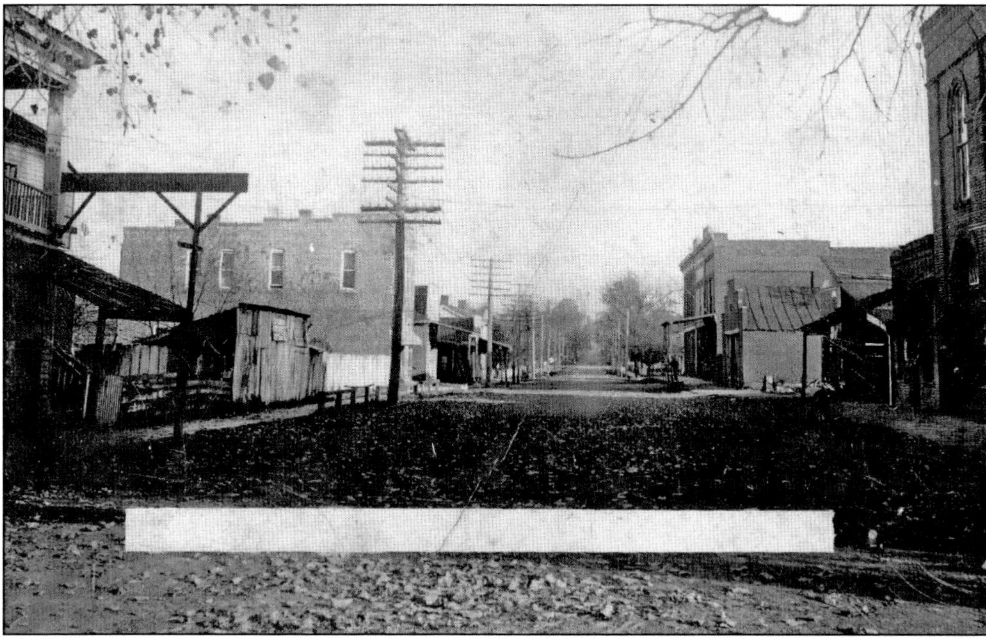

An old postcard shows the view from the Ohio River down Court Street in Smithland. Some of the businesses identified on the left include the Tipton Building, Smithland Bank, Shelby Wilson Building, Larcen Yancey Building, and Bunton Grocery. Establishments on the right are C. C. Seyster (later Reynolds Grocery), Bridges Store, and Dycus Store, with the post office and law offices upstairs.

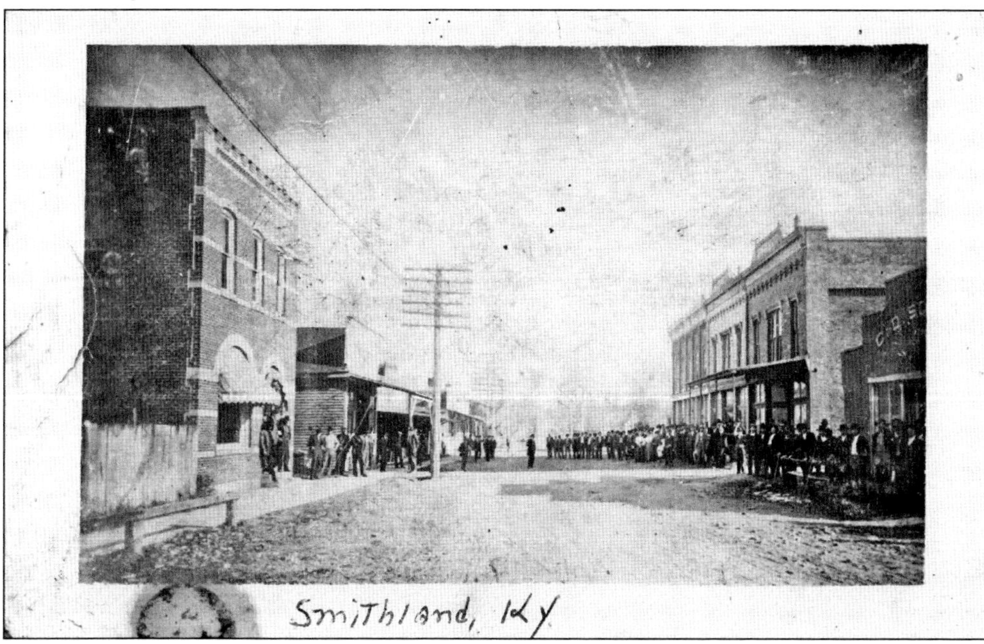

This postcard shows lower Court Street in 1907. The big celebration is of the opening of the Smithland/Livingston Bank, formerly the First Southern Bank of Kentucky during the 1850s. Notice that everyone dressed in suits for any celebration, as compared to currently dressing in jeans and T-shirts.

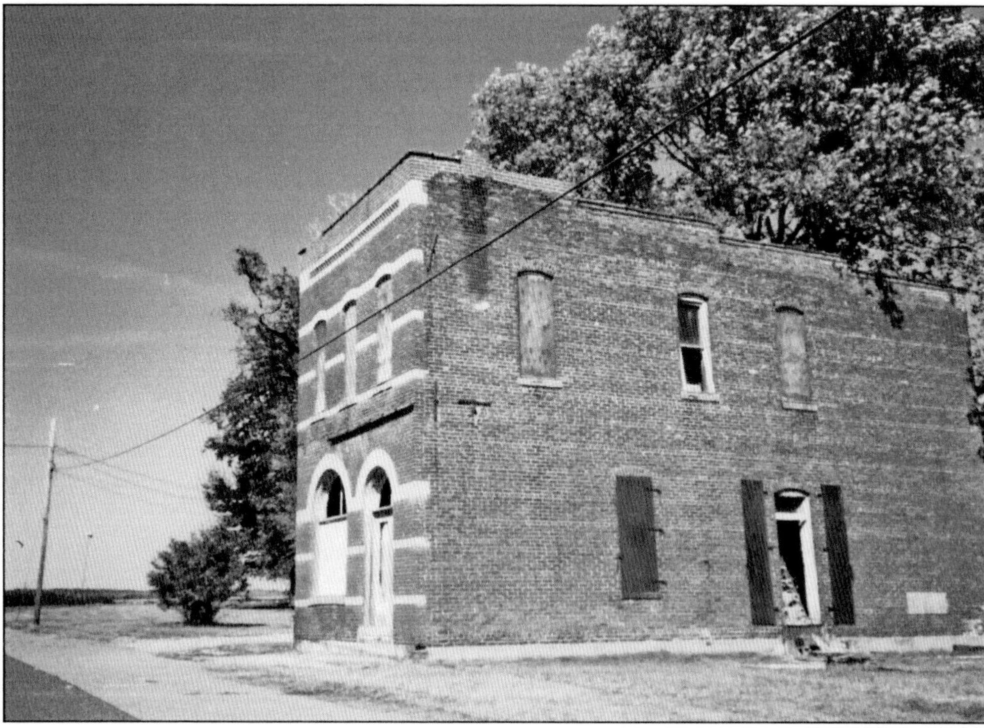

This photograph of the old Smithland Bank was taken in 1998. The first floor still has the ornate teller cages with wooden columns and latticework of iron. The second floor was used in the 1940s for the Smithland Telephone Exchange and as an apartment for the telephone operators. The building has since been renovated into a residence to remain a part of the heritage of Livingston County.

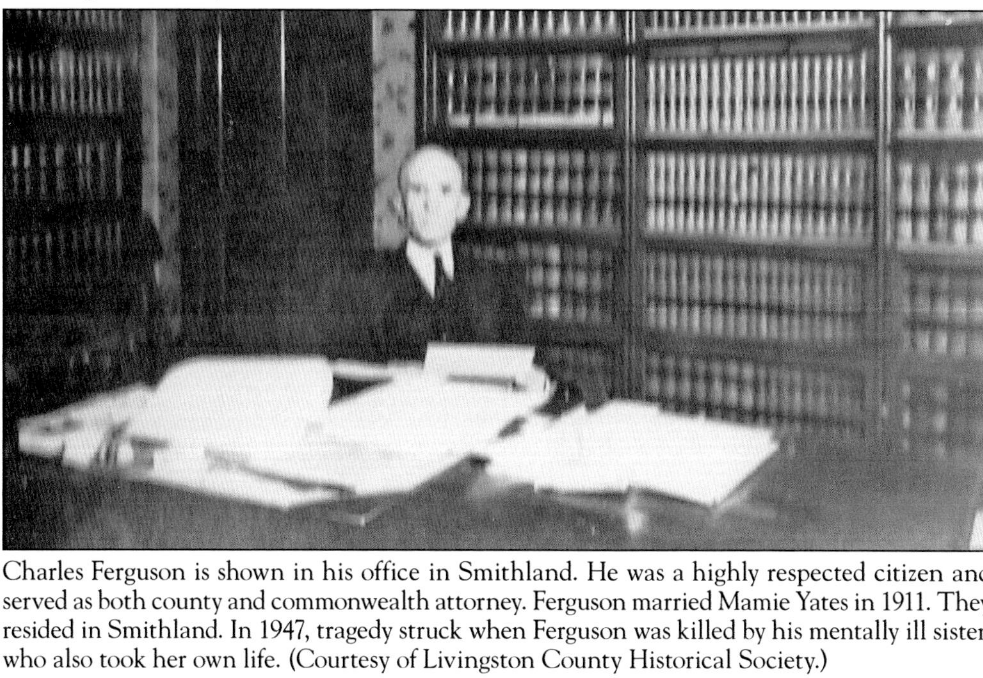

Charles Ferguson is shown in his office in Smithland. He was a highly respected citizen and served as both county and commonwealth attorney. Ferguson married Mamie Yates in 1911. They resided in Smithland. In 1947, tragedy struck when Ferguson was killed by his mentally ill sister, who also took her own life. (Courtesy of Livingston County Historical Society.)

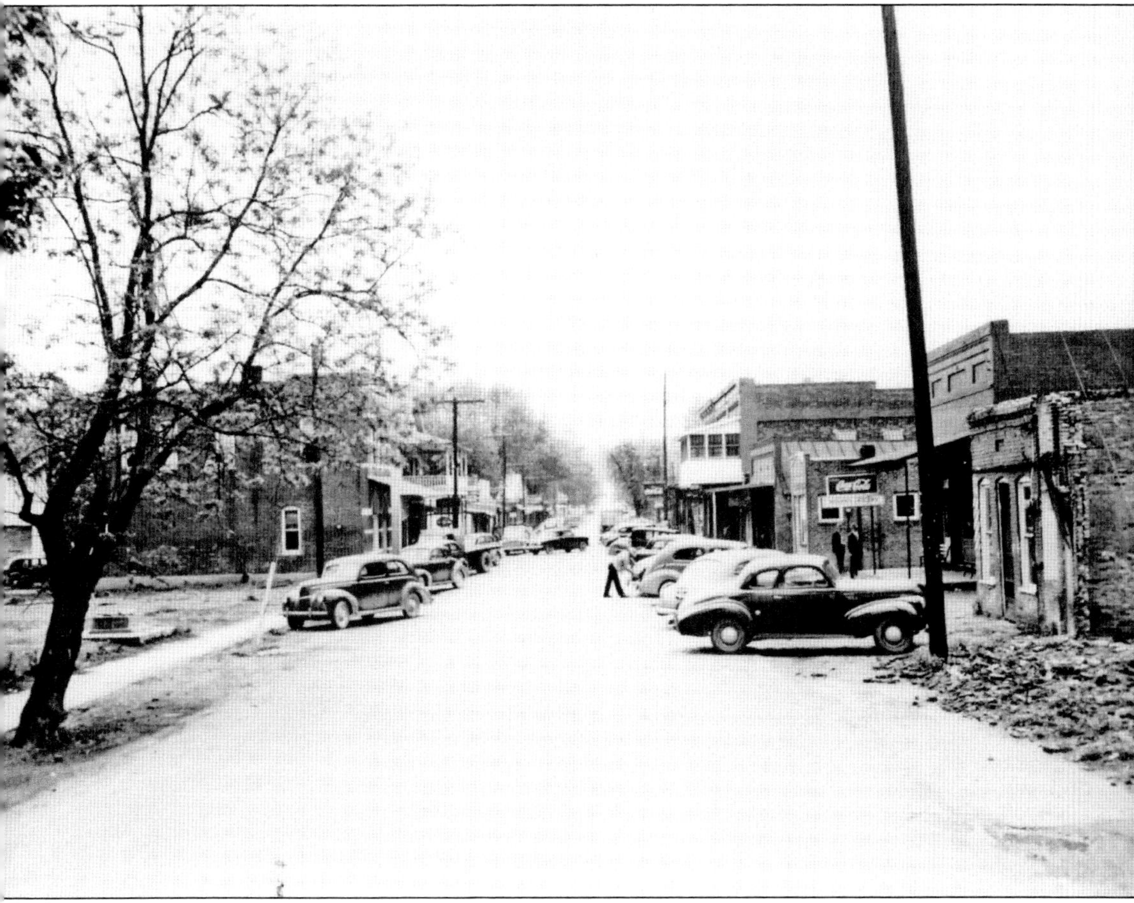

Seen around 1939, lower Court Street is becoming the main business section of Smithland. Cars have mostly replaced the horses and wagons and buggies. After the 1937 flood, businesses that were located on the riverfront began moving toward what is now Adair Street or Highway 60. The land of Smithland was owned by Zachariah Cox, who was a member of the Ohio Land Company. He named the town after his close friend, James Smith, a young man from Pennsylvania who was raised by northern Native Americans and escaped during a battle in Canada. There have actually been three Smithlands known to its inhabitants. The first Smithland was located three miles below the present site and is believed to have slid into the river. It was known as the lower town. Middle and upper towns were formed later. Today only part of the middle one remains, and the upper one is the main section of town. In 1860, the Englishman Thomas Ache wrote, "Smithland is situated on a high cliff rock about 200 feet above the level of the Ohio River. It contains 150 houses and has 27 mercantile stores. The staple commodities are cattle and corn. It is a lively place for business and the inhabitants enjoy good health." (Courtesy of Livingston County Historical Society.)

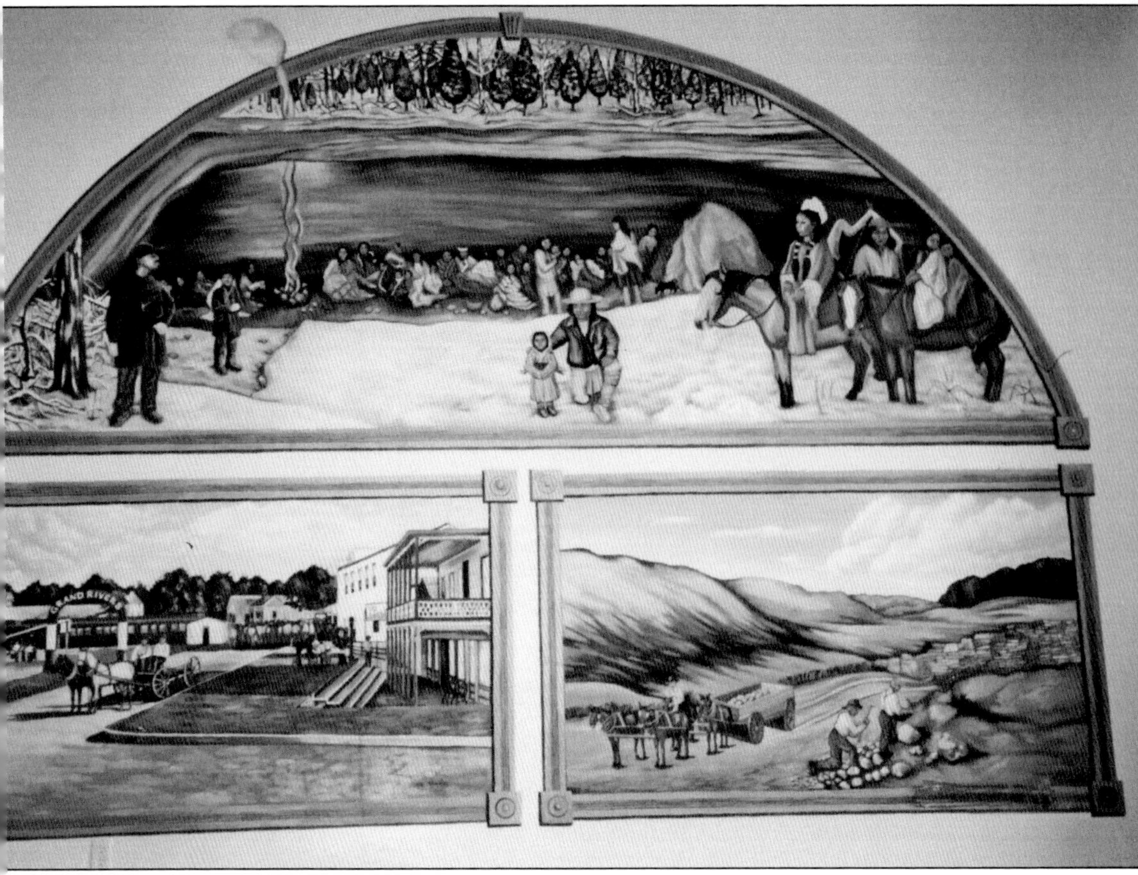

Tiline artist Dana Aguilar has done several murals in the historic courthouse depicting scenes from Livingston County's past, including the scene pictured above, which portrays the Native Americans at Mantle Rock, a stop on the Trail of Tears. The lower left shows the prospering Grand Rivers community in 1898, the heyday of Thomas Lawson's iron foundry, when the railroad ran through the center of town. The lower right portrays the early beginning of the limestone rock quarries in this county. Aguilar has done murals covering the east wall of the upstairs courtroom in the county's historic courthouse and around the entrance way downstairs. One mural shows a Civil War scene at Fort Smith, the remains of which are on a hill behind the high school in Smithland. Another painting shows the Klondike fluorspar mine southeast of Salem. The murals are unique and help preserve some of the rich heritage of the county.

Three

SOUTH LIVINGSTON COUNTY

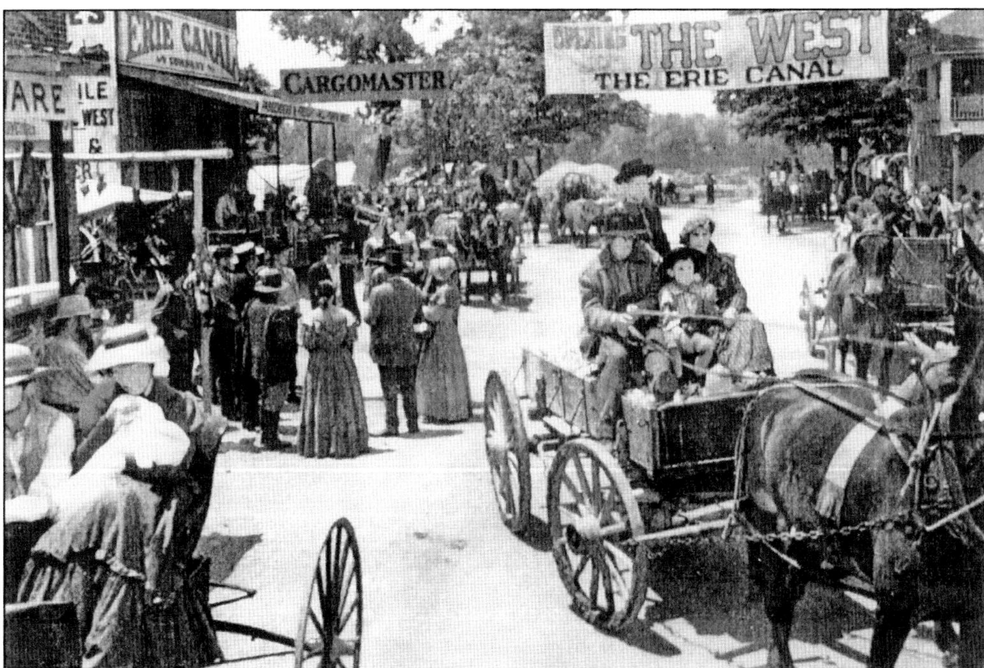

In 1961, Smithland became Albany, New York, as it was in the 1830s, when the movie *How the West Was Won* was filmed. This scene was almost to the riverfront on Court Street, with many local people as extras and stand-ins. On the left are Charles Babb and Anna Lois Mitchell holding baby Steve. On the right are Frank and Elva Rudd with grandsons Glenn (left, back) and Van Rudd (right, front). (Courtesy of Livingston County Historical Society.)

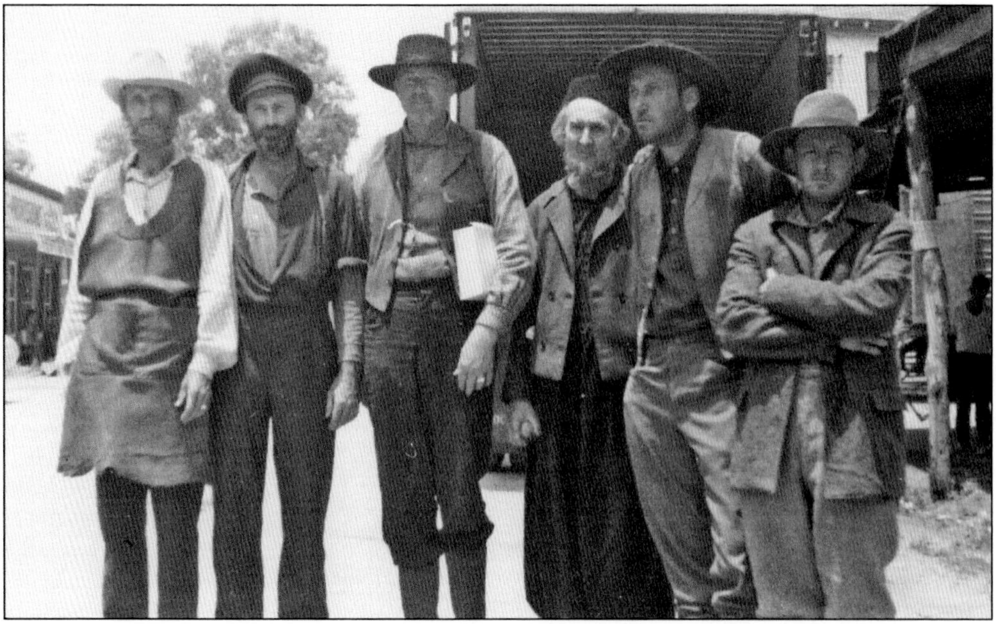

These men served as extras or stand-ins for the filming of *How the West Was Won*. From left to right are Ernest Driskill, Harry Flannery, Charlie Brasher, Hugh Harvey, ? Jones, and Owen Hurley. Among the cast of stars in Smithland were James Stewart, Debbie Reynolds, Carl Malden, Agnes Morehead, Carol Baker, Lee J. Cobb, John Wayne, Andy Devine, Walter Brennan, and Henry Fonda.

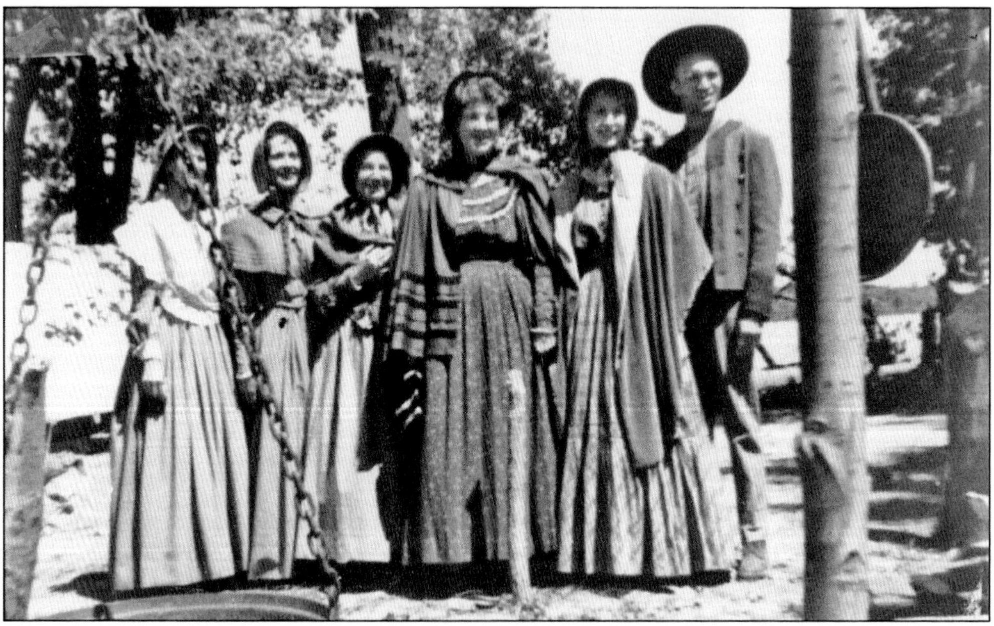

Shown in a 1961 photograph are a group of citizens of Livingston County in full costume for their parts in *How the West Was Won*. From left to right are two unidentified, Lois Mahan, Kathleen Alderdice, unidentified, and Wayne Harvey. During the filming, thousands of onlookers jammed the space behind the roped-off section of the set hoping to get a glance of the cast of stars. (Courtesy of Livingston County Historical Society.)

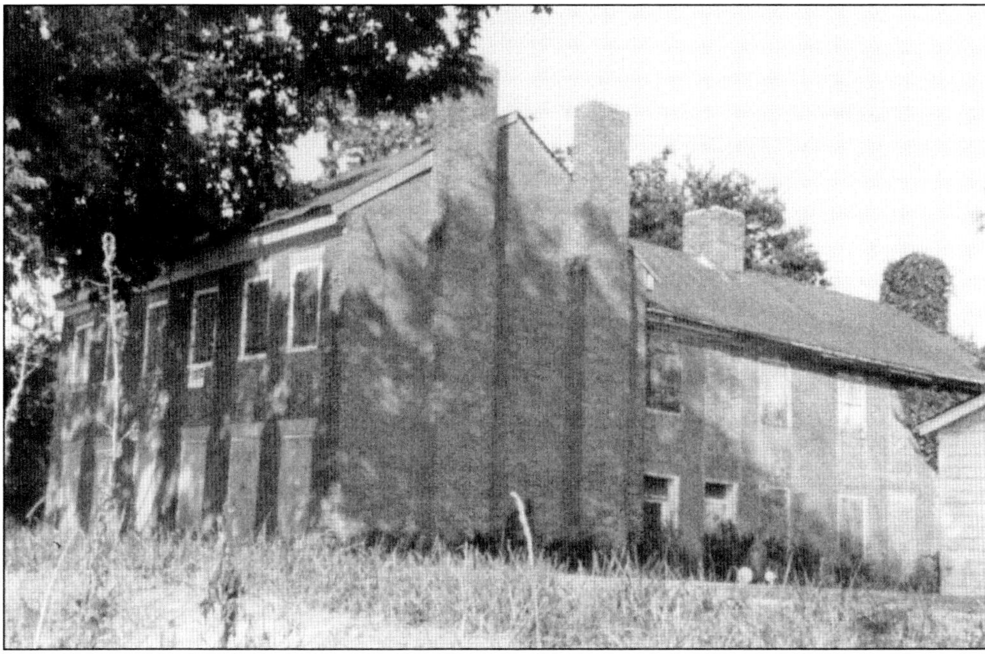

At the confluence of the Cumberland and Ohio Rivers in Smithland sits one of the most fabulous inns between Louisville and New Orleans—the Gower House. It was once called Bell's Tavern but was renamed when it was bought by Stanley P. Gower in 1836. A cellar under the house, joining a tunnel, is believed to have been a part of the Underground Railroad for escaping slaves who were seeking their freedom.

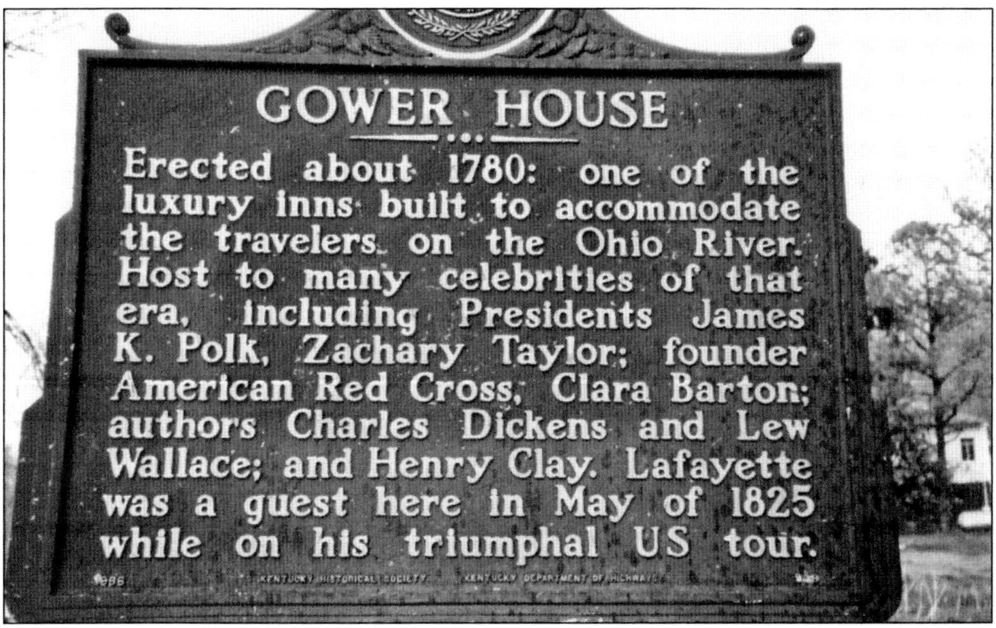

This sign tells of some of the famous guests that have stayed at the Gower House in Smithland. Some of the outstanding guests believed to have visited were Aaron Burr, Abraham Lincoln, James Audubon, Benedict Arnold, Jenny Lind, James K. Polk, Zachary Taylor, Charles Dickens, Andrew Jackson, Clara Barton, and Henry Clay.

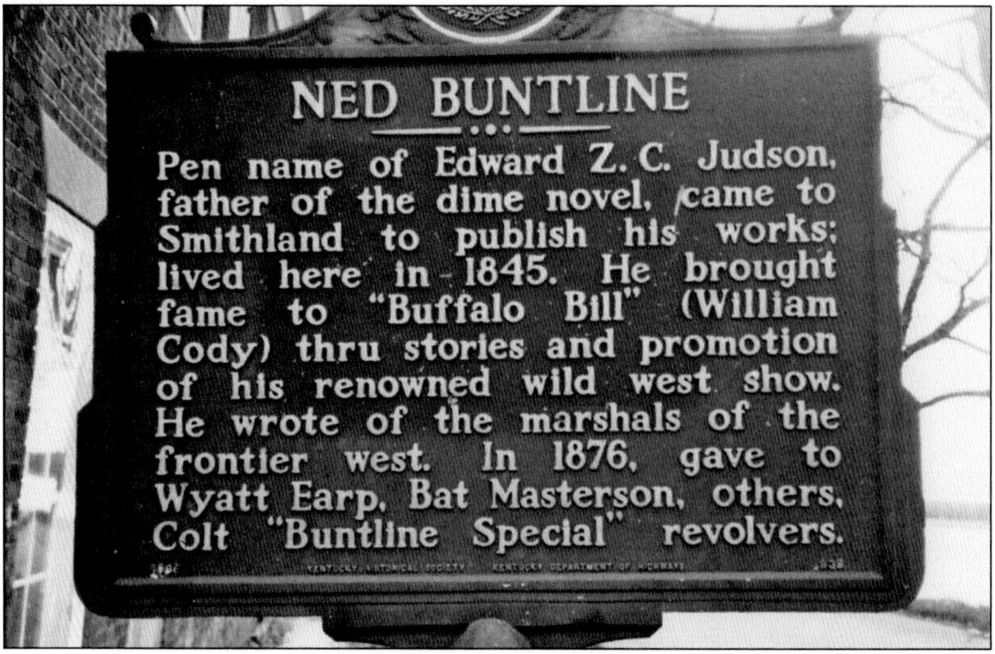

This sign tells the history of Ned Buntline, the pen name of Edward Z. C. Judson, who was an adventurer as well as an author. He moved to Smithland in 1845 with his lovely Spanish wife and later disappeared, leaving her heartbroken. She died and was buried on Cemetery Hill in an unmarked grave. Buntline wrote more than 400 dime novels, serials, and plays.

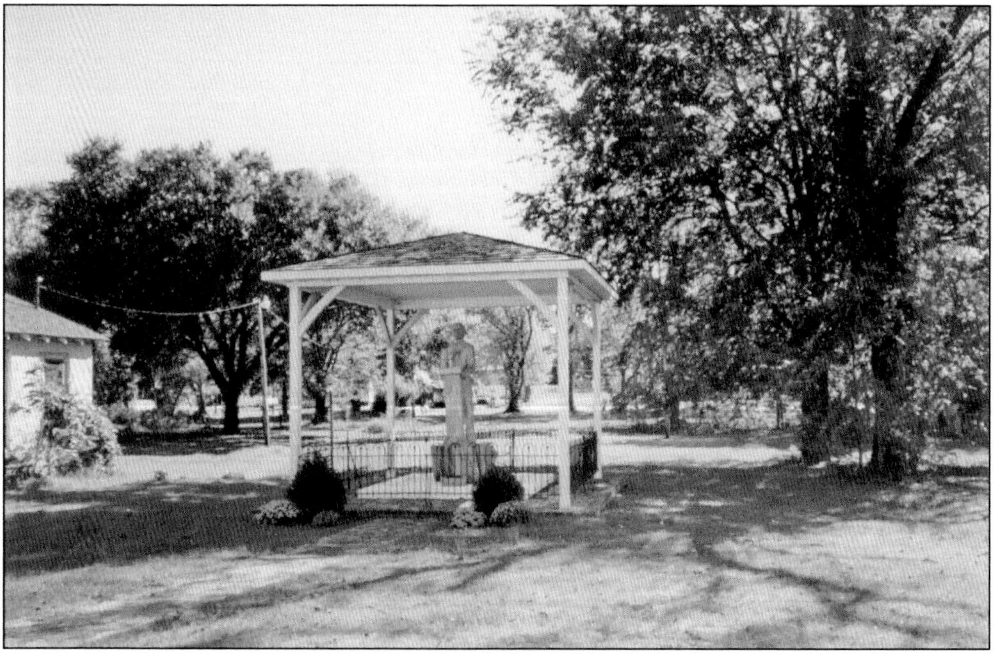

County court was held under a huge Dutch elm tree known as the Judge Elm, standing in front of the Gower House. Justice usually came swiftly, and if the sentence called for hanging, it was done on the spot. When the old tree died in 1994, the Roberts family had a statue of Henry Clay carved out of the tree. That statue now stands on Smithland's historic riverfront.

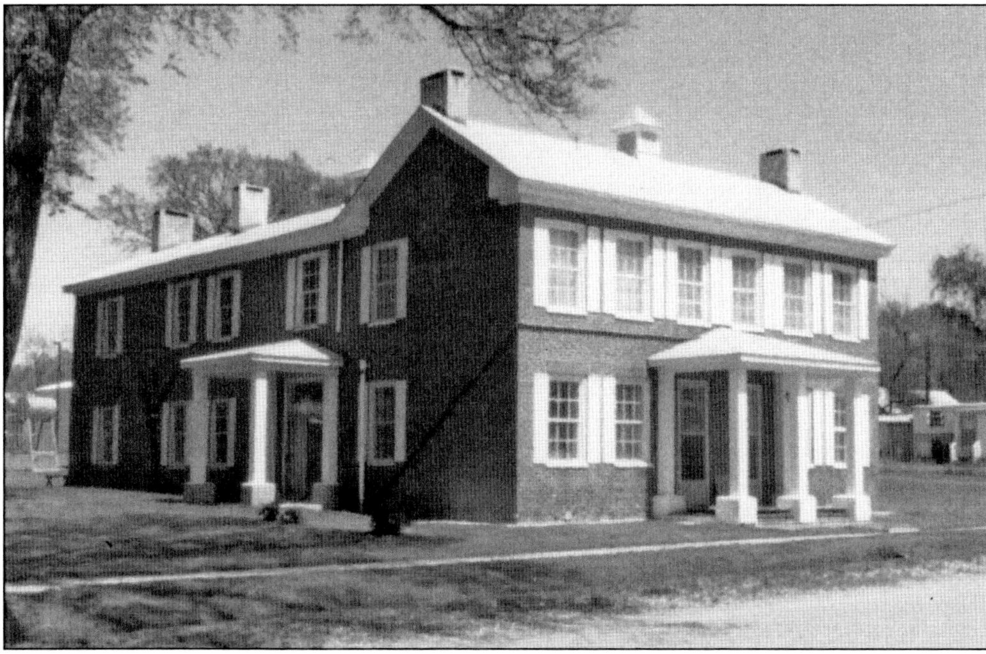

The James L. Dallam House, or Bush House, is owned by Tommy and Doris Cothron. It is located on Mill Street in Smithland and was once owned by a well-known attorney, John W. Bush, who was a captain in the Union army. The Bush family owned the home from 1881 until 1947, when it was sold to the Cothron family. This pre–Civil War home is designated a Kentucky landmark.

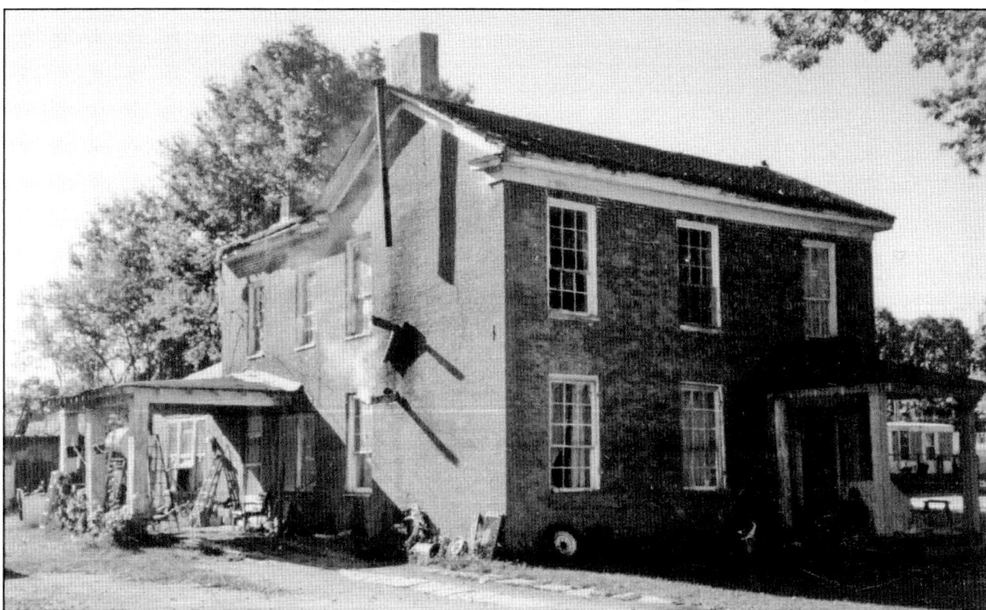

The home of Gen. Lew Wallace while he was stationed in Smithland during the Civil War was torn down in 1988. General Wallace lived in the brick house on Charlotte Street when he commanded Fort Smith, which was on a high hill overlooking the Ohio and Cumberland Rivers. After the war, General Wallace was appointed governor of the New Mexico territory and later was U.S. minister to Turkey.

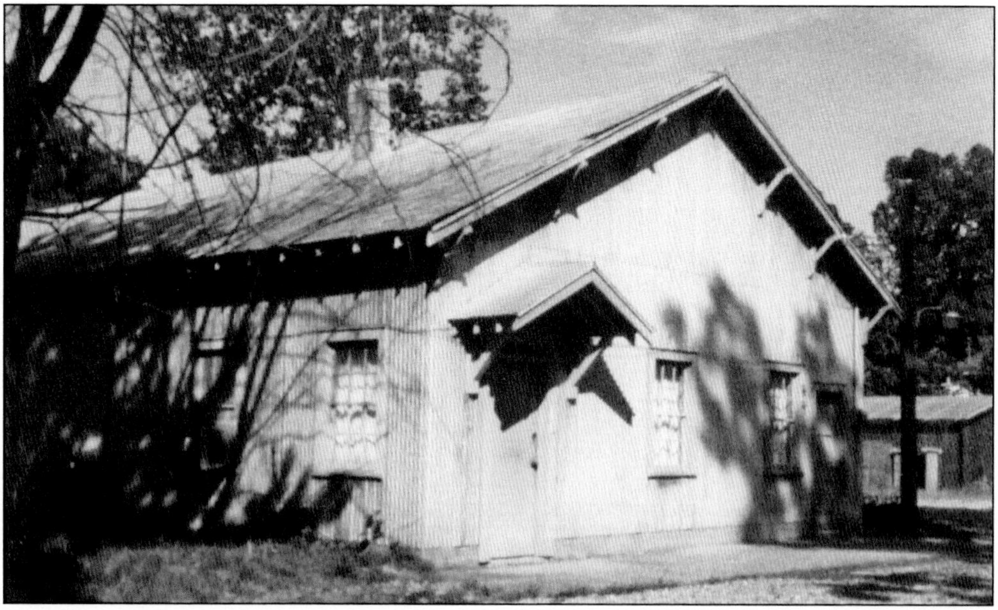

This photograph was taken in 1986 and shows the old WPA (Workman's Progress Administration, created by Pres. Franklin D. Roosevelt) Office and supply building. C. C. Brasher was the timekeeper. The building was later used as the Public Assistance Office, Food Distribution Center, and Disaster Emergency Services. It still stands on Mill Street in Smithland.

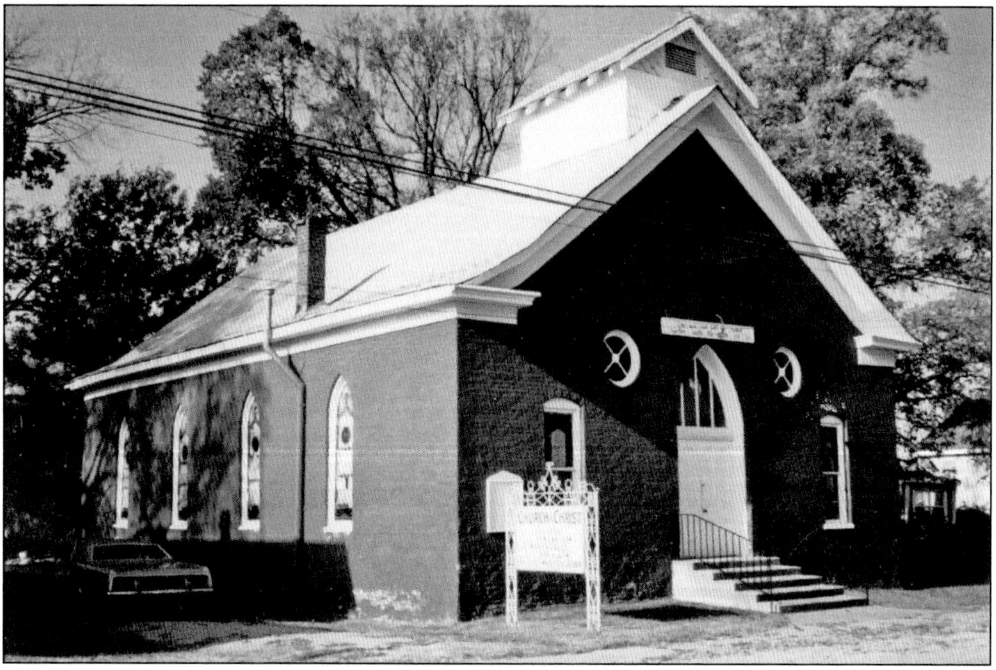

The Methodist church is believed to have been built in the late 1840s. There was a fire in 1886, and it was rebuilt with beautiful stained-glass windows. In the 1937 flood, the water was almost to the roof of the building and destroyed all the pews and the piano. In 1939, the congregation built a new church and sold the old one on Mill Street to the Church of Christ, which used it for 60 years.

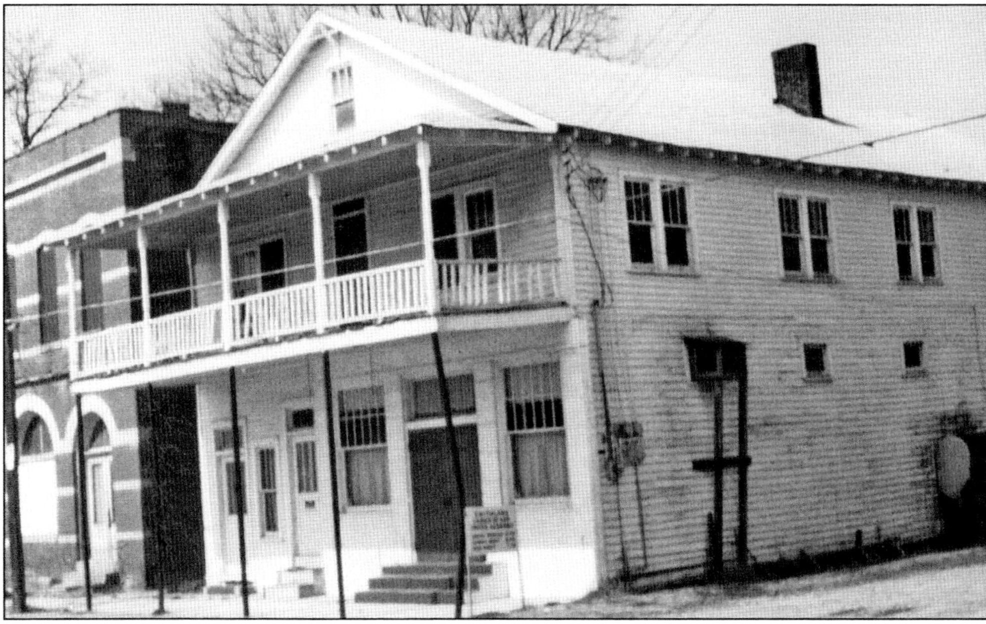

The old Hale Hotel was on Court Street in Smithland. The owners were Harold and Flora Hale. The Hales came from Arizona in 1924 and developed the hotel, which later became the biggest one of its kind in Western Kentucky. While boarders stayed on the second floor, a restaurant on the first floor became famous. Indeed people came from several states to enjoy the fabulous Sunday dinner.

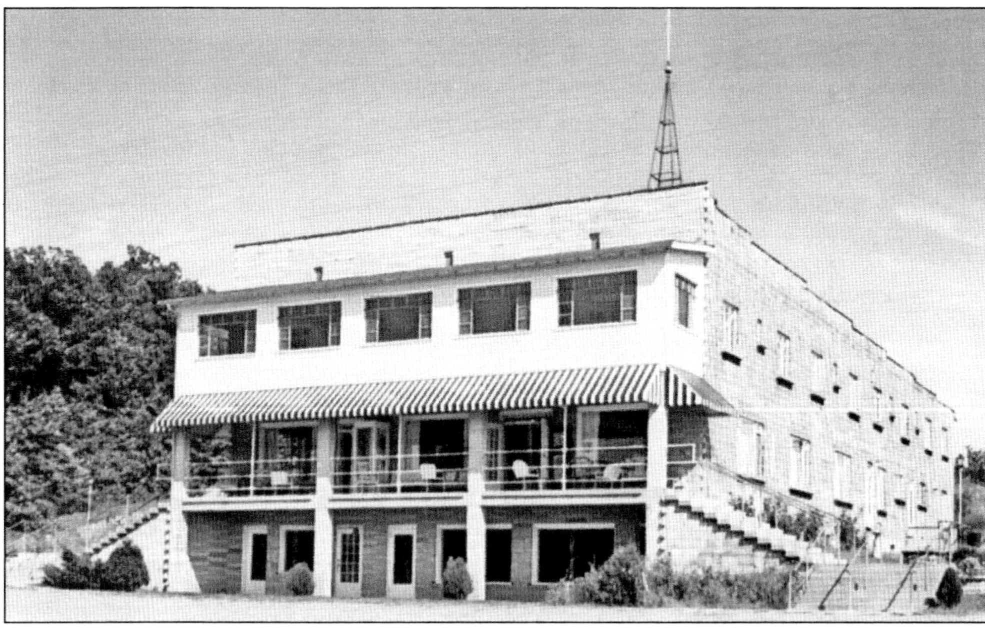

This postcard shows the new Hale Hotel, which was built in 1956 on Highway 60 to be safe from floodwaters. The building had 25 rooms and 14 baths to accommodate boarders. The dining area could seat 185, but one Mother's Day, the restaurant fed around 900 people, some waiting hours. Flora Hale fed the Hollywood stars of the movie *How the West Was Won*. The building was razed in 1992.

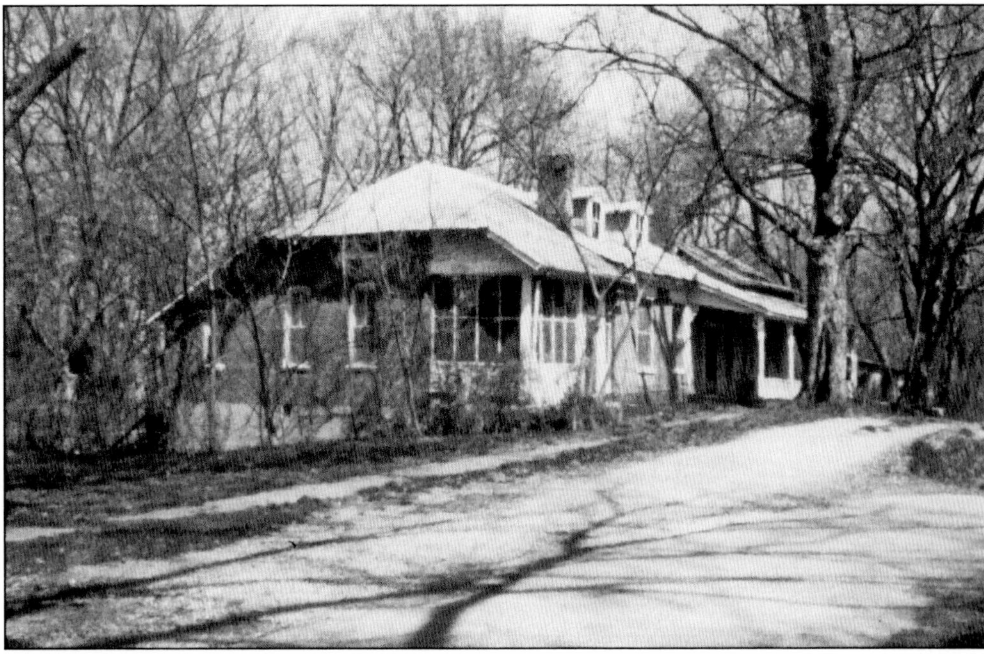

The Massey House on Charlotte Street is believed to be the oldest in Smithland. It was built in 1799 by Thomas Ballard. A door that appears to be part of the wall opens into a closet with a trapdoor in the floor. From there, a tunnel dug to the river allowed slaves to escape by boat. This was said to be part of the Underground Railroad during Civil War times.

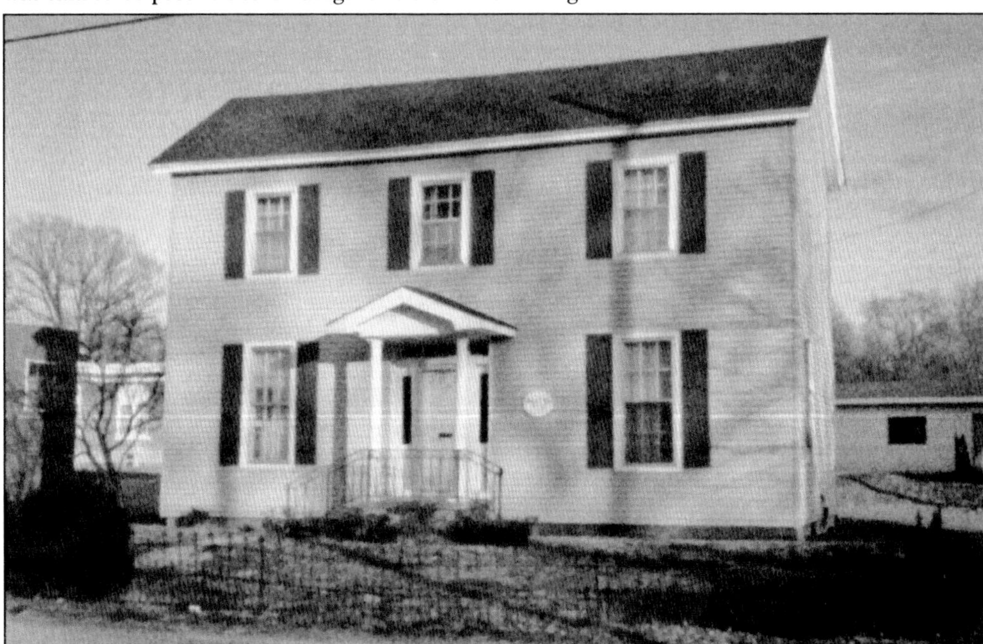

This historic building on Highway 60 in Smithland is now the McGee Law Office with attorneys William F. and Billy McGee, a father-and-son business. Billy's grandfather, attorney Raymond Dycus, used the office for many years. Other former occupants of the house were Dave and Minnie Webb. Dave was the Livingston County court clerk for many years.

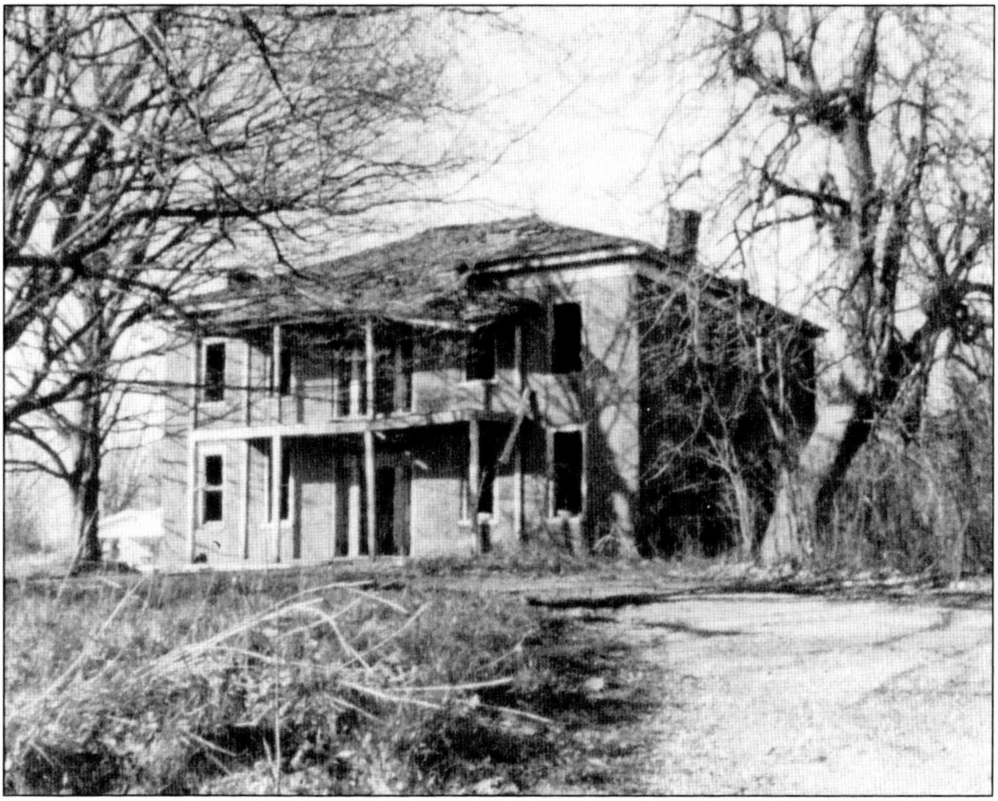

The Wilson House on Mill Street in Smithland was torn down in 1988. Dr. Will Saunders built it for a residence and office in 1834. When the first stages of the Civil War began to unfold, Dr. Saunders converted it into a hospital for wounded soldiers. One of the legends concerning the house is that there was an incinerator behind it to burn bandages and body parts.

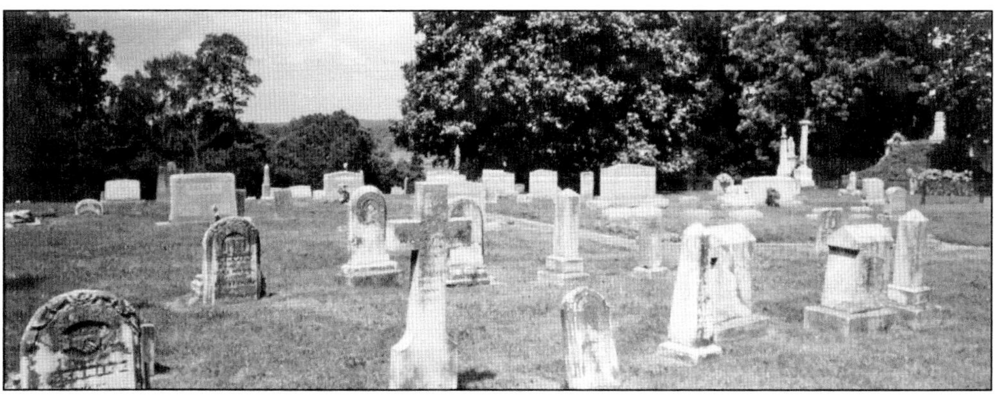

The Smithland Cemetery is located on a high hill overlooking the Ohio and Cumberland Rivers. During the Civil War, Gen. Ulysses Grant built a gun emplacement within the cemetery to control river traffic to and from Nashville. The oldest readable tomb is dated 1844, but many are believed to be much older. Smithland Cemetery is the resting place for W. Courtney Watts, author of *Chronicles of a Kentucky Settlement*.

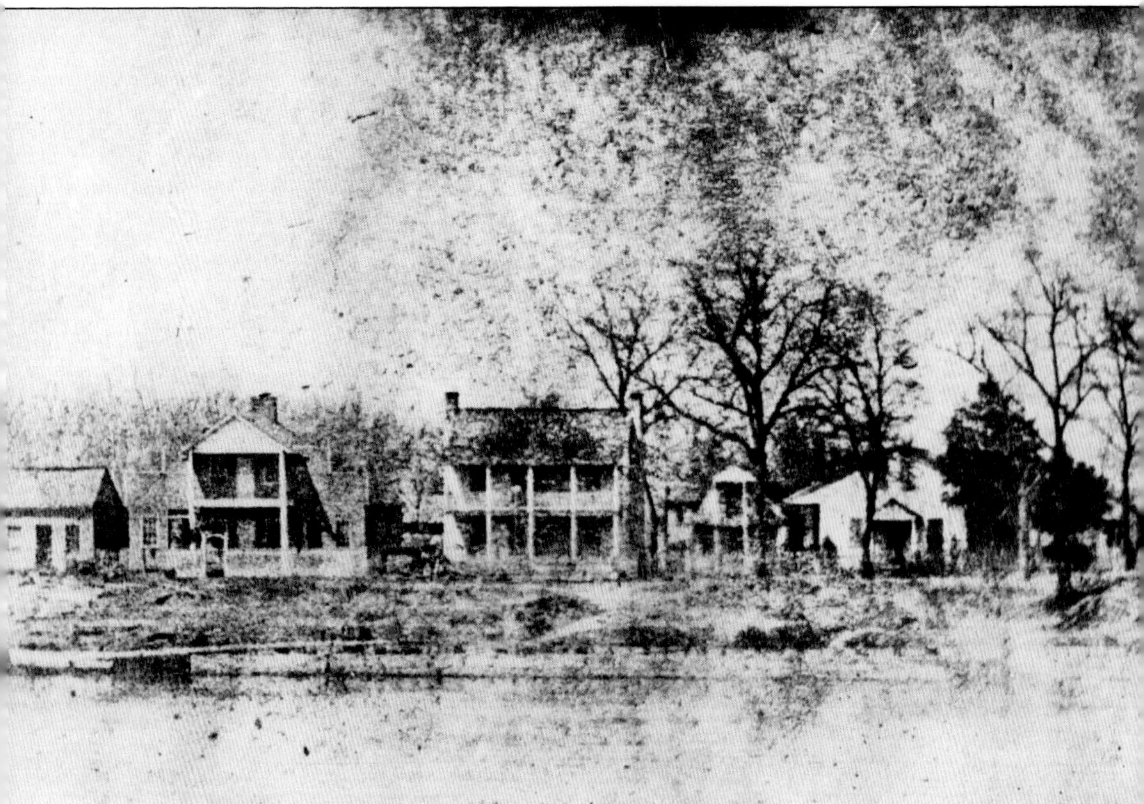

On July 22, 1811, Gustavious Brown moved the court to establish a town named Westwood directly across the Cumberland River from Smithland. This was a part of the first entry of land given for Revolutionary War service in the name of William Brown in 1784. This photograph has the Dannell family names written on the back with dates in the 1800s. From left to right are Grandma's storage and smokehouse, grandma's house (Sarah Ward Dannell), great-grandma's house (Opha Wheeler Dannell), Dean's house, Wants's house, and the house in which aunt Columbia taught school. The man in the picture is Charles Maureen Livingston Dannell, son of John and Eunice Wheeler Dannell. He was born on February 26, 1817, in Smithland and died on September 24, 1860. The young boy shown is Hugh Dannell, who was born on December 23, 1848, and died in April 1862. (Courtesy of Livingston County Historical Society.)

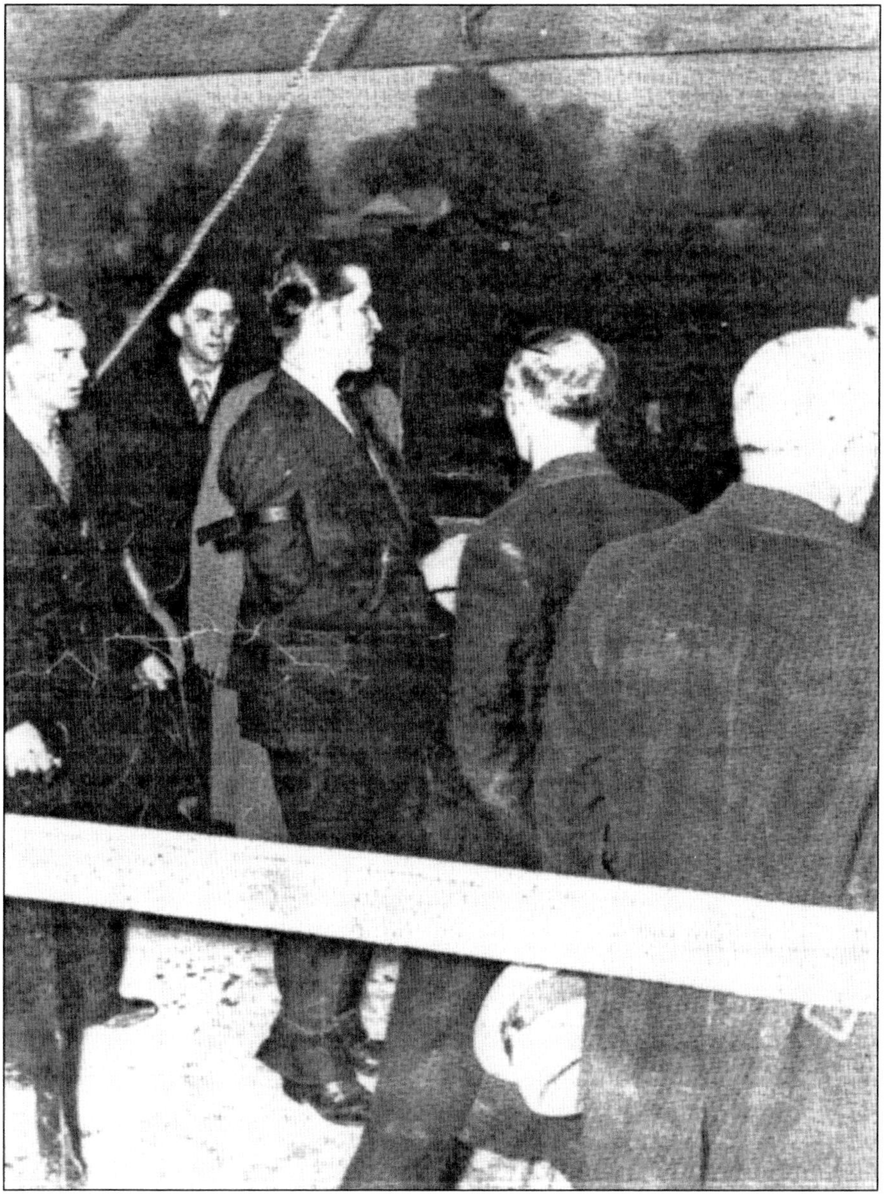

This image shows one of the biggest events in Livingston County history, the hanging of William Deboe on April 19, 1935. Deboe was arrested in June 1934, and a grand jury returned an indictment on two charges of rape and three charges of robbery. More than 200 citizens were interviewed before a jury was selected for the trial. Deboe was found guilty on July 20, 1934, after only five minutes, and the jury ruled that he must die. On April 18, 1935, Gov. Ruby Laffoon said he would not extend executive clemency in any form for Deboe. Sheriff George Heater swore in more than 100 deputies to assist six state policemen to keep order among the large crowd expected. All roads were blocked coming into Smithland, and the gallows were placed in the courtyard in readiness. When guards led Deboe to the scaffold, his sister and father walked behind him. For 45 minutes, Deboe launched an impromptu, scathing attack against the woman whose testimony brought him a death sentence. He declared he was guilty of the robberies but not the rapes. Two doctors pronounced him dead, and his funeral and burial were held in McCracken County.

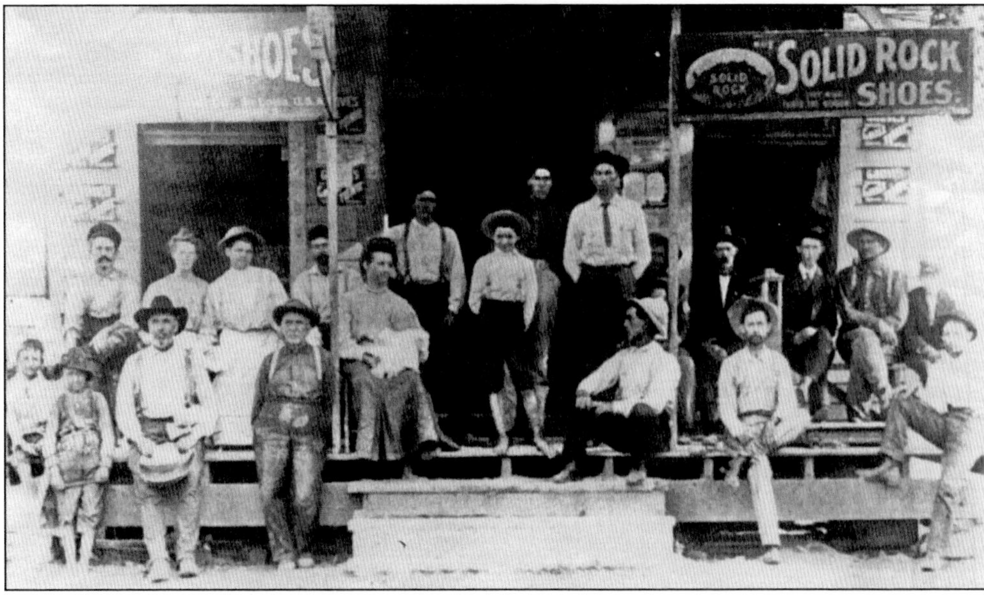

Local residents of Tiline pose for a photograph on the porch of the R. H. Smith General Store in 1910. From left to right are (first row) Jesse Bennett, Frank Smith, B. Paris, John Long, Iva Smith (holding baby Phillip Smith), unidentified, Stoke Thomas, Billy Smith, and Press Cruce; (second row) Tom Smith, Dorene Lee Smith, Fannie Smith, Henry Smith, Corbett Paris, Ollie Paris, R. H. Smith, unidentified, Preacher Bennett, Arch Moreland, W. T. Ward, and Homer Smith. (Courtesy of Livingston County Historical Society.)

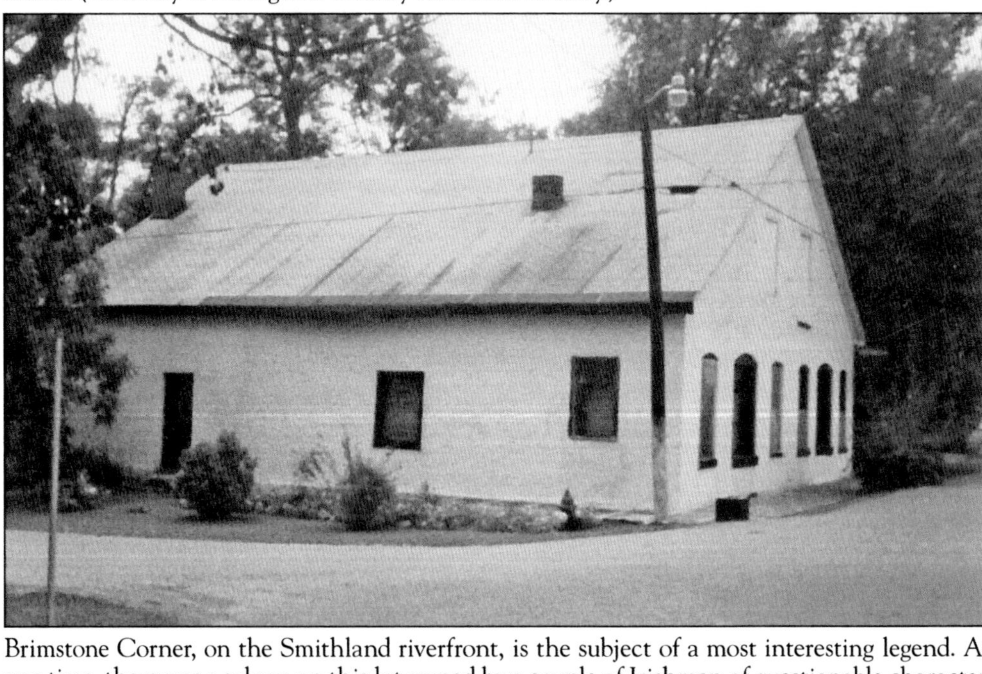
Brimstone Corner, on the Smithland riverfront, is the subject of a most interesting legend. At one time, there was a saloon on this lot owned by a couple of Irishmen of questionable character. When a stranger came in, his drink was drugged, and he was robbed, murdered, and dropped through a trapdoor into a tunnel. Then an unknown doctor dissected his body in the name of science, and the remains were taken by skiff to a nearby island for burial.

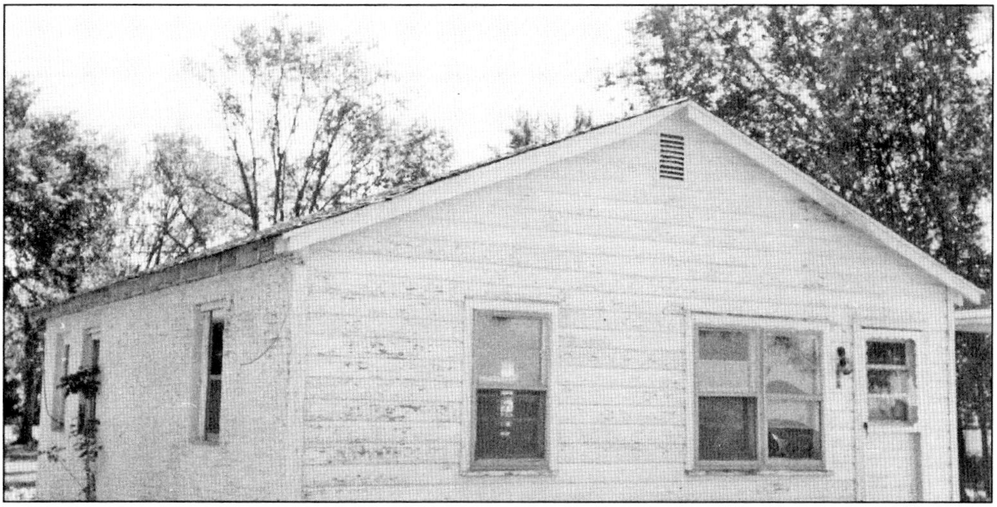

The Brandstetter house sat on the riverfront in Smithland and was bought in 1857 by Isadore Brandstetter, who was a gunsmith and shoemaker from Germany. The Brandstetter descendants also operated a tavern on the riverfront. Some of their buildings were lost in the 1937 flood, and part of the building shown was destroyed by fire.

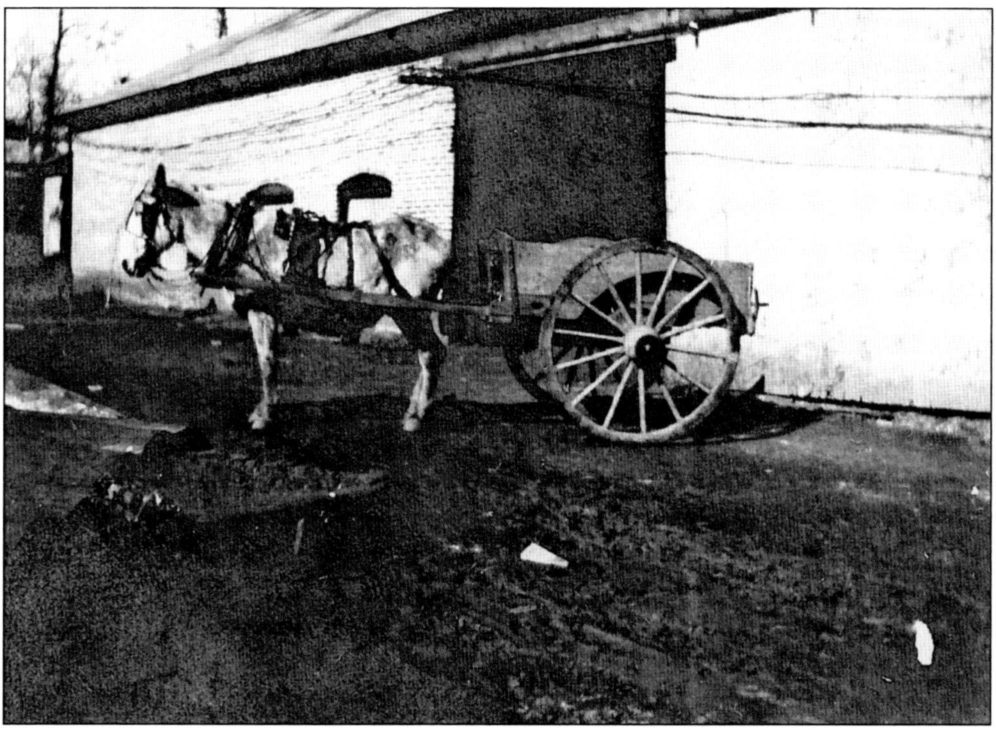

This quaint old photograph has written on the back, " 'old Gray' Colliery 'C' at West Kentucky Coal Company, 3-06." The history of Grand Rivers shows that the West Kentucky Coal Company was there during the time period of 1906. Therefore, old Gray was probably there working hard. (Courtesy of Livingston County Historical Society.)

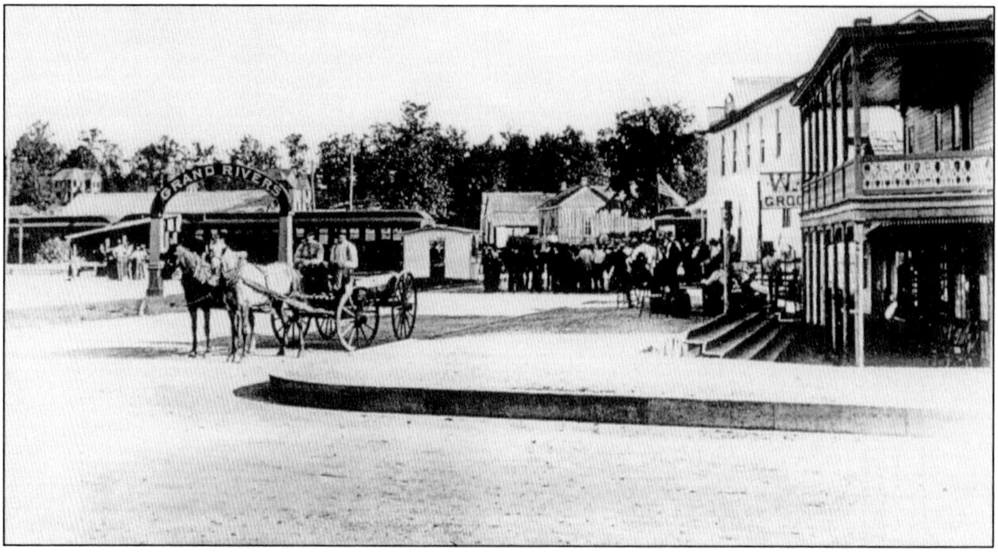

Pictured is a view of Grand Rivers at the intersection of Dover Road and Cumberland Avenue in the 1880s. As is shown, the citizens took great pride in their town. Grand Rivers offers vacationers a trip into the past with antique decor and serious shopping at the many unique specialty shops. (Courtesy of Livingston County Historical Society.)

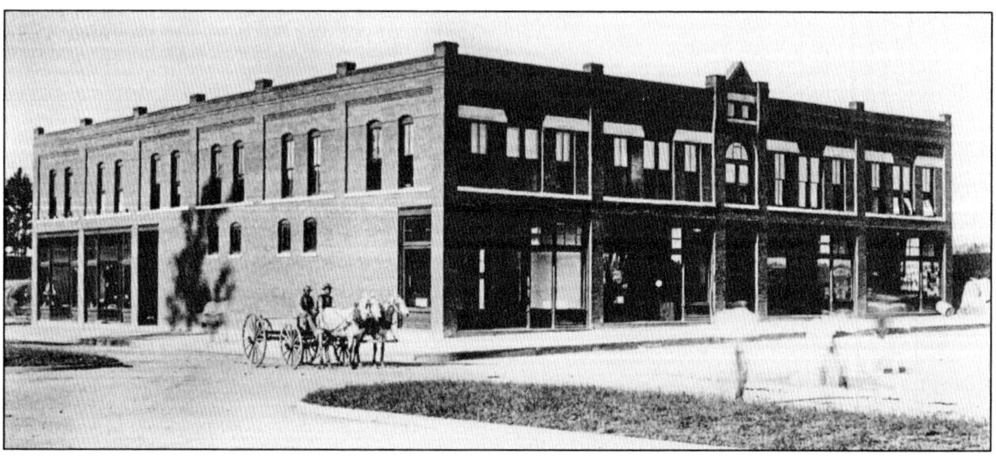

Located at the corner of Dover Road and Cumberland Avenue in Grand Rivers, this facility was known as the Boston Block. It covered a city block and had 28 rooms upstairs and six downstairs, used mostly for business purposes. It burned in 1944, and the Iron Kettle Restaurant was built on a section of that city block. (Courtesy of Livingston County Historical Society.)

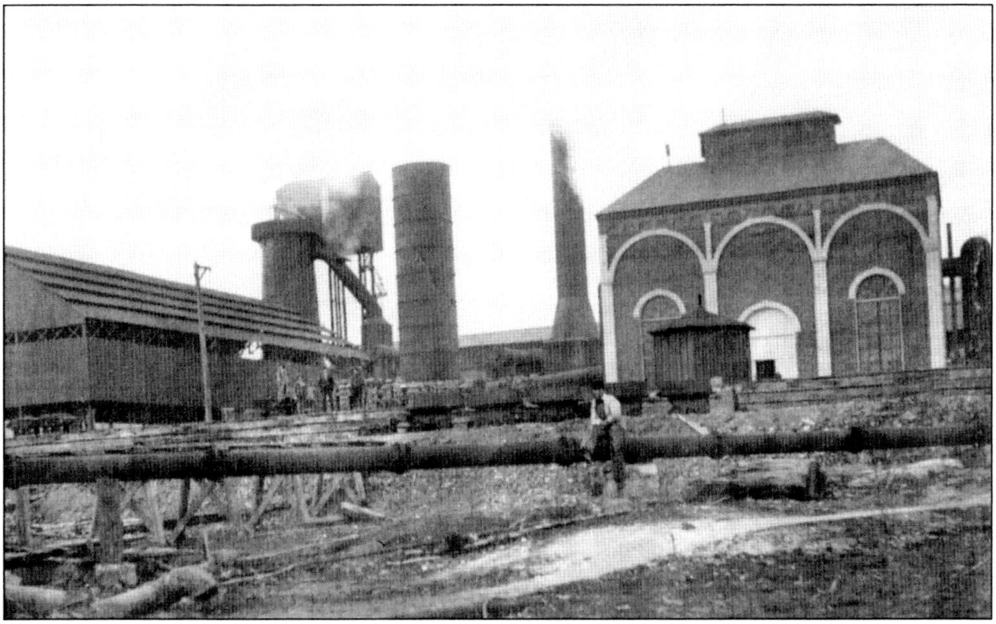

This photograph was made in 1902 of the foundry/furnace that was to be joined by railroad to a major line. It was sent to the historical society by Bob McCloy from Pennsylvania and was taken by his grandparents, William and Lucy McCloy. William worked as a surveyor and construction engineer for the railroad in Grand Rivers. (Courtesy of Livingston County Historical Society.)

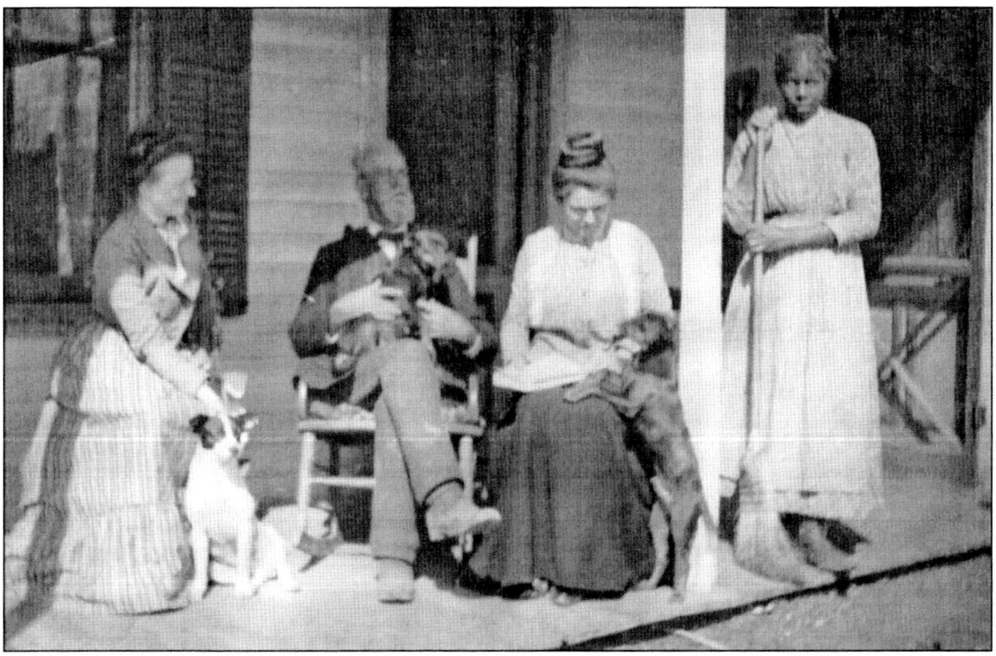

This photograph was sent to the historical society by Bob McCloy. It was taken when his grandparents lived in Grand Rivers in 1902. From left to right are Lucy McCloy, ? Ferriman and his wife, and hired girl Osie. The McCloy family boarded with the Ferriman family while William McCloy worked as a surveyor and engineer for the railroad. (Courtesy of Livingston County Historical Society.)

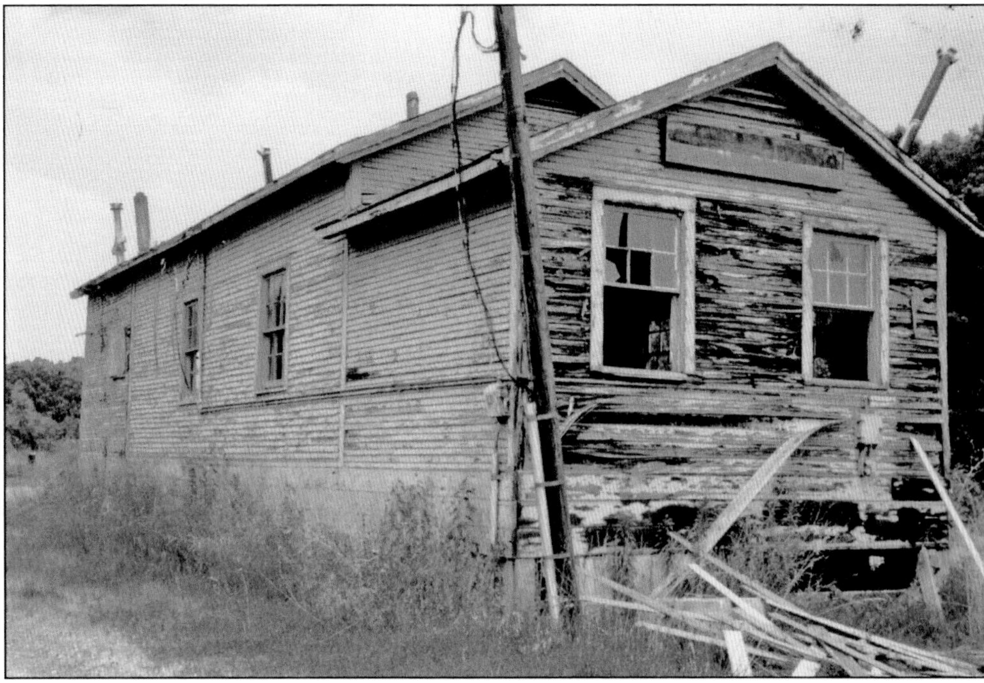

The old Grand Rivers Depot is pictured in 1991. As early as 1850, there were permanent residents in the area between the rivers, then known as "the Narrows," where the Cumberland and Tennessee Rivers nearly converge and where Grand Rivers stands today. The railroad offered a connection to the outside world and brought prosperity to the community.

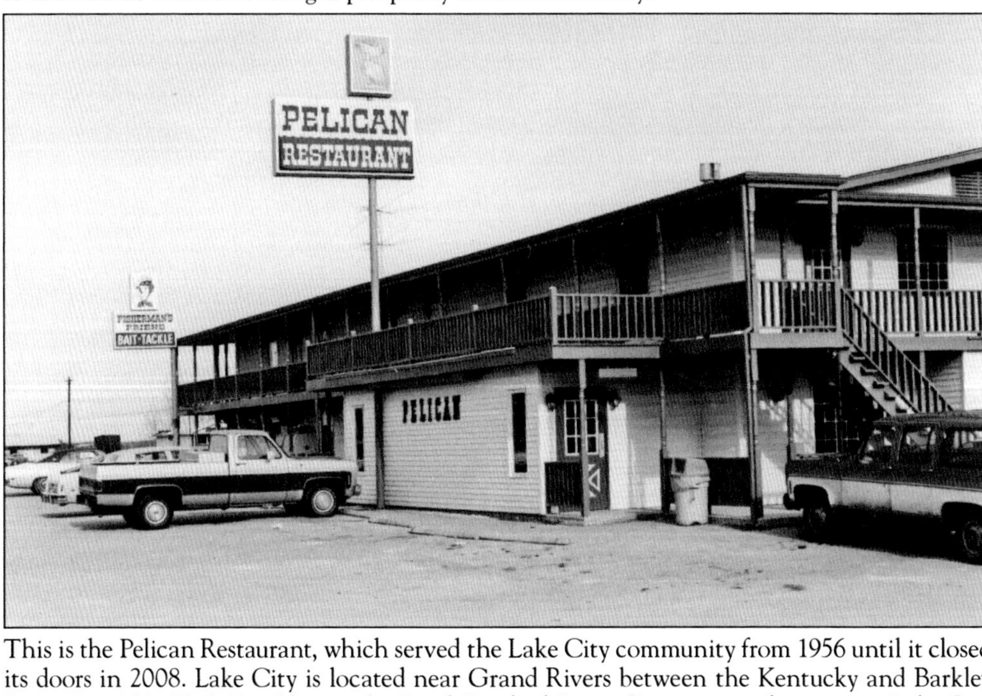

This is the Pelican Restaurant, which served the Lake City community from 1956 until it closed its doors in 2008. Lake City is located near Grand Rivers between the Kentucky and Barkley Dams. In 1950, Clyde Reed began the Reed Crushed Stone Company, and as it grew, Lake City prospered. (Courtesy of Livingston County Historical Society.)

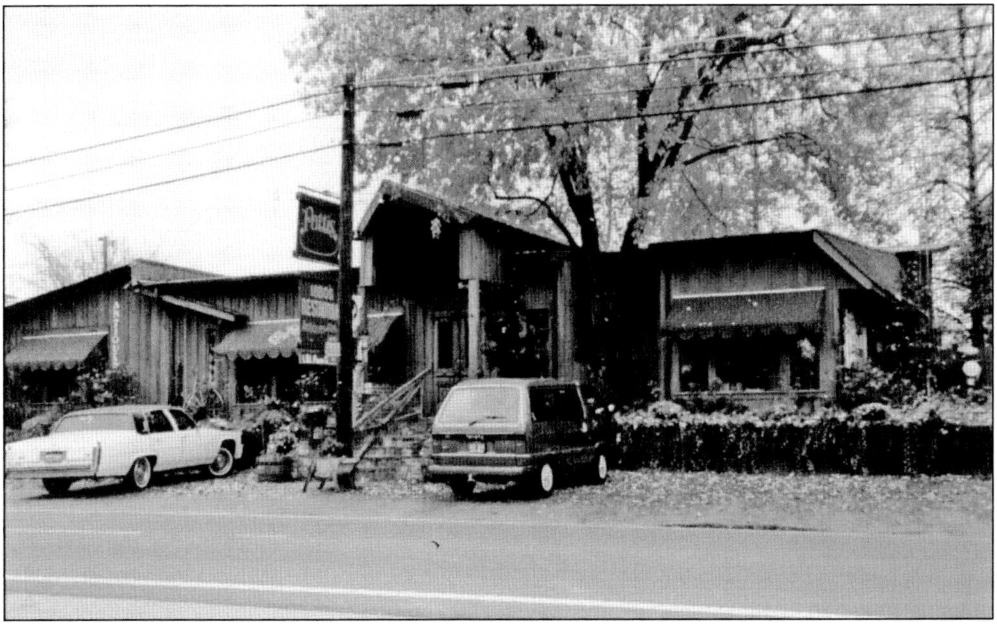

Patti's 1880s Restaurant in Grand Rivers has changed considerably since this 1986 photograph. This restaurant evolved from Patti's Ice Cream Parlor, which started in 1977 with 20 seats. Bill and Patti Tullar moved from Florida with their sons and have done their part to re-create the history of the area. Bill's Restaurant was built behind Patti's, allowing for a seating capacity of several hundred when their menus and buildings were later combined.

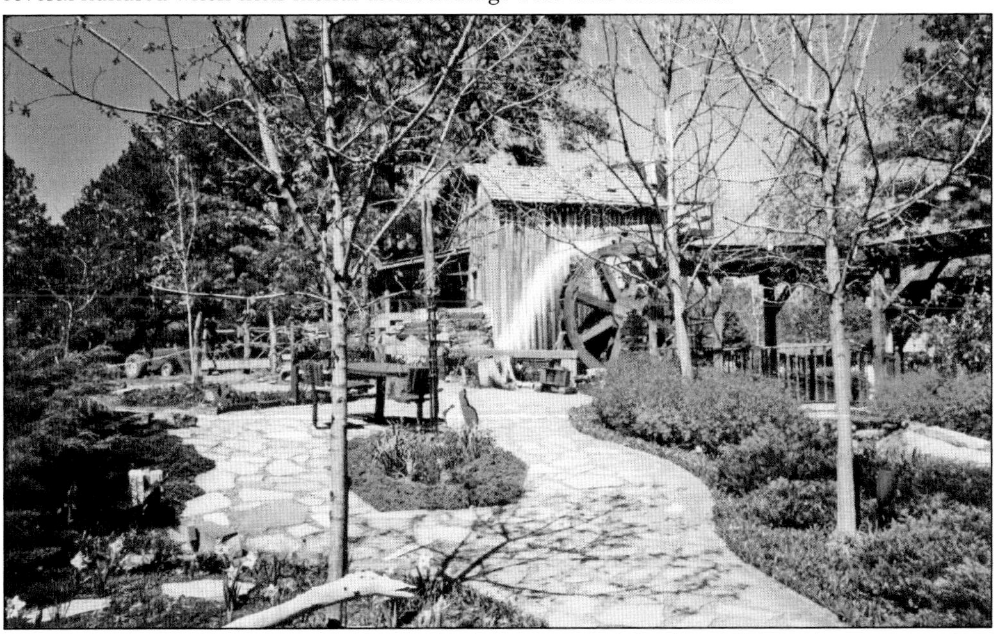

Taken in 1998, this photograph shows the beginnings of the beautiful gardens surrounding Patti's 1880s Restaurant. An outside dining area was added in 2008. All the house specialties offered inside, such as the 2-inch-thick pork chops, mile-high meringue pies, flowerpot bread, and whipped strawberry butter, are also served on the patio. The festival of lights, featured during the Christmas holidays, makes this garden a winter wonderland.

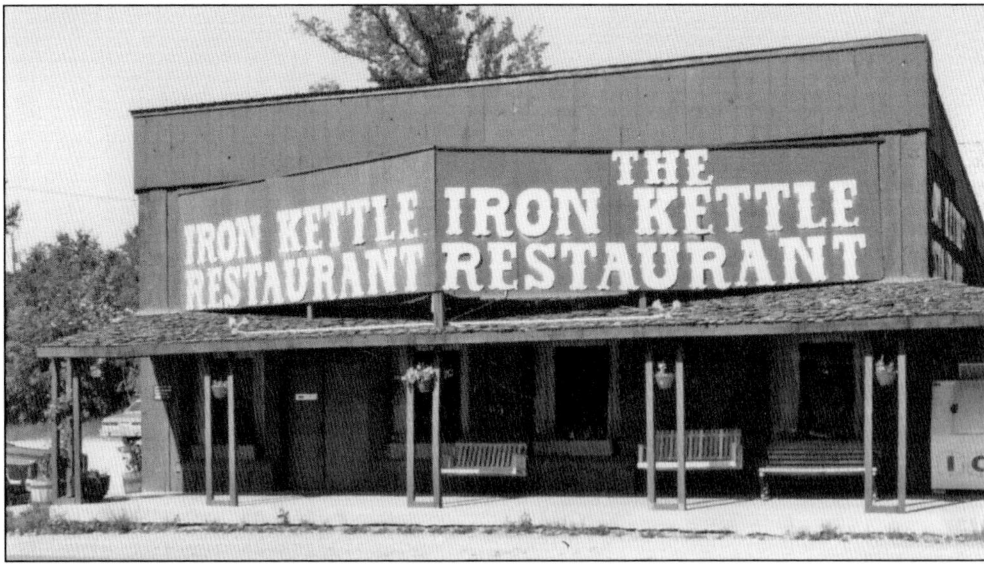

Until fire destroyed it in the spring of 2008, the Iron Kettle Restaurant was located at one end of what was once the Boston Block in Grand Rivers. It offered a pleasant family-type atmosphere where customers could fill their plates from the old-fashioned, cast-iron stoves as many times as they liked. This restaurant was also owned by the Tullar family, and they plan to rebuild it. (Courtesy of Livingston County Historical Society.)

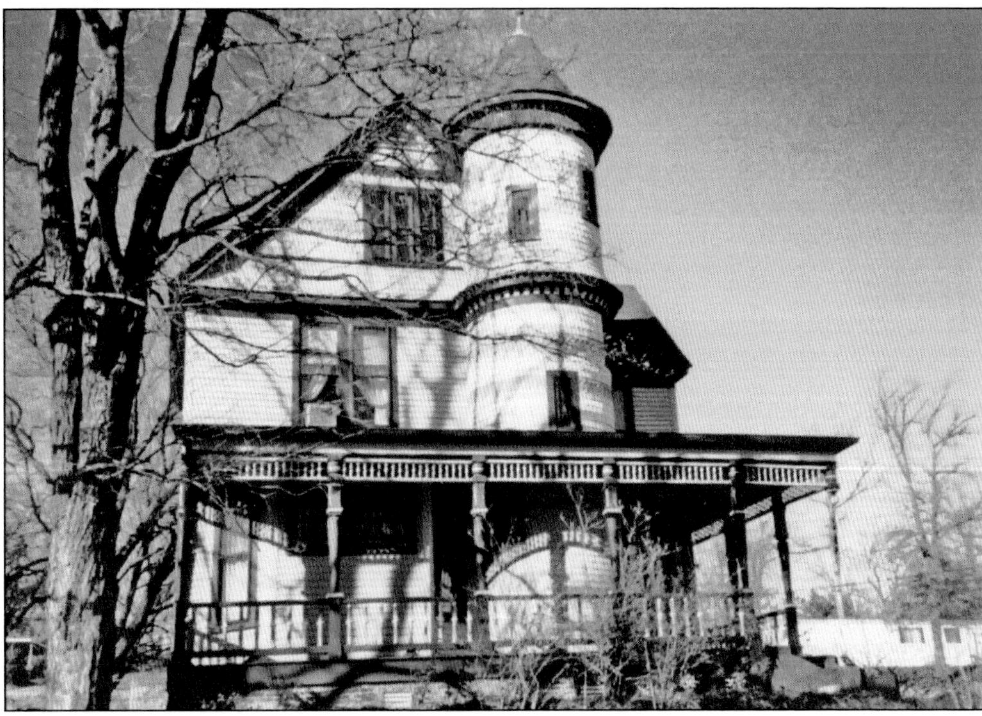

On the National Register of Historic Places, this heritage home has a Queen Anne architectural style. Thomas Lawson, a millionaire from Massachusetts, came to a new town called Grand Rivers (formerly called Nickell Station) in 1890 and built this beautiful house. The Tullar family owns it now and keeps it well maintained.

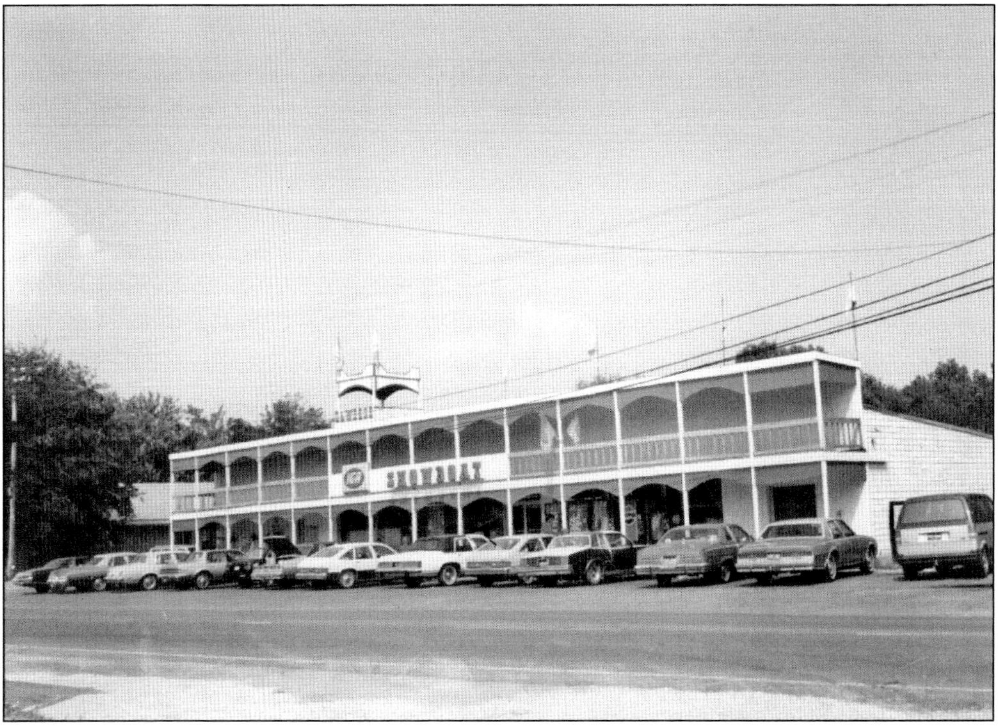

This photograph shows the DeWeese IGA in Grand Rivers as it looked for more than 20 years. J. L. and Nelda Dunkerson DeWeese and several other citizens of Grand Rivers traveled on a tour to Georgia around 1970. The group decided to make their town resemble showboat times. This resulted in the DeWeeses' store being transformed, with "SHOWBOAT" painted on with the help of local kids. A new store was built in the 1990s called Jeff and Emily IGA, and it is still owned by the DeWeese family.

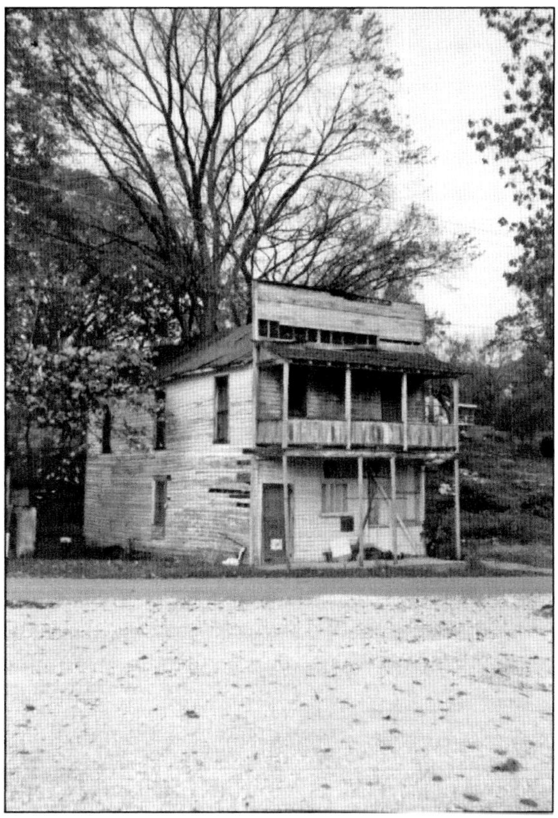

This old post office in Grand Rivers served its patrons for many years. In the 1700s, people began to move westward. People of Scottish, Irish, and German ancestry established farms and settlements in the land that became known as "between the rivers." This community first became known as Nickell Station, named after a prominent local family given a Revolutionary War land grant in the area.

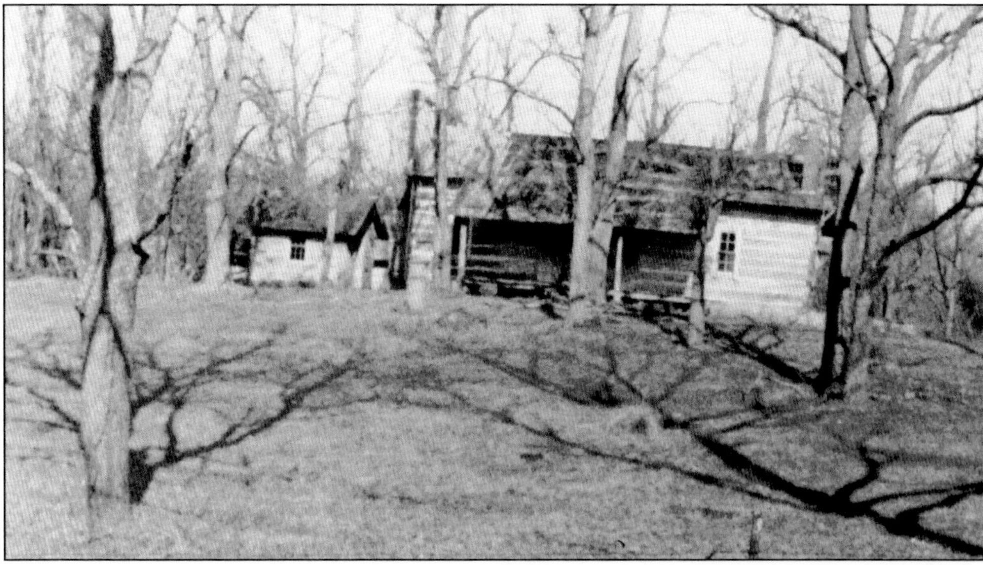

Taken in the 1940s, this photograph shows the Wallace log house. Originally, the house was on the Bond Farm on Highway 133 near the 137 junction between Joy and Lola. The log house was moved behind the Days Past Antique on J. H. O'Bryan Avenue in Grand Rivers.

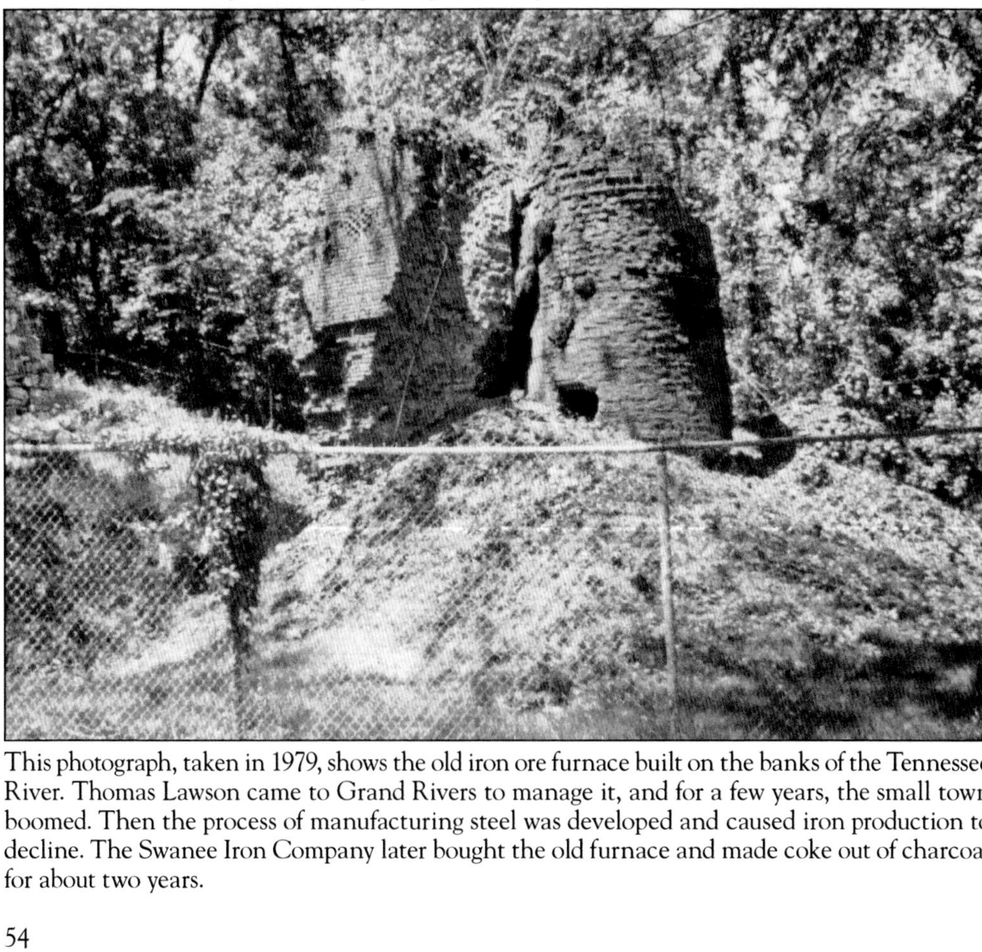

This photograph, taken in 1979, shows the old iron ore furnace built on the banks of the Tennessee River. Thomas Lawson came to Grand Rivers to manage it, and for a few years, the small town boomed. Then the process of manufacturing steel was developed and caused iron production to decline. The Swanee Iron Company later bought the old furnace and made coke out of charcoal for about two years.

Four

North Livingston County

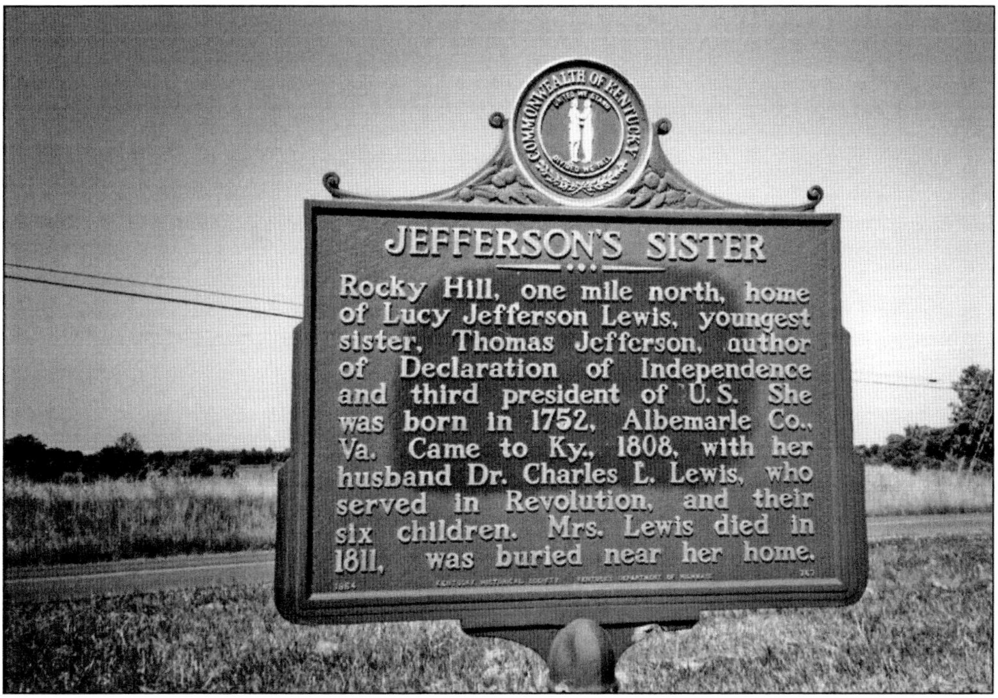

As the sign states, Lucy Jefferson Lewis, sister of U.S. president Thomas Jefferson, lived near the town of Birdsville on Rocky Hill. Her husband, Col. Charles L. Lewis, was a Revolutionary War hero, and his brother was Meriwether Lewis, a pioneer explorer. The Lewis family came to Kentucky from Virginia in 1806. Lucy Lewis died in 1811 and is buried near her home.

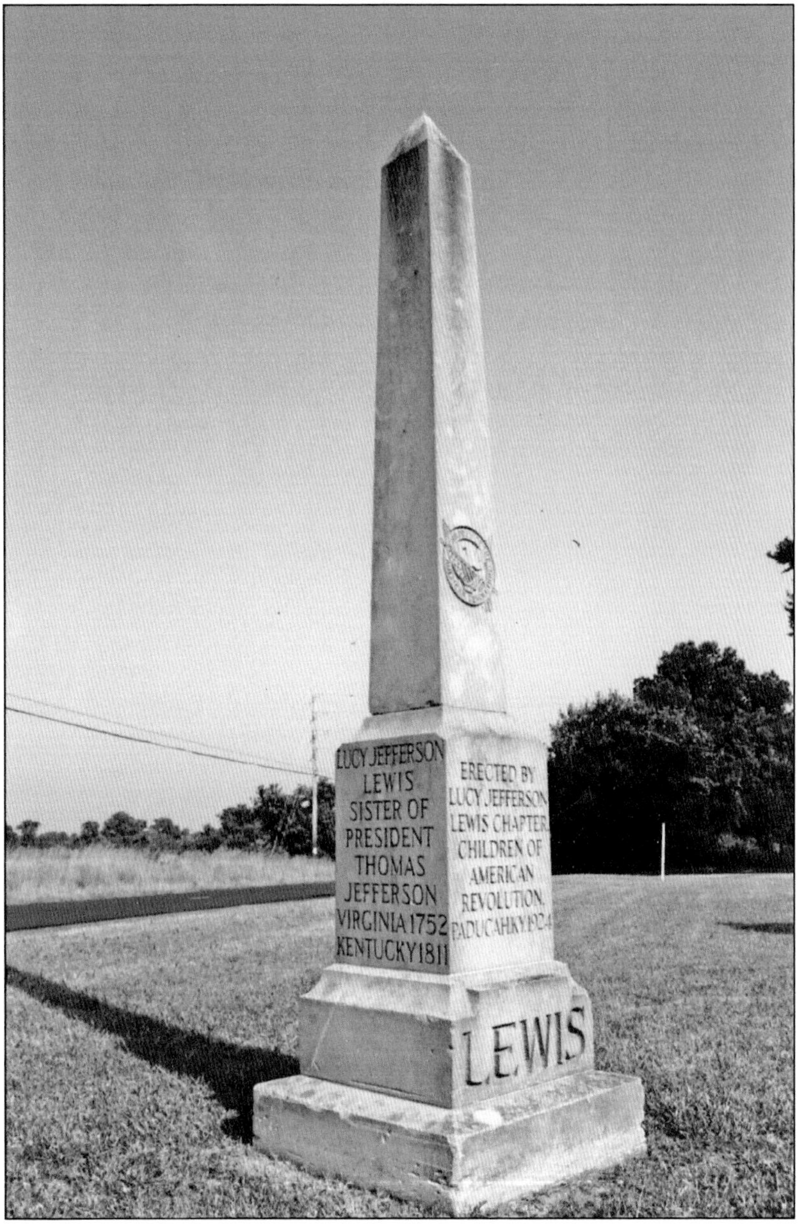

This monument erected by the Daughters of the American Revolution in honor of Lucy Jefferson Lewis is at the junction of Highways 60 and 137. The bridge over the Cumberland River in Smithland is also named for her. Two of Lucy's sons, Lilburne and Isham, played a prominent role in the plans for the town of Westwood, which was built on the point across from Smithland. But they were known for their drunken sprees, and in 1811, they brutally murdered a slave for breaking a pitcher. They dismembered the body with an axe and burned it in the fireplace, hoping to eliminate the evidence. While the slave's body parts were burning, the first shocks of the famous earthquake of 1811 were felt, and the chimney collapsed. A few months later, a passerby saw a dog chewing on a head and reported it to the law. A jury presented a true bill for Lilburne and Isham, but they were released on bond. Lilburne accidentally killed himself, and it scared Isham so much that he later escaped jail and disappeared completely.

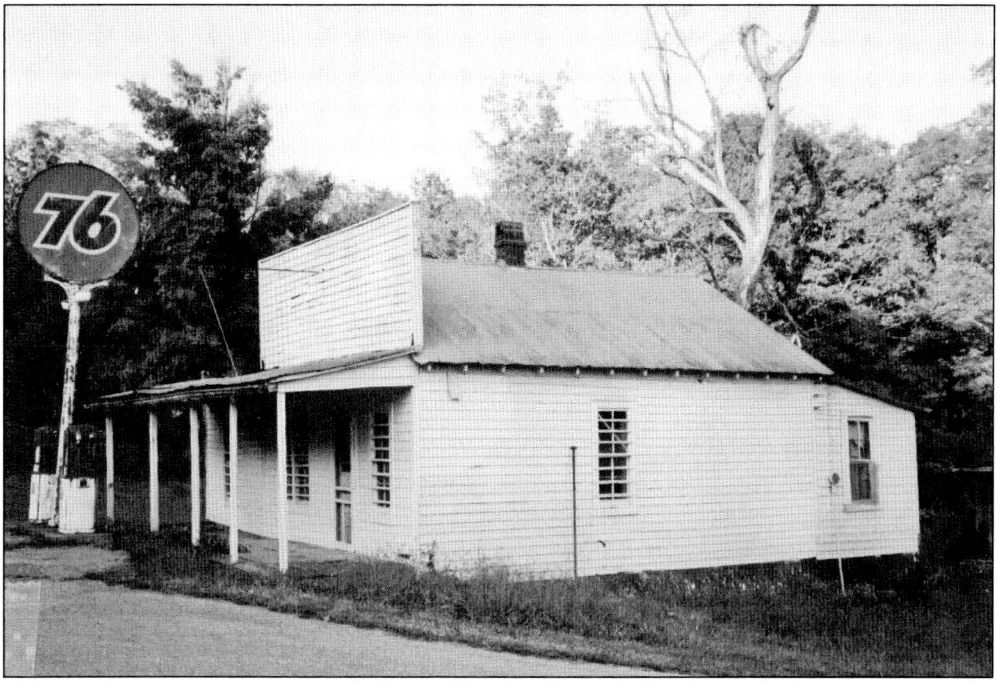

Uncle Bud Loyd's Store in the Dyer Hill community, near Burna, was the place to visit and trade from the 1930s through 1955. A bologna sandwich and soda drink could be bought for 5¢ each. Uncle Bud died in 1955, and his son, Freeman, kept the store until his death in 1971. The store now stands empty, but fond memories remain.

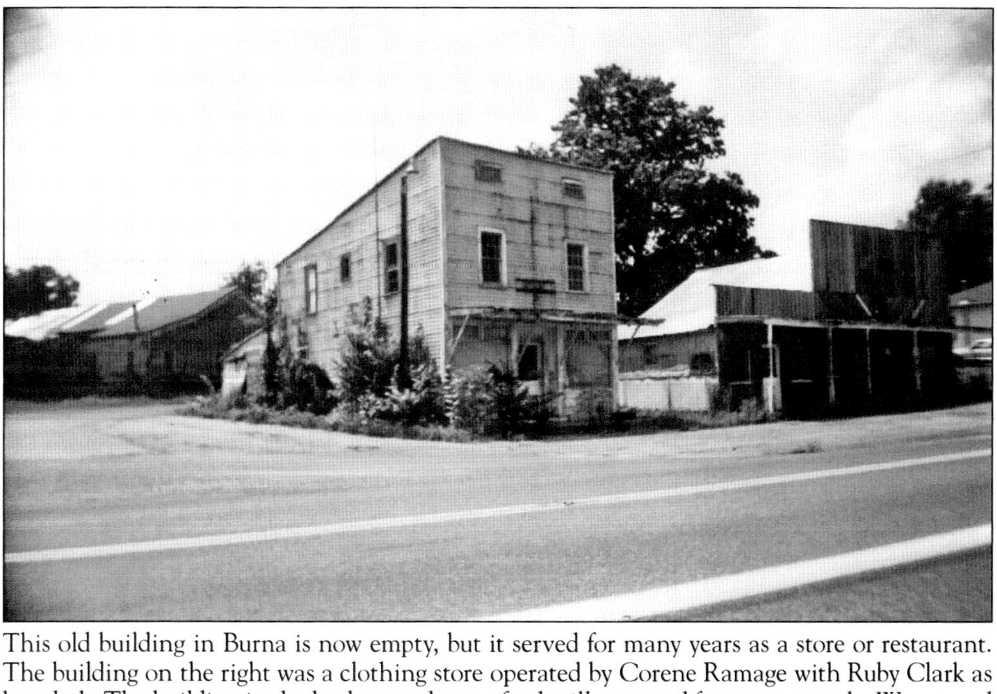

This old building in Burna is now empty, but it served for many years as a store or restaurant. The building on the right was a clothing store operated by Corene Ramage with Ruby Clark as her clerk. The building in the background was a feed mill operated for many years by Wayne and Mildred LeVan.

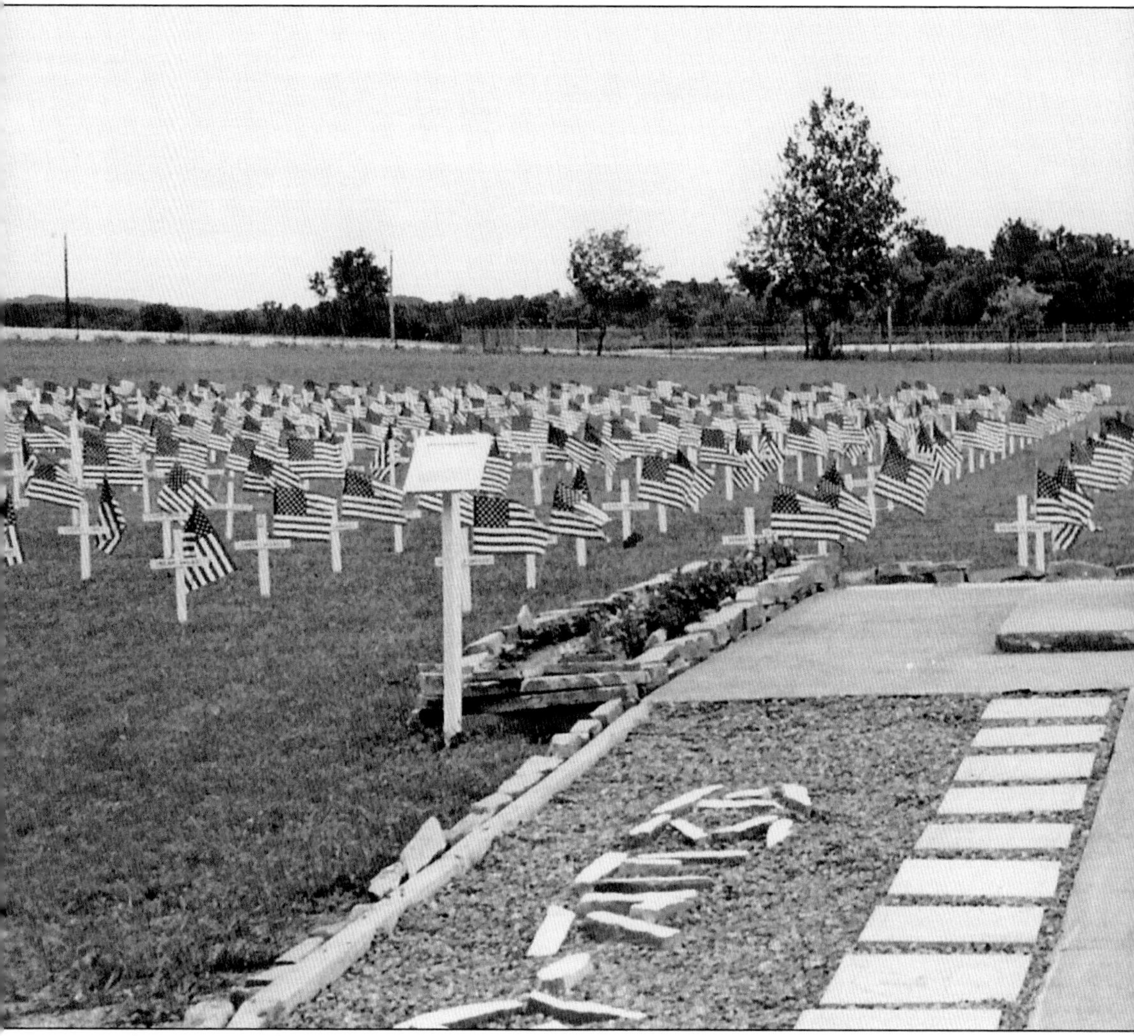

The Logan E. Clark American Legion Post 217, near Burna, displays these crosses for their garden of memories each year on Memorial Day. Each white wooden cross has the name of a Livingston County service man or woman who has served his or her country and died since World War I, whether killed in action or dead of natural causes. There is always a guest speaker on Memorial

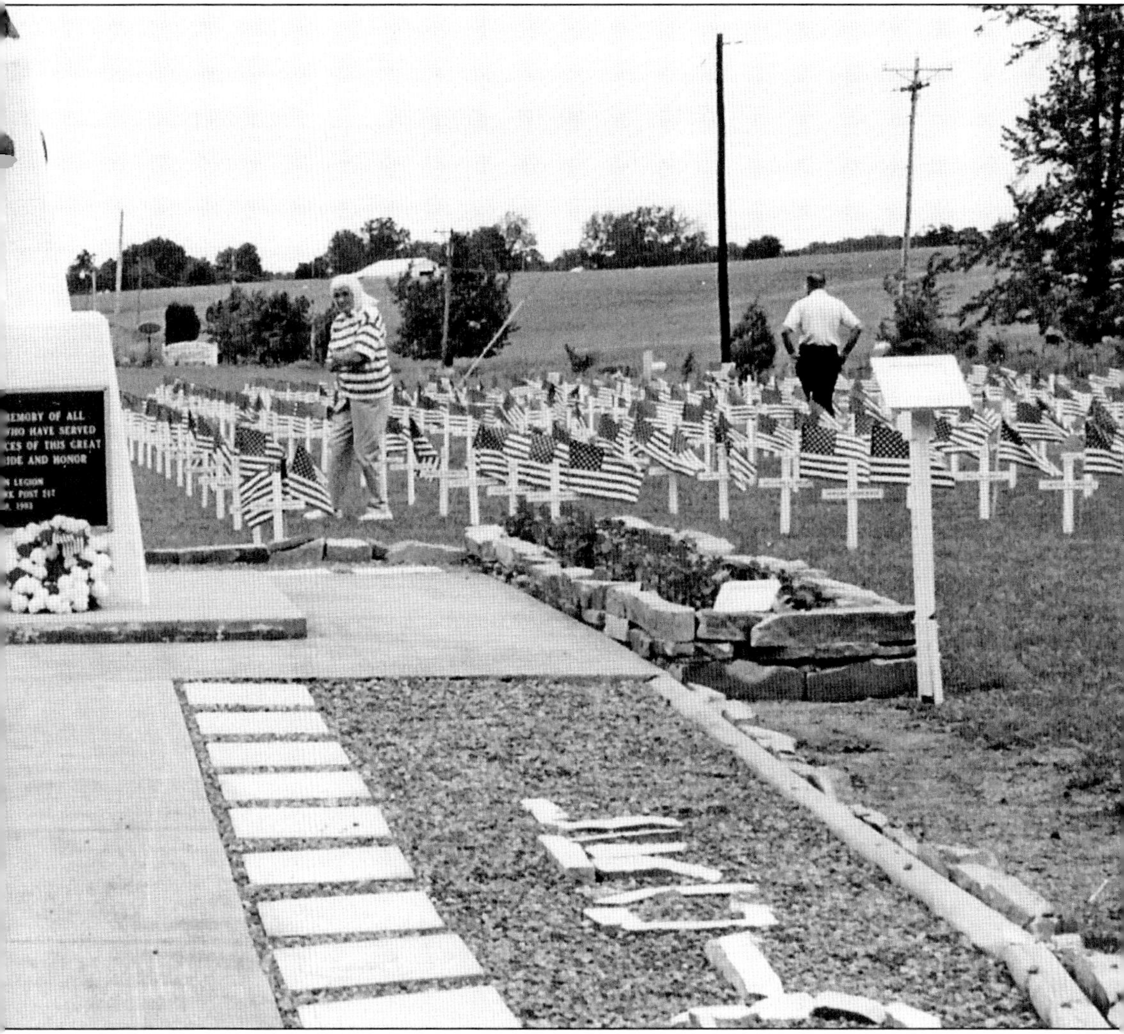

Day, and the field beside Post 217 is in perfect order, adding new crosses each year since 1939. In 2008, there were around 1,800 crosses and flags in the magnificent and informative display. Veterans should be thanked often for their service to their country, which ensures freedom on a daily basis.

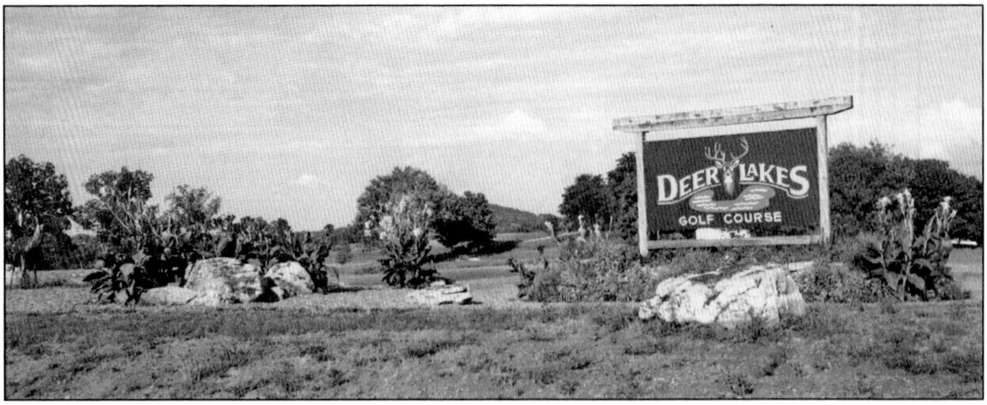

The photograph above shows the entrance to Deer Lakes Golf Course in Salem. The course is owned by George Malcolm. The photograph below shows a historic old bridge that was installed in 1898 over Sandy Creek on the old Lola–Salem Road. This road was often called the Golconda Road because it was a part of the Dover, Tennessee–Golconda, Illinois, stagecoach line. The bridge was moved to the nearby Deer Lakes Golf Course in 2000 and was narrowed down for a walking bridge. Historian Hazel Robertson suggested this, and the community was receptive to the idea.

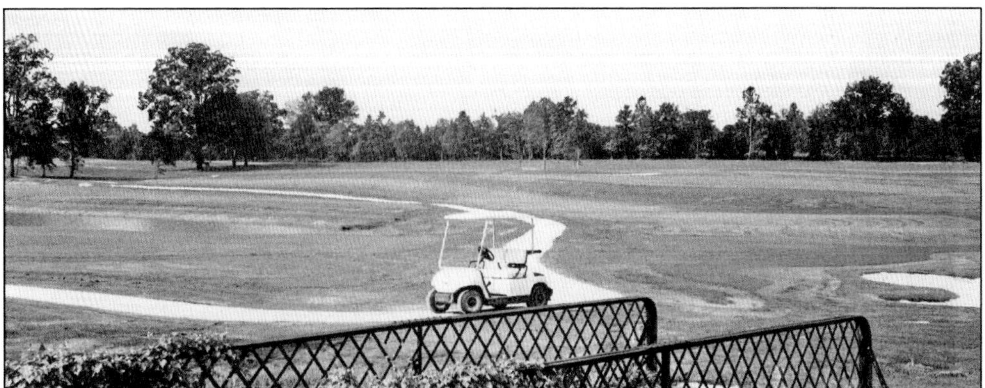

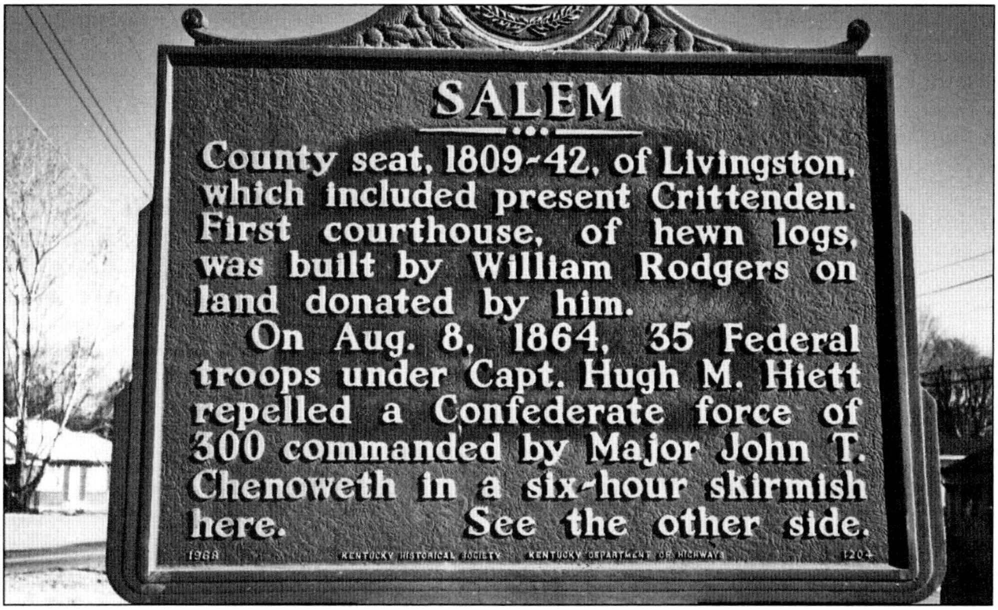

As one enters Salem on Highway 60, this sign tells of the years 1809 to 1842, when the county seat was located there. Settlers from Virginia, the Carolinas, Tennessee, and eastern Kentucky came to this beautiful valley to establish homes by the early 1800s. The courthouse was the setting for the Lewis brothers' trial. Slave auctions, especially of runaways, were common at the courthouse door.

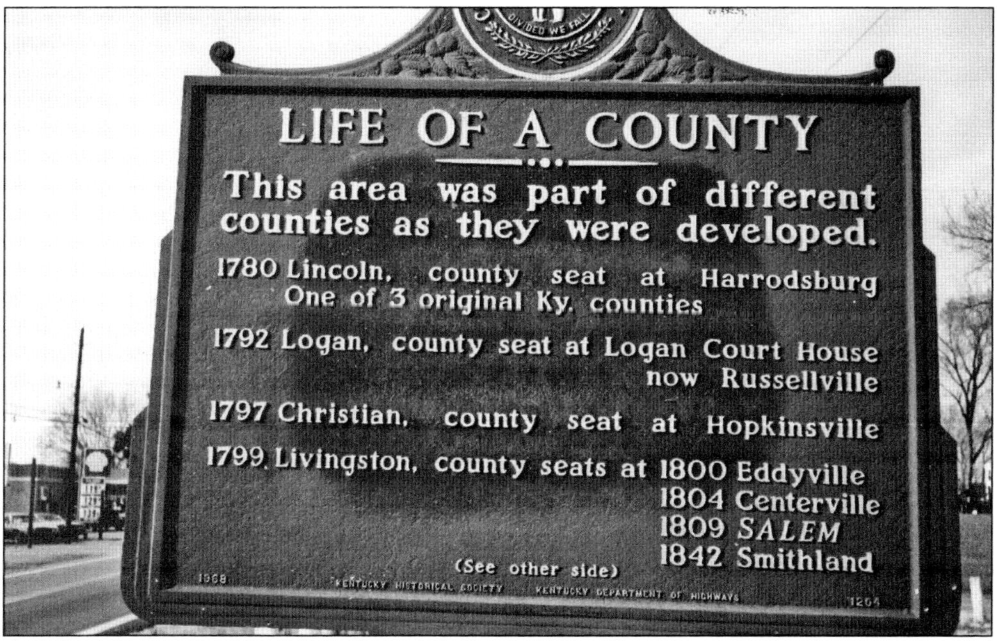

This is the back of the sign pictured above. Kentucky County, Virginia, was divided into three counties in 1780: Jefferson, Fayette, and Lincoln. After the Revolutionary War, Kentuckians turned their thoughts toward statehood. Many conventions were held in Danville to consider the separation of Kentucky from Virginia. On January 1, 1792, Kentucky became the 15th state of the Union, and this portion of the state developed, as the sign implies.

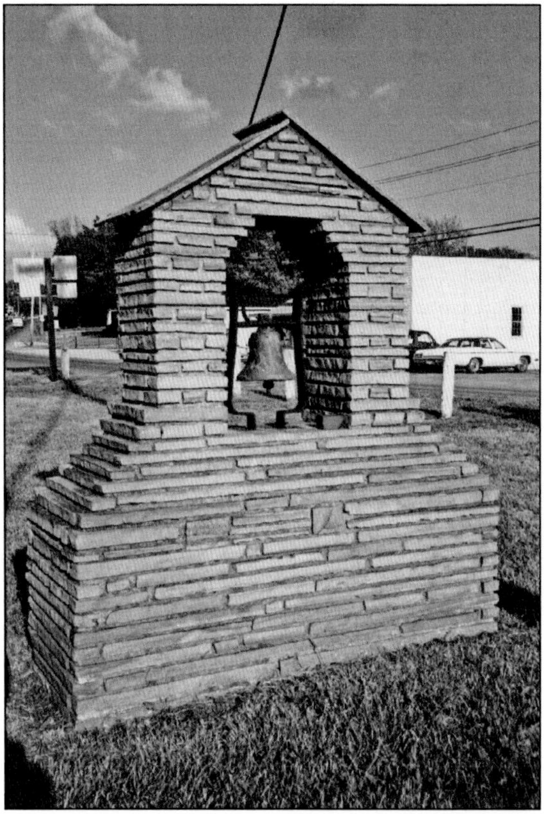

Travelers through Salem will see this old courthouse bell in the Y at the junction of Highways 133 and 60. The bell came from the Salem Courthouse, built in 1810. During the Civil War, the courthouse was occupied by the Union army. One day, the rebels found the courthouse unguarded and started to burn it, but the people begged them not to. The rebels let them tear it down instead.

Methodists have been in the area from the early years of the 19th century, but they were usually organized into societies rather than churches. The Salem Methodist Episcopal Church, South, was organized in 1889, and services were held in the Union Church. A new church was built in 1955, and in 1968, the church united with the Evangelic United Brethren Church, thus changing the name to the Salem United Methodist Church.

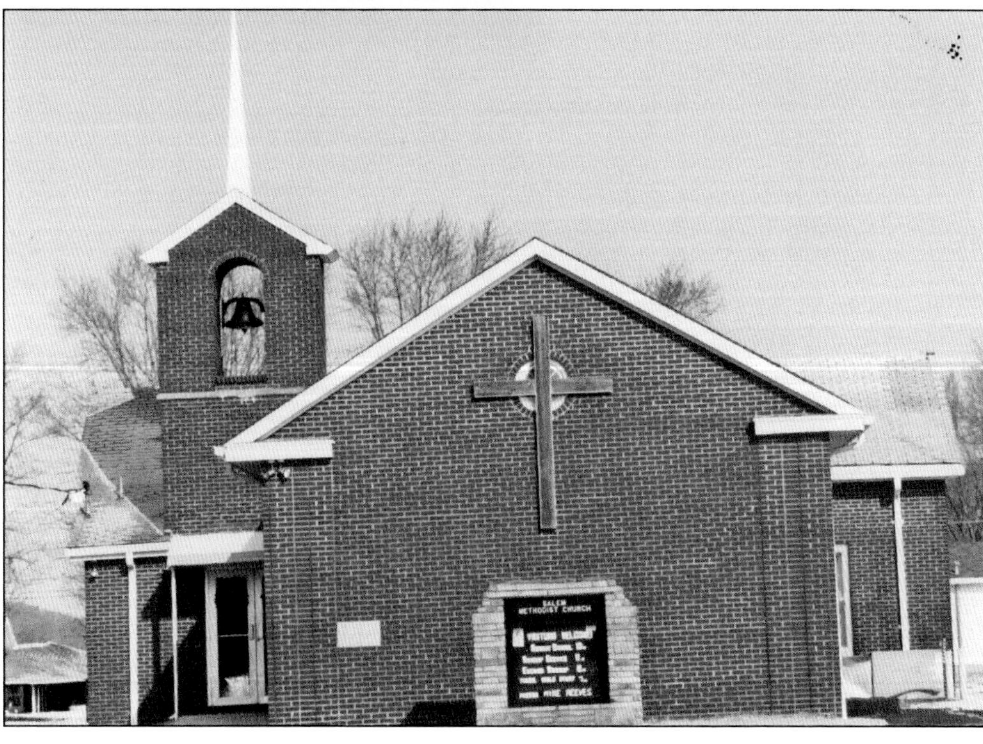

The Salem Baptist Church was built in 1910 from hand-molded blocks on the ground. They church members had been meeting at the Union Church until land was donated by Duke Roney and Fleeta Barnes. Additions to both the sanctuary and the educational facilities were made in 1932, 1948, 1953, and 1960. This church was torn down in 1979 after a new church was built in 1975.

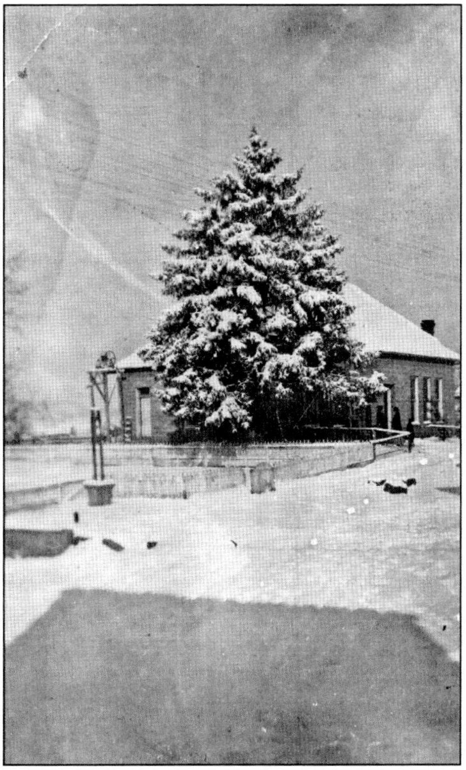

The current Salem Baptist Church was built in 1975, after adjoining property was purchased from the Wright McDaniel family. The church has had five parsonages. The present one stands on property acquired from the Harry Martin family. An antebellum home formerly used as the parsonage was torn down to make room for the new home.

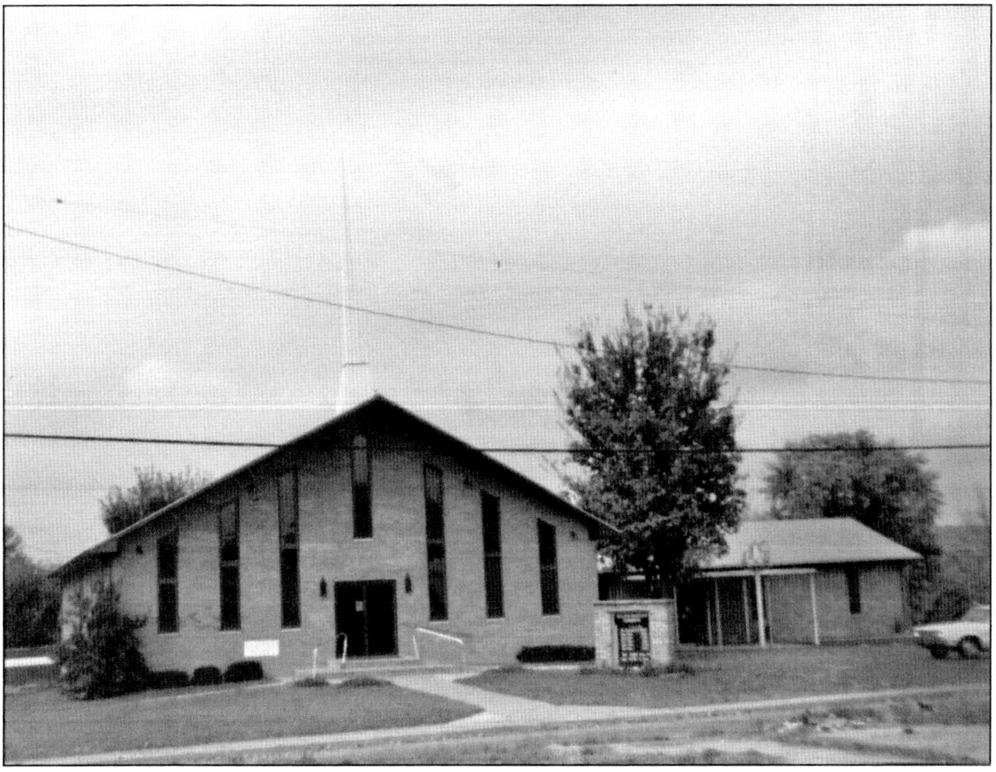

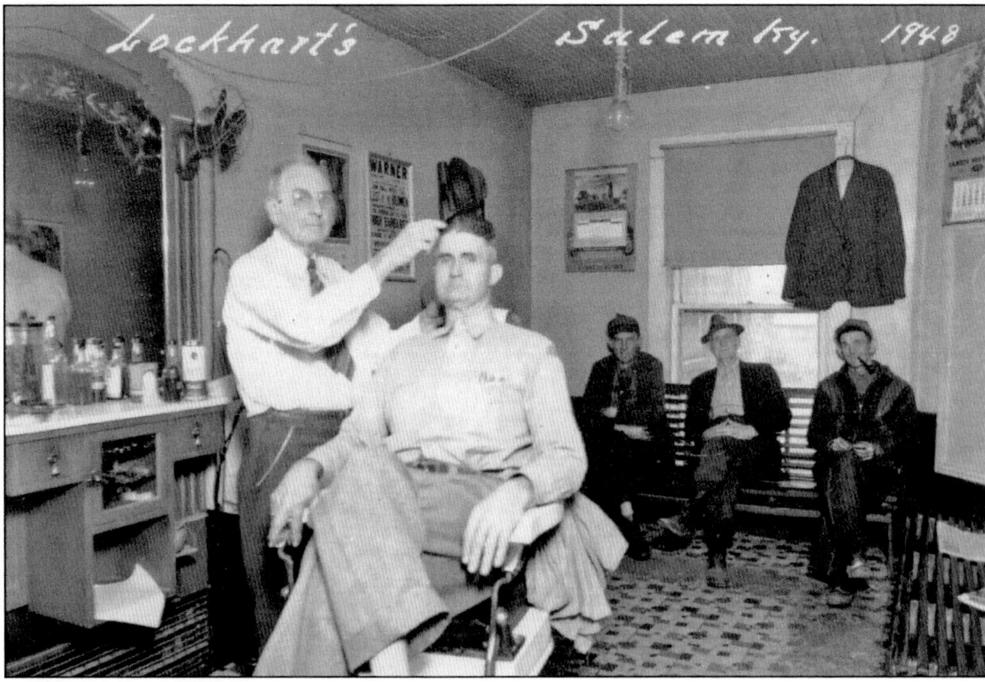

This 1948 photograph of the Lockhart Barber Shop shows William T. George in the chair and barber Perce Lockhart. In the background, seated from left to right, are Carl Waddell, Cleve Linley, and Bill Null. The shop was on Highway 60 in Salem.

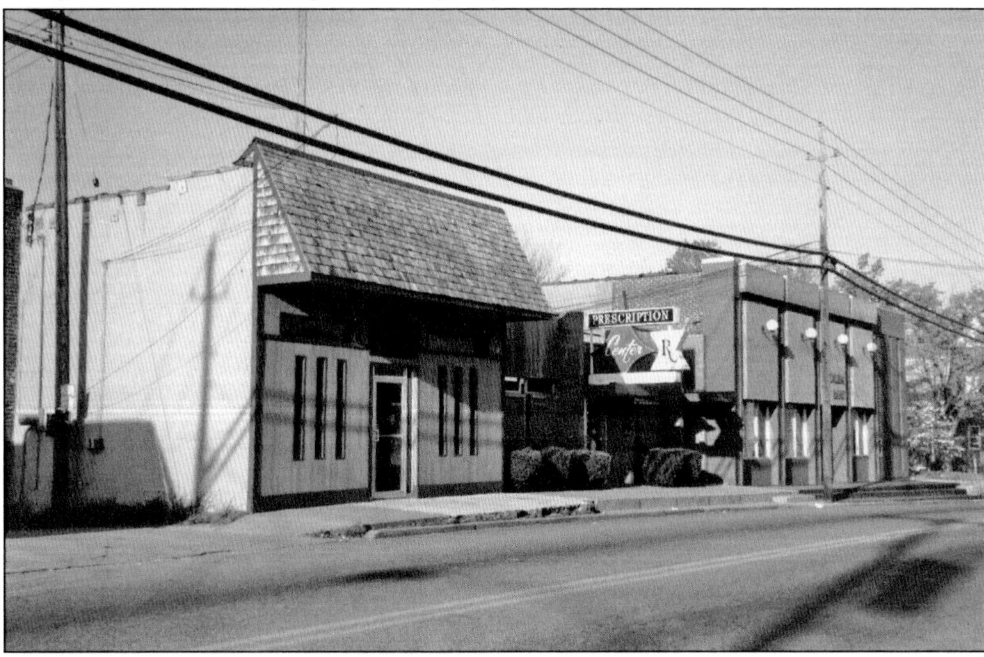

The building on the far right is the Salem Bank as it was in 1987. The Salem Bank incorporated in 1902, and the new building was constructed in 1924. In 1958, the Smithland Bank was merged with the Salem Bank. It is called Regions Bank now. The building on the left is the Prescription Center, which was built in 1965 and is operated by Norris Glenn.

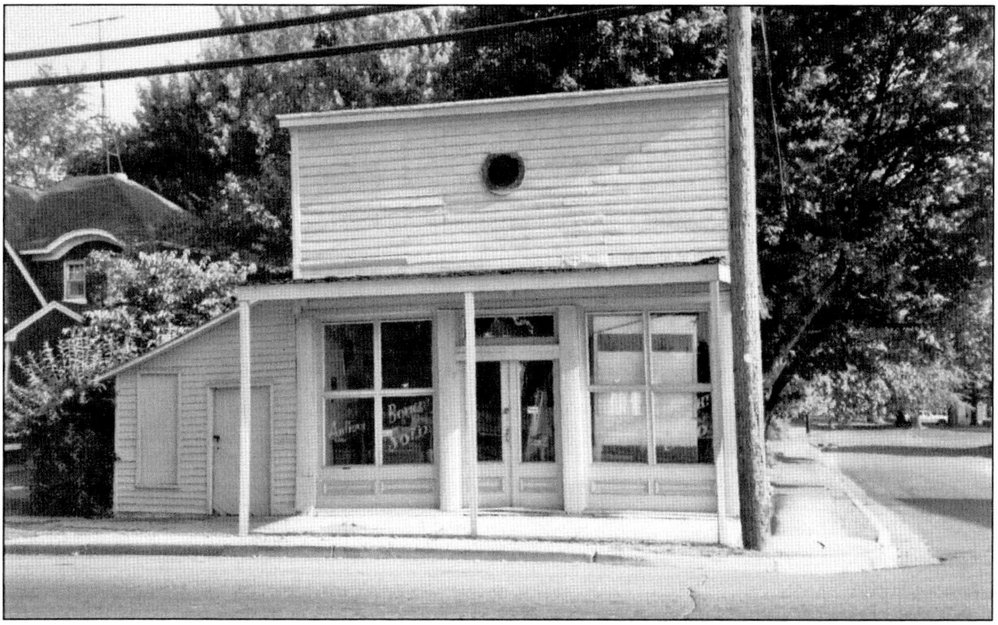

The old Boyd Building is shown in this 1991 photograph. Bob Boyd had a store here for a number of years around the beginning of the 20th century. He sold caskets among a collection of general merchandise. Other businesses were a light plant supplying limited electricity for the town by dynamo, a cleaning establishment, and Jim LaRue's antique store. The building was destroyed by fire sometime after 2000.

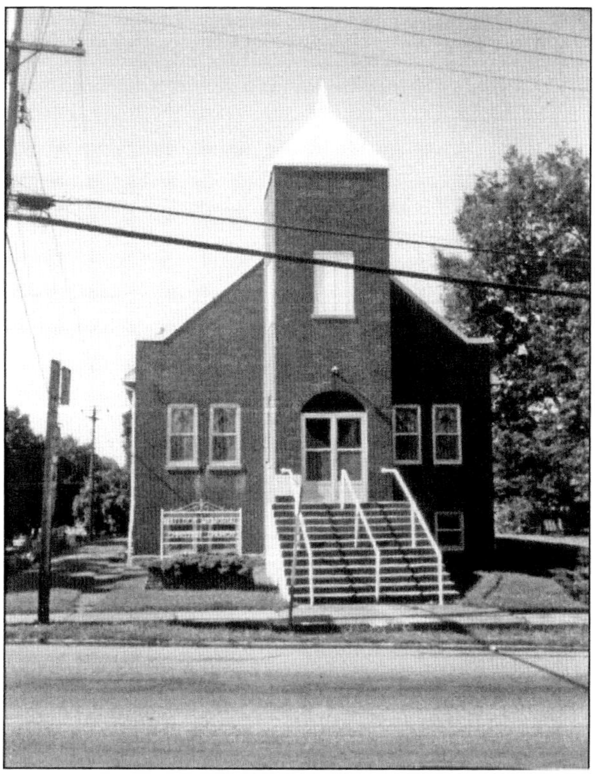

The Salem Christian Church was organized by the Shelby family, and other original members were Farris, Grassham, Matlock, and Hayden. From 1889 to 1941, the members met in the old Union Church. A new church was completed in 1941 on Highway 60. The sign outside this building now reads the Miracle Word Church.

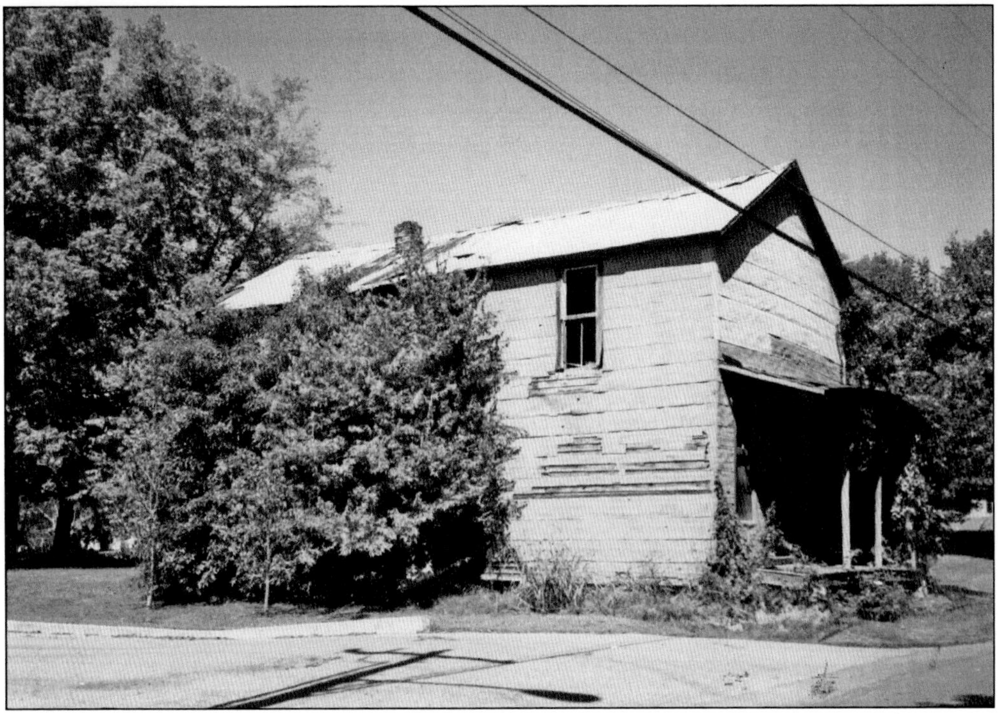

The old Salem Masonic Lodge Hall on South Hayden Avenue was at one time a rather active black lodge. It is the first building on the right heading out of town on Pinckneyville Road.

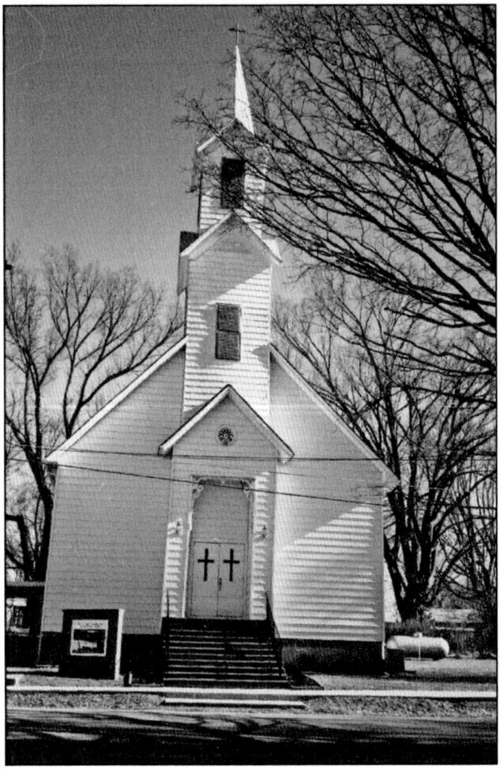

The historic Cumberland Presbyterian Church stands on Church Street in Salem. The church was built in 1889 and was called the Union Church, because four denominations held services there. After the Baptist, Methodist, and Christian congregations all built new churches, the Presbyterians renovated the historic building. The original bell remains in the 70-foot steeple.

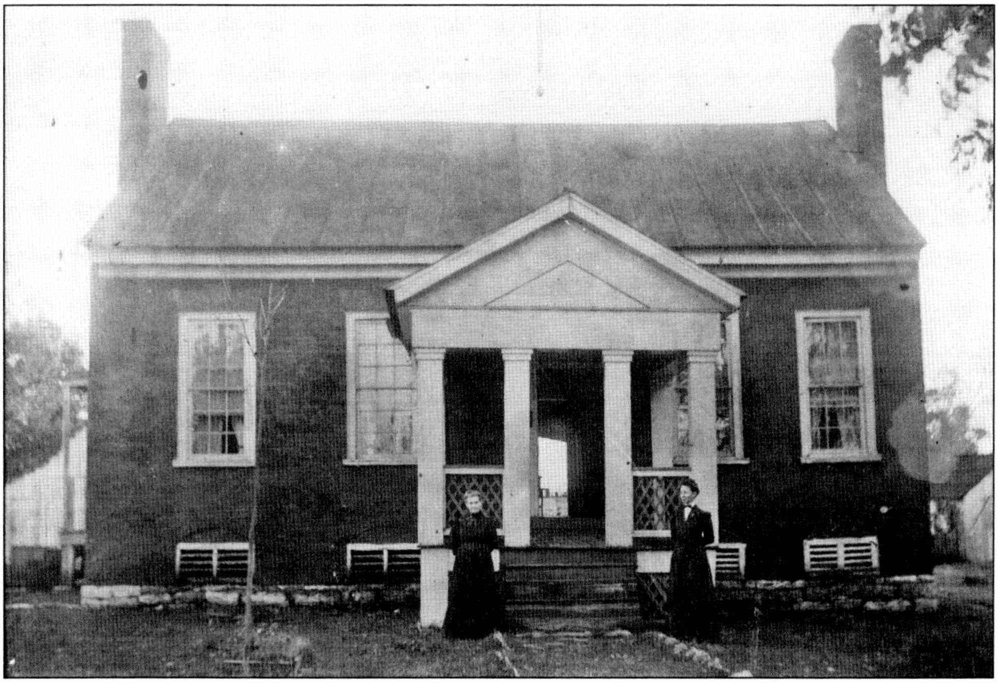

This photograph was made just prior to World War I, when Mable Alvis and daughter Electra were the only occupants of this house. The house is believed to have been built around 1800. It has some structural designs and inside trim identical to the Old Kentucky Home. For many years it was occupied by Asa and Mable Alley Alvis, their six children, and some of the 10 children from Asa's previous marriage.

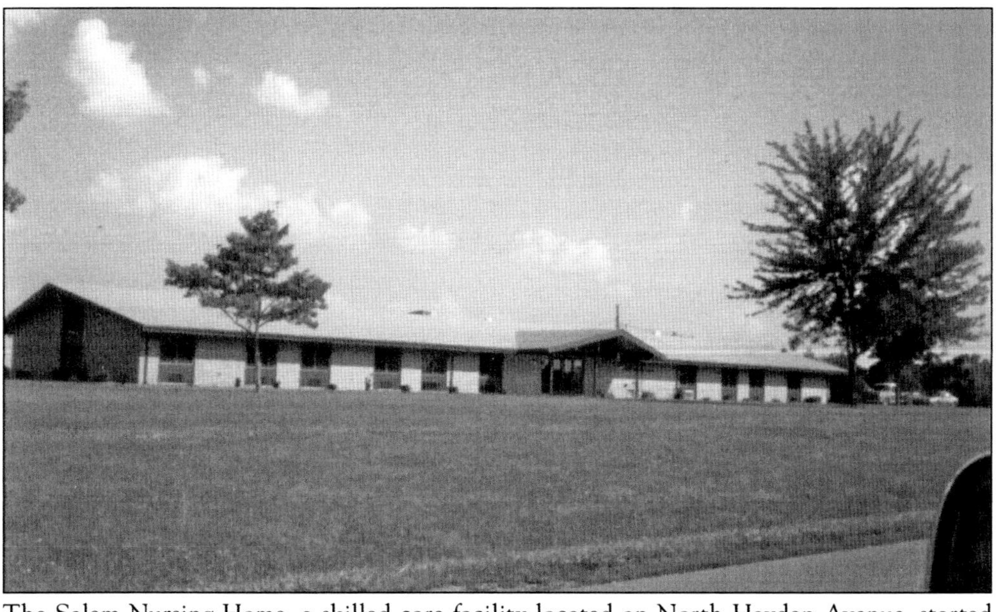

The Salem Nursing Home, a skilled care facility located on North Hayden Avenue, started operation in 1967. The formation of the home was spearheaded by Dr. Stephen Burkhart, and he later purchased the facility in 1988. This photograph was taken in 1985; the building has since been torn down and replaced by a new home called the Salem Springlake Care Center.

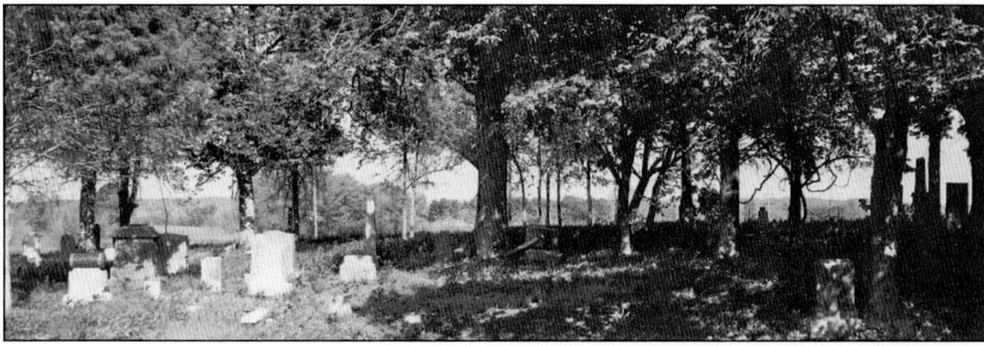

The Salem Mills Pioneer Cemetery has early settlers buried here of the Watts, Philips, McCollums, Rutters, Dallams, Haynes, and Fords families. Some relatives of Isaac Shelby, first governor of Kentucky, are here. In the early 1960s, a Shelby descendant placed a large Shelby monument here with much Shelby genealogy on all sides, seen on the left of the photograph.

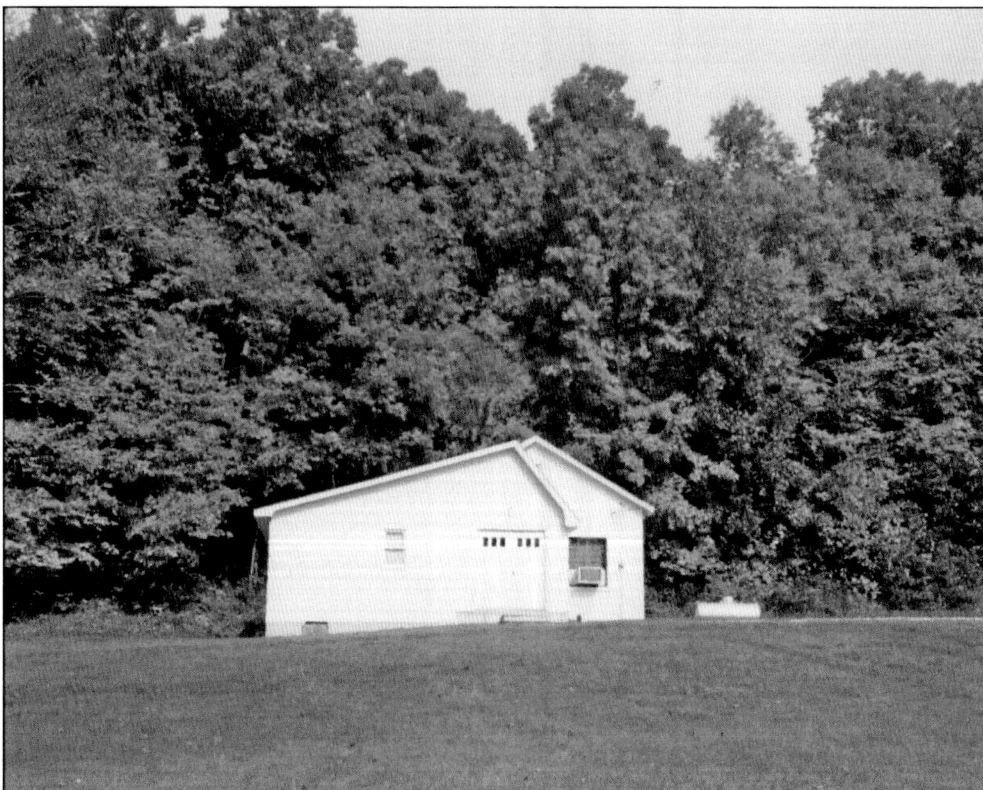

Maranatha Baptist Church is on Cedar Grove Road near Salem. Originally, it was the site of Beech Grove School, which was the last black school in Livingston County. The church has been renovated and additions have been made since this 1994 photograph.

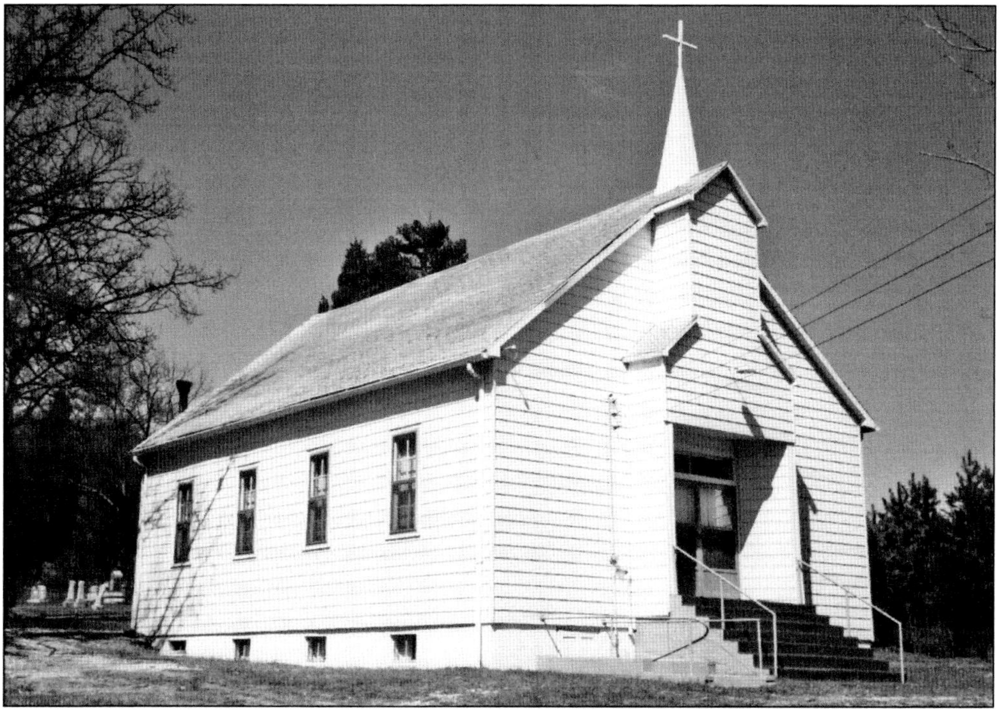

Cedar Grove Methodist Church is located a few miles southwest of Salem. An old church known as Little Bethel was the first place of worship and is believed to have burned. Built in the early 1900s, the church in this 1990 photograph had a basement dug beneath it in 1954, creating a kitchen, dining room, classrooms, and restrooms.

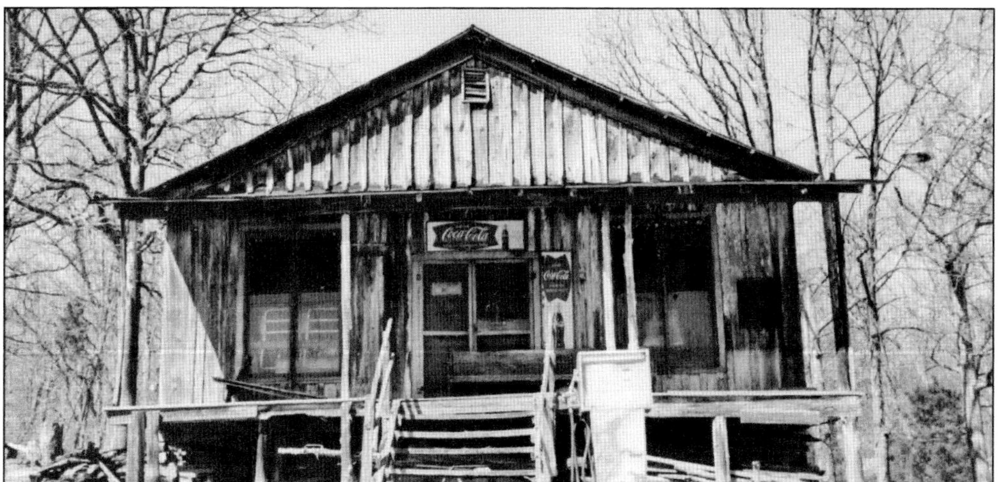

The Parker Store was started by Leonard and Earl Parker in the early 1900s. Leonard ran the store, and Earl hauled freight in wagons from Moxley's Landing on the Cumberland River to the store. T. R. Peck bought the store in the late 1940s and operated it until the 1970s. The Parker Store is located in the Cedar Grove community, where the Klondike and Hudson Mines once employed around 400 men.

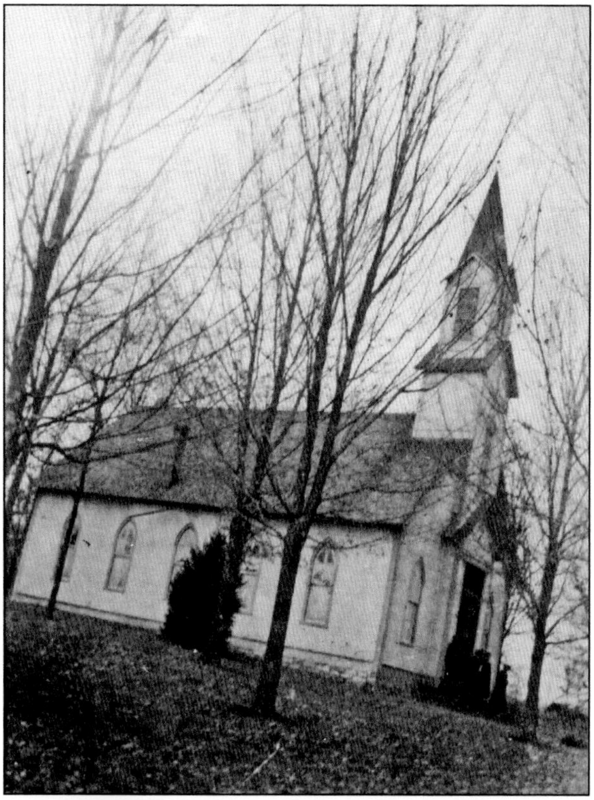

Pinckneyville Baptist Church was built in 1888 at a cost of $1,646.10. T. C. Guess and his wife, Mary Elizabeth, donated the 4 acres of land it was built on. In 1896, the church purchased 1 acre of ground from J. A. and Sarah Deboe for a cemetery. J. A. Deboe was the first person buried in the new graveyard.

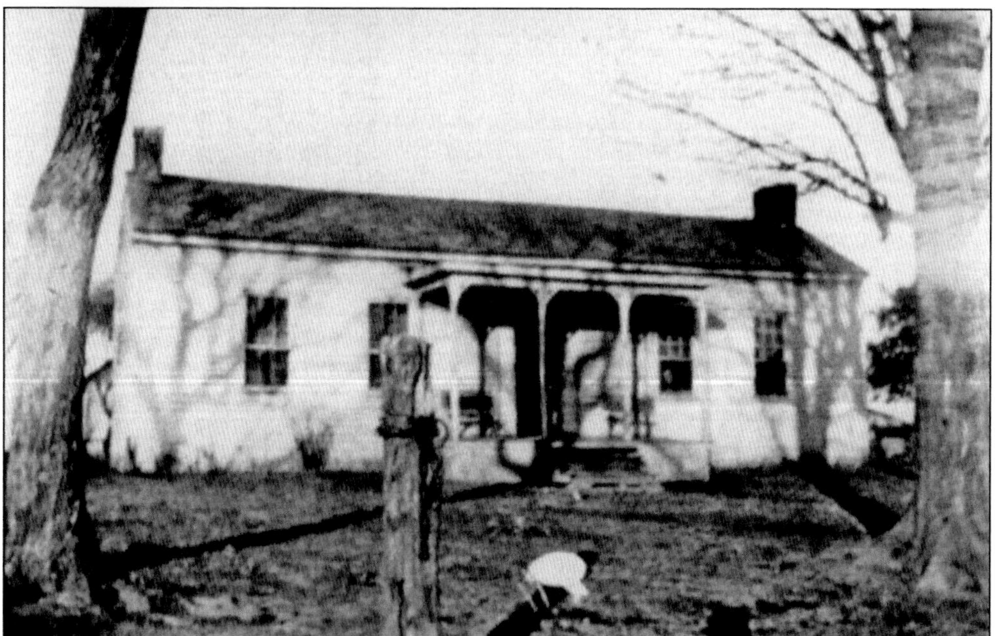

This is the James R. Ryan house, just behind the Pinckneyville church on the Farris Bridge Road. The photograph was probably taken around the mid-1920s. The Ryans both died in 1922. The home was later occupied by their son, Burnett Ryan, and his family.

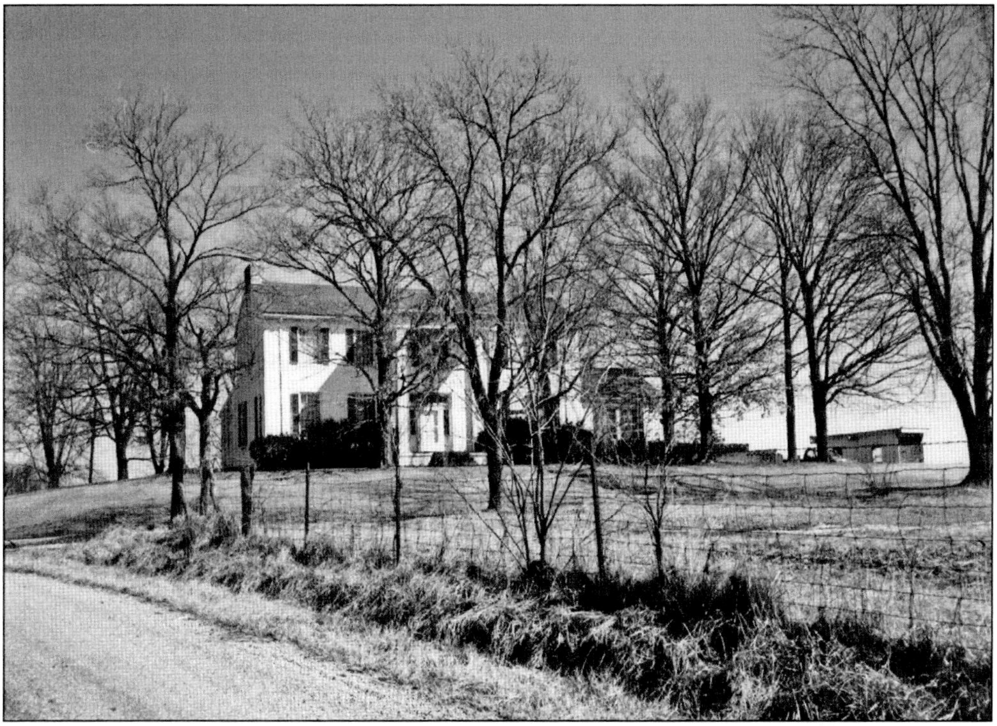

The Miles or Maddux House, located 5 miles south of Salem, was built in 1832, according to a cornerstone of the house. It was built by Richard A. Miles, the great-grandfather of Louis Maddux. The Maddux family did extensive restorations, making it the beautiful home shown in the photograph above. After the deaths of the Madduxes, Phillip and Sandy Barnes purchased the house and made more improvements.

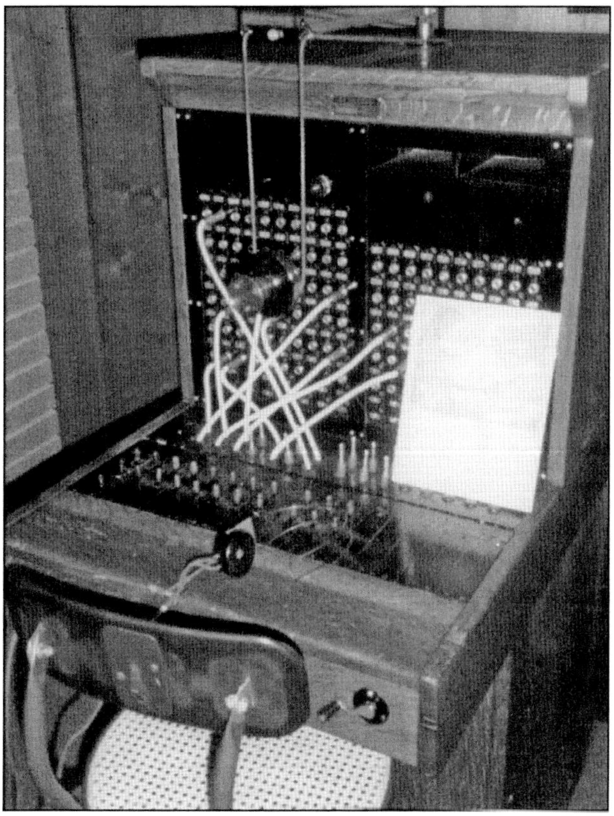

The old common battery switchboard of the Salem Telephone Company was used until the dial system was installed in 1962. The office was opened in 1911 by the Shelby family, and they sold it to William and Lillian Boswell and W. B. Butler in the 1940s. This photograph was taken in 1984 when the old switchboard was restored by William Thomason.

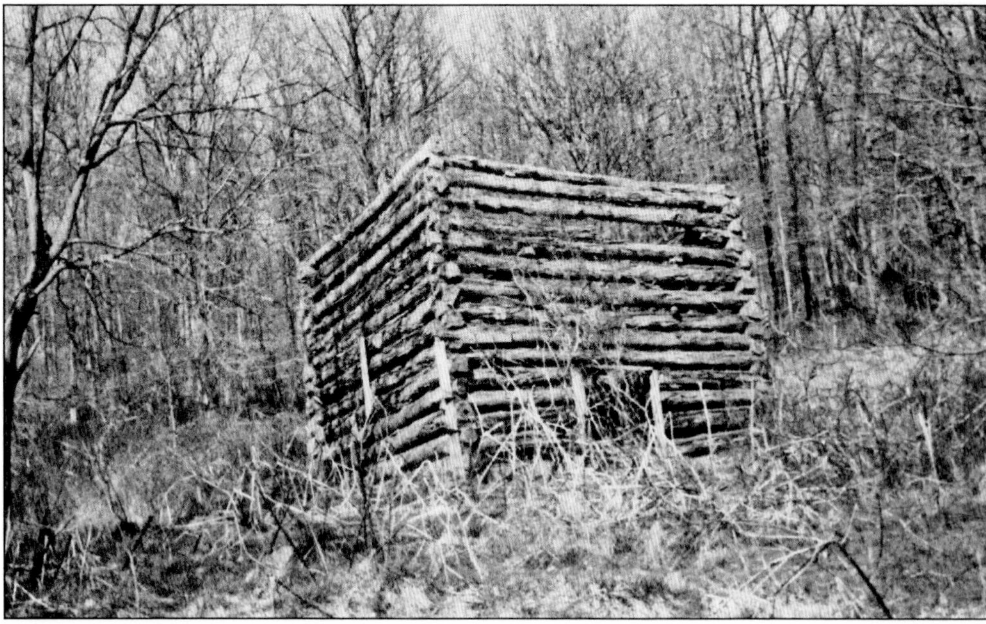

Augustus and Adeline Shear Alley came from North Carolina about 1850 and moved into a small log house, where they built this two-story crib. In later years, "Jesse James" was carved on a log in the upper part, so it was assumed that Jesse has spent a night there some time. The old crib was removed around 2000 to make space for a home on Highway 133 north of Salem.

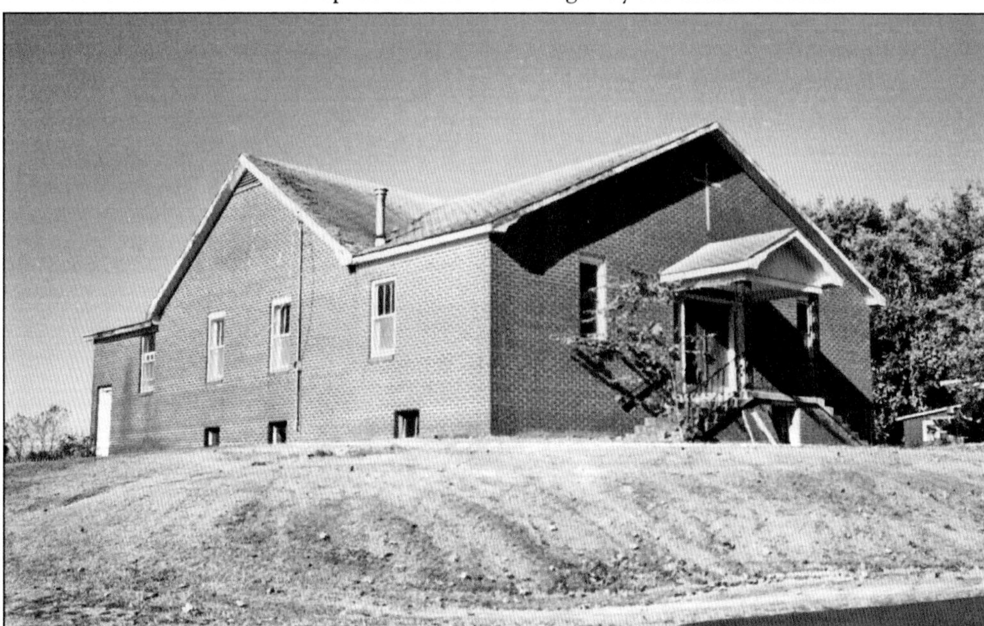

The Lola Pentecostal Church had its beginning in the early 1900s when the congregation worshipped in brush arbors and individual homes. Property was bought in 1915, and the first church was erected. In 1952, the original church building was moved, and another sanctuary was built on the same site. The building in this photograph was torn down in the 1990s after a new, modern building was finished in 1988.

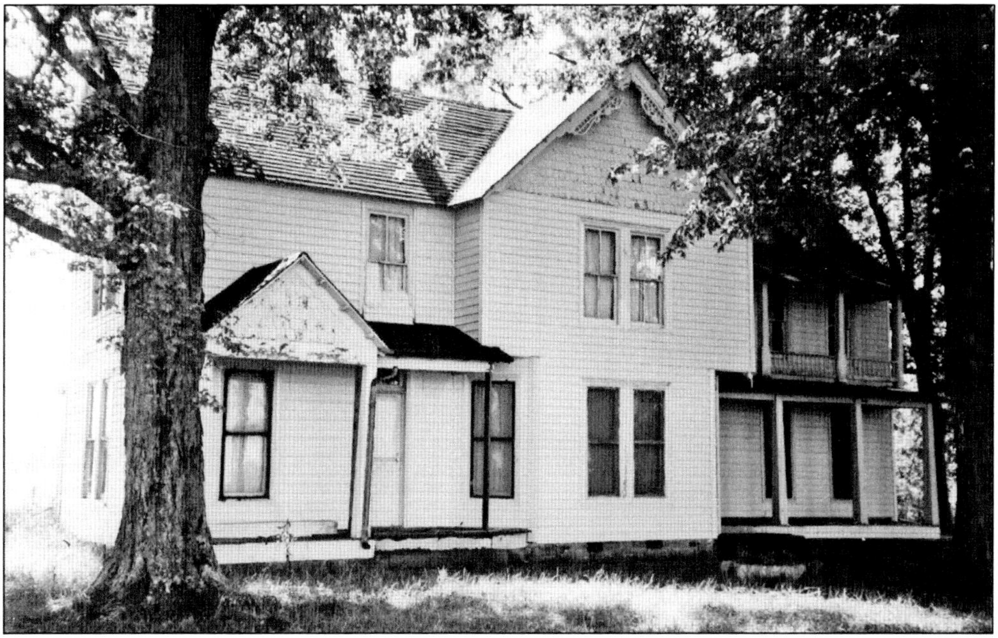

This old house is still standing on the edge of Lola near Highway 133. It was known through the years as the Gardner, Kennedy, and Johnson homes. Lola was once a bustling town with several stores, a hotel, a telephone office, and the first government-supervised distillery. The government authorities came in and stamped the barrels of whiskey to be sold by the quart on the side of the street.

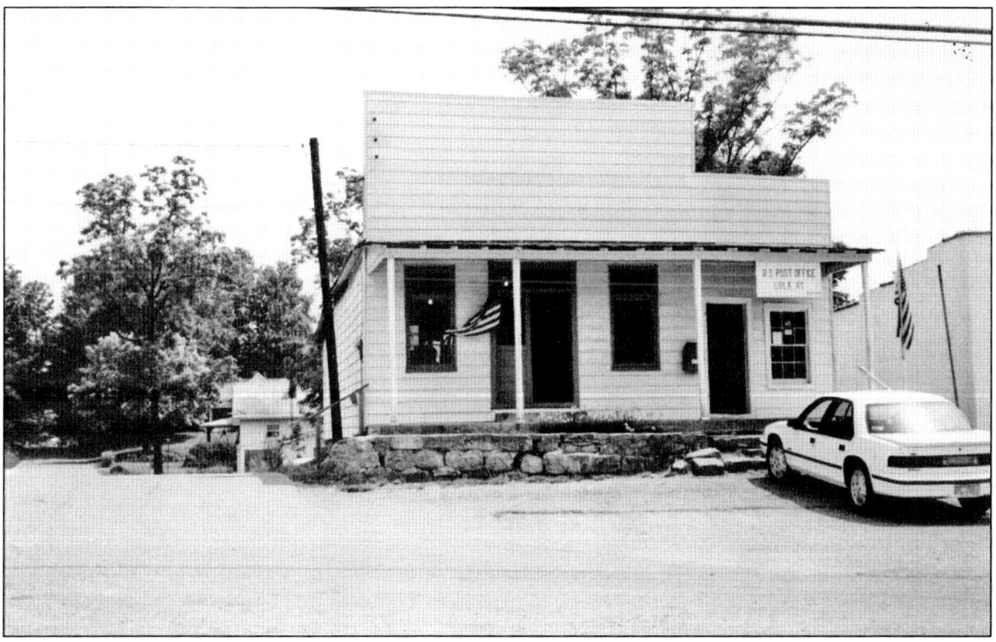

The Lola Post Office was closed in the late 1990s. Some of the postmasters were Davis, Mitchell, Perrin, and Cooper. Lola boasted of several famous people: Paul Gossage was an American League baseball pitcher, former governor of Kentucky Keen Johnson attended school in Lola, and Tom Robinson rode with the Quantrill gang during the Civil War and knew Frank and Jesse James.

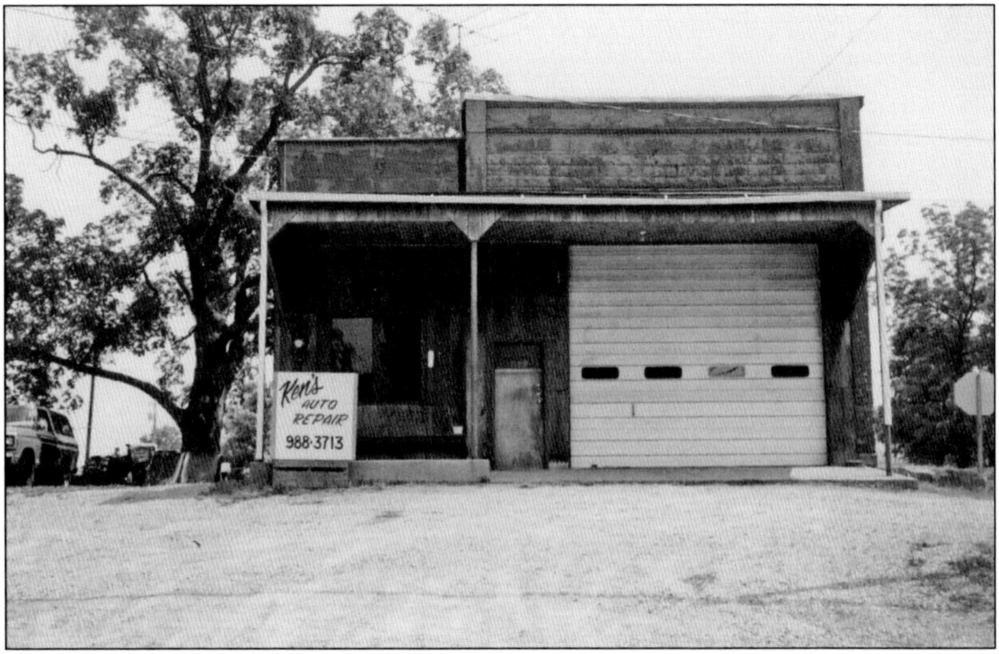

One of the oldest buildings in Lola was a general store owned and operated by Tommie May for many years. Built in 1896, this building was constructed with brick from an old kiln. In this photograph, taken in 1994, the store has been converted to a garage. By 2008, the building was vacant.

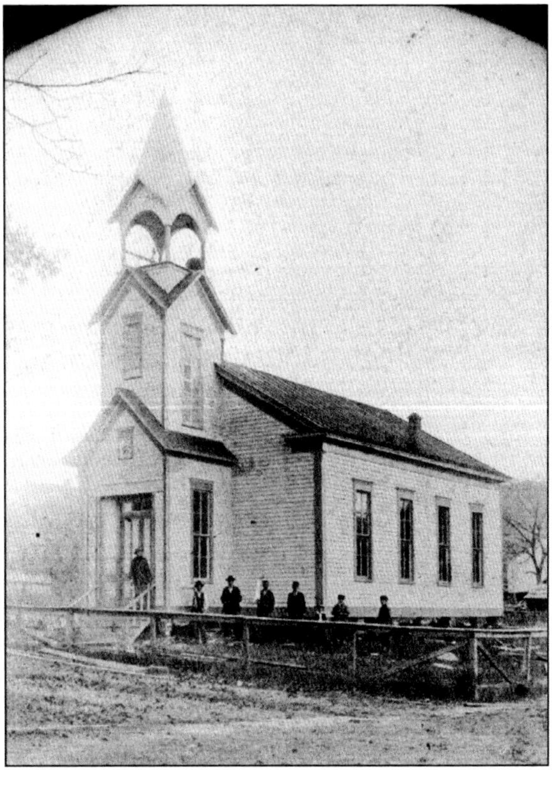

Carrsville Presbyterian Church was built in 1875 and was purchased by a Methodist congregation in 1950. This photograph was taken around 1900. Roger D. Morris, a local artist who has won many awards, had his Rivertree Studio there for years. It later housed a toy museum.

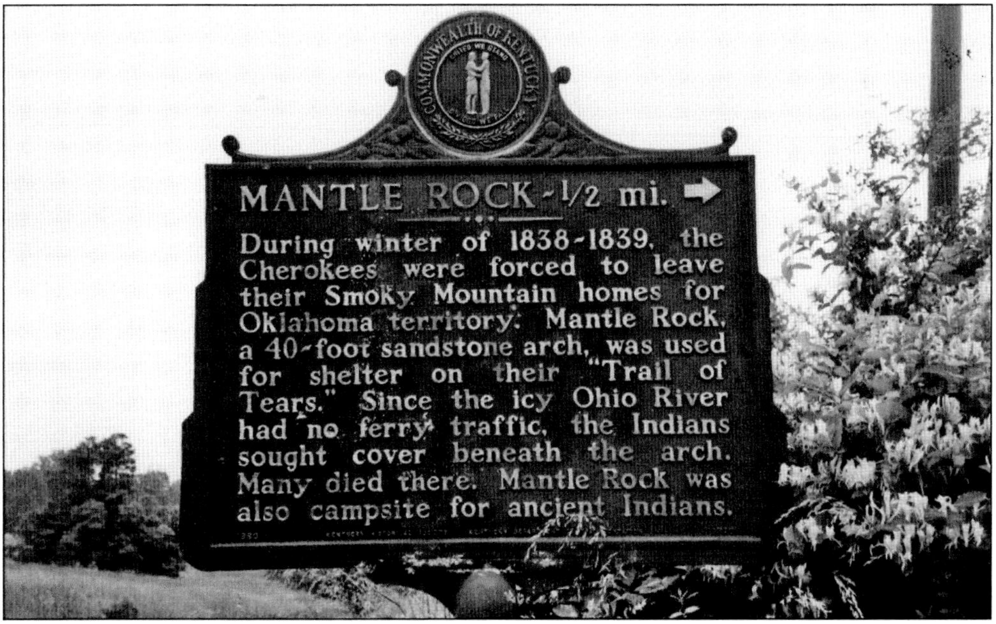

This Kentucky historical marker, on Highway 133 near Joy, designates the importance of Mantle Rock during the winter of 1838–1839 when the Cherokees were driven from their homes to the Oklahoma territory. Mantle Rock has a natural bridge 40 feet high and about 180 feet long that sheltered the Cherokees while they were waiting for the Ohio River to thaw enough to cross at Berry's Ferry. Vast numbers were buried there.

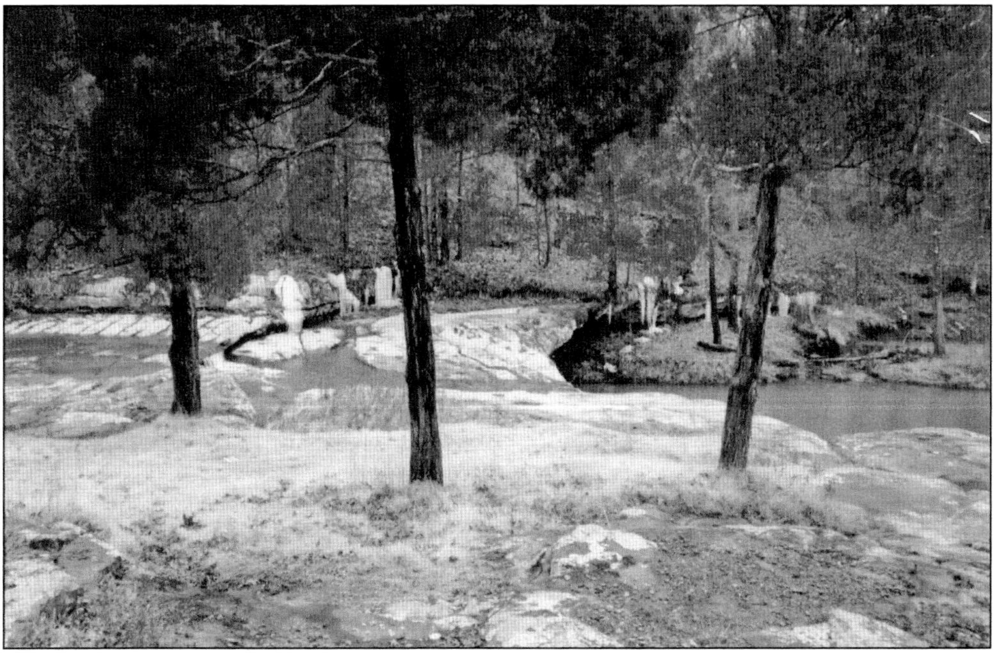

Mandy Falls is a beautiful waterfall where the Cherokees got fresh water while camping at nearby Mantle Rock. Many Native Americans have visited the area through the years because it is customary to pay homage at their ancestors' graves. Mandy Falls is one of the few waterfalls in western Kentucky.

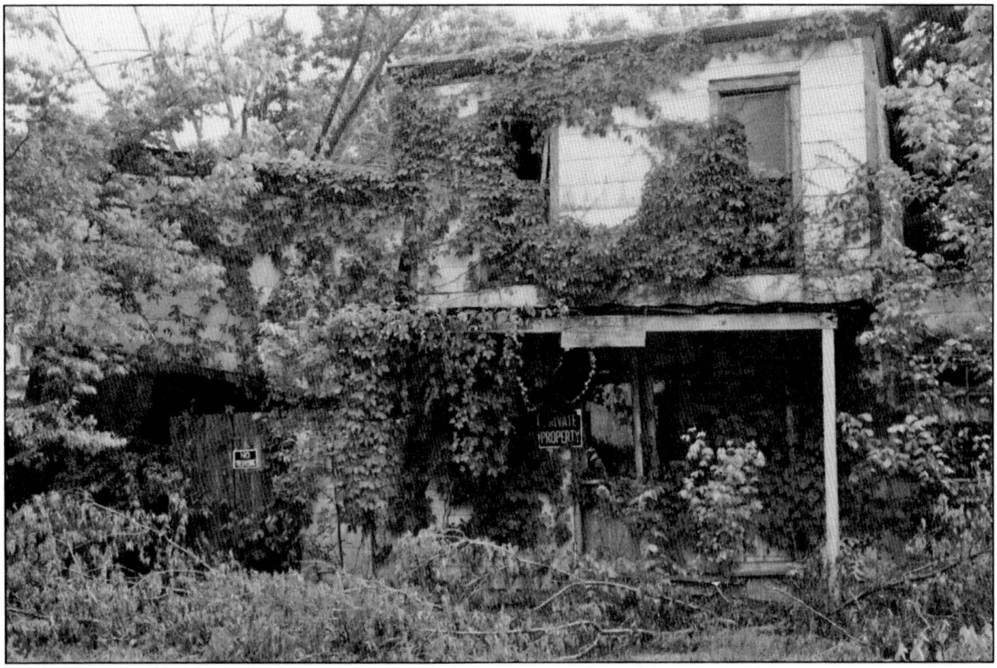

This building was first known as Earl's Store, then Shell's Store, and later as the last post office in Carrsville. Evelyn Whitecotton was the postmaster when it closed in 1981. This photograph of the old historic building was taken in 1993. The first post office was established in Carrsville in 1854.

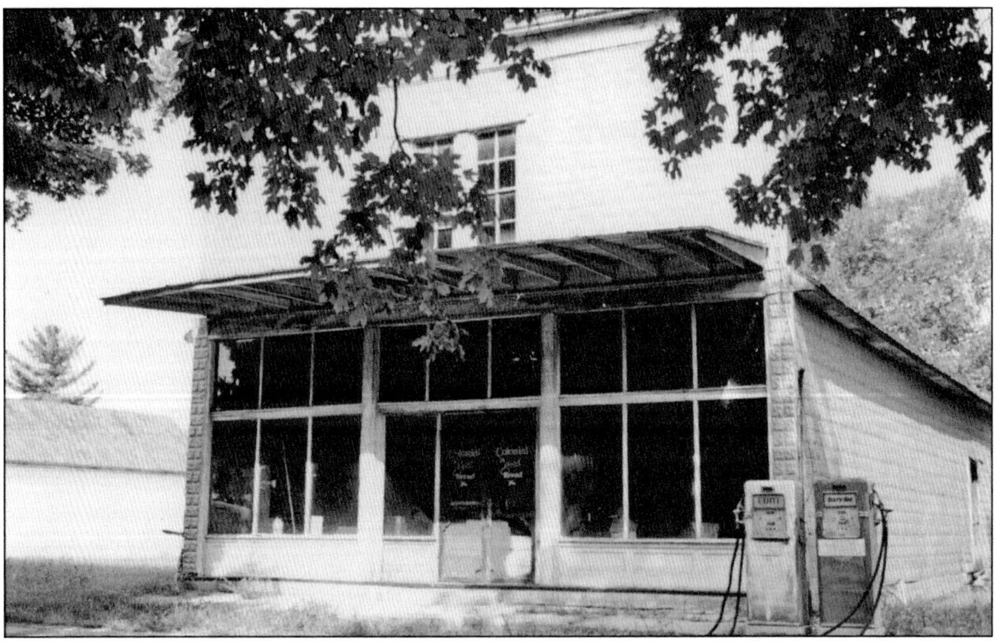

Ernest M. and Cozette Casper owned and operated this general store and post office in Hampton for 40 years. The historic building stands empty now. Hampton was named after Gen. Wade Hampton, a noted officer of the Confederate army who was stationed in the small settlement during the Civil War. Several businesses in Hampton were destroyed in a big fire in 1914.

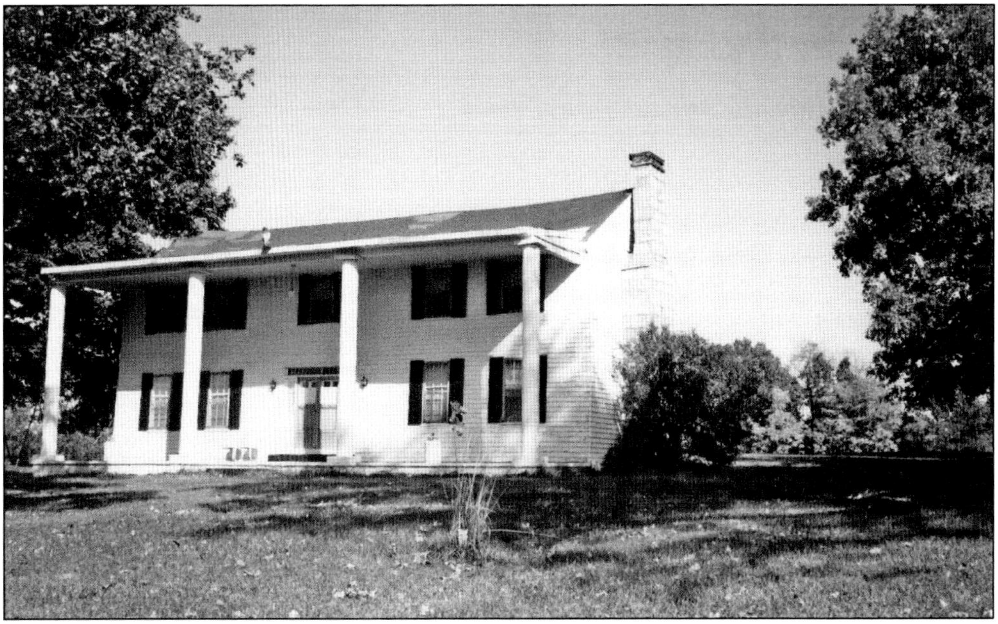

W. A. and Elizabeth Duley Chipps were married in 1862. They received an original land grant from the governor of Virginia during the Civil War. Taken in 1992, this photograph shows the remodeled original home built on a bluff near Bayou. W. A. took part in the California Gold Rush in 1849 and kept a diary of the daily adventures, which became a valuable part of the Chipps family history.

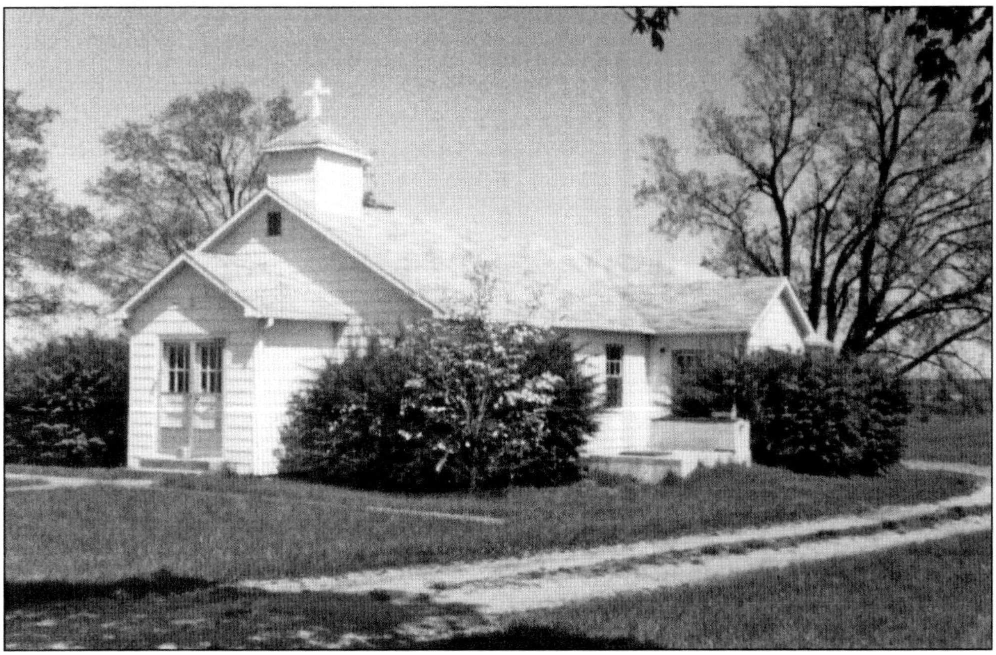

Pictured in 1983, the McMurray United Methodist Church was dedicated in 1958. It replaced the original one, built in 1912. T. A. McMurray moved to the Bayou area from Union County, Kentucky, in 1903. He donated land for the church. The church is still an active part of the Bayou community.

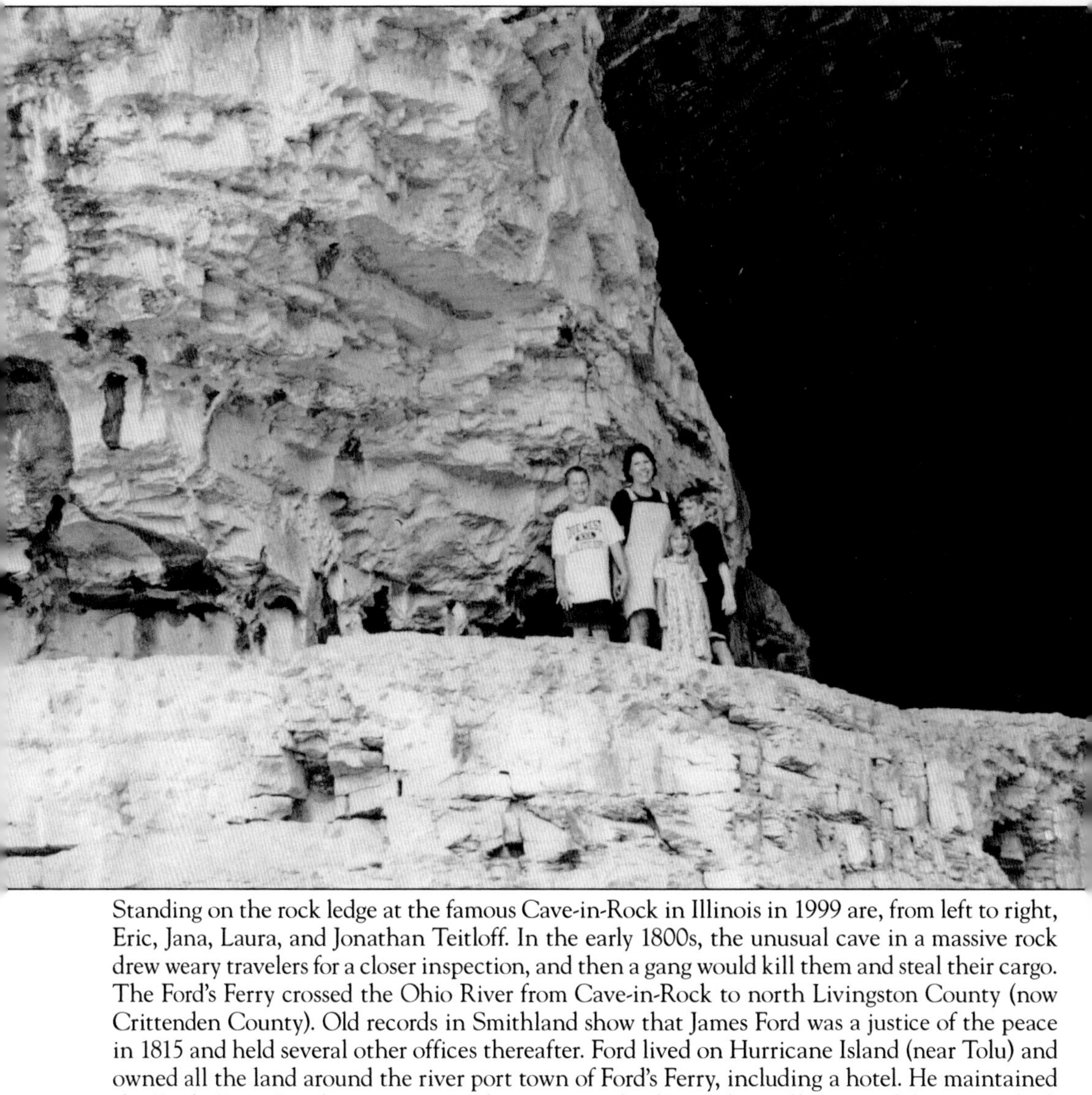

Standing on the rock ledge at the famous Cave-in-Rock in Illinois in 1999 are, from left to right, Eric, Jana, Laura, and Jonathan Teitloff. In the early 1800s, the unusual cave in a massive rock drew weary travelers for a closer inspection, and then a gang would kill them and steal their cargo. The Ford's Ferry crossed the Ohio River from Cave-in-Rock to north Livingston County (now Crittenden County). Old records in Smithland show that James Ford was a justice of the peace in 1815 and held several other offices thereafter. Ford lived on Hurricane Island (near Tolu) and owned all the land around the river port town of Ford's Ferry, including a hotel. He maintained the Ford's Ferry Road to attract travelers to cross the ferry, where all traces of them vanished. Nothing has ever been proven about Ford being the leader of the Ford's Ferry Gang, but it all ended in 1833 when he was murdered. (Courtesy of Faye Teitloff.)

Five

EDUCATION

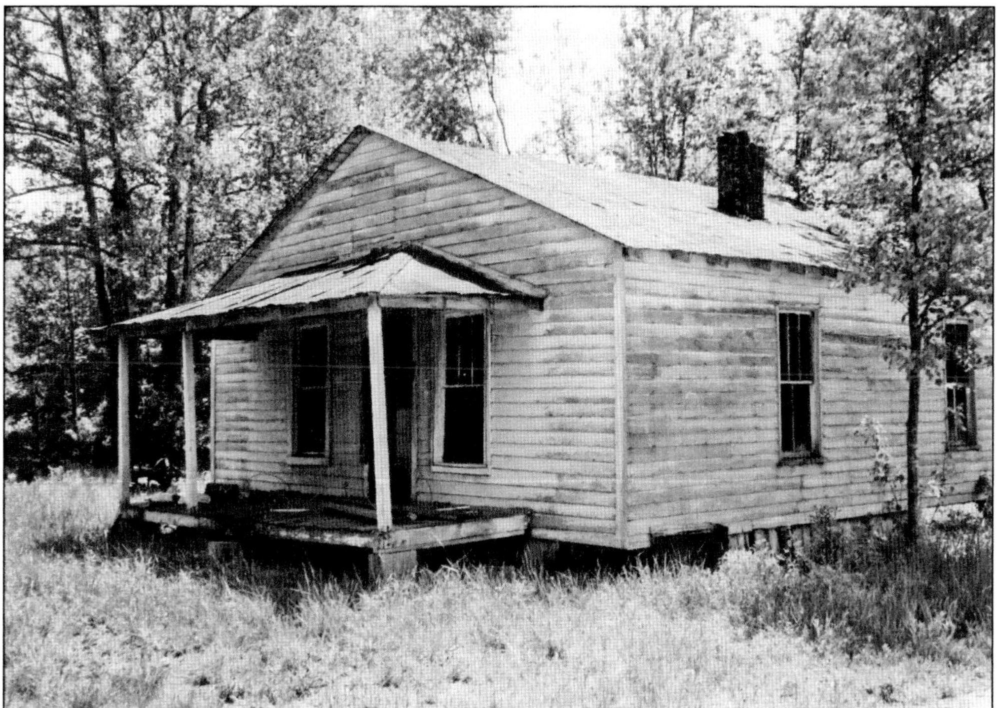

Known as the Lick Skillet School, this one-room school was moved from a hill on Lick Skillet Road to Highway 133 near Salem. It was then called the Barnett School and was closed as a school in about 1940. There were many one-room schools since everyone had to walk to class no matter what weather conditions existed.

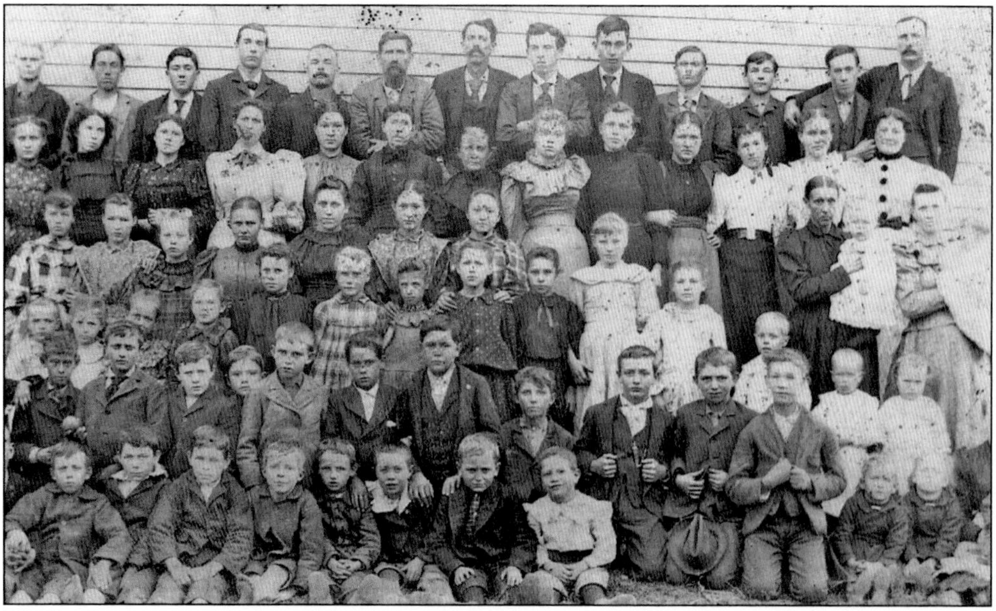

The students at Gum Springs School in 1896 are, from left to right, (first row) Shird Hale, Aubrey Haley, Orel Champion, Forrest Champion, Murvin Haley, ? Stringer, ? Lee, Horace Driskill, and ? Clark; (second row) Jewell Driskill, Clarence Driskill, Tiller Hale, Charley Stringer, Samual Ferren, Clarence Ferren, Will Bennett, Dick Lucas, Horace Haley, Will Stringer, Gordon Ferren, Harve Champion, Virgil Driskill, Salen Driskill, and Vera Driskill; (third row) Dora Rudd, Ida Stringer, unidentified, Maude Champion, Irene Ferren, Mate Hill, ? Stringer, Nora Lucas, Rosa Lee, Rene Ramage, and Mary Cooper; (fourth row) Jettie Wright, Lulu Stringer, Emma Hale, Vade McQuigg, Helen Dycus, Abbie Stone, Ada Driskill, and Martha Jones; (fifth row) Lydia Coffer, Cora Coffer, Mag Driskill, Manda Bridges, Minnie Howerton, Manda Moore, Jo Hopper, Eva Jones, Sarah Rice, Lizzie Ramage, Mag Scott, Bettie Smith, and Emma Lucas; (sixth row) John Hale, Huey Driskill, Henry Lucas, Byrant Bennett, Tom Champion, Doze Driskill, Roland Bennett, Zed Bennett, Oscar Driskill, Henry Hale, Clarence Champion, Will Scott, and Finis Lantrip. The women holding babies are ? Driskill, ? Clark, ? Haley, and Mollie Bennett. (Courtesy of Livingston County Historical Society.)

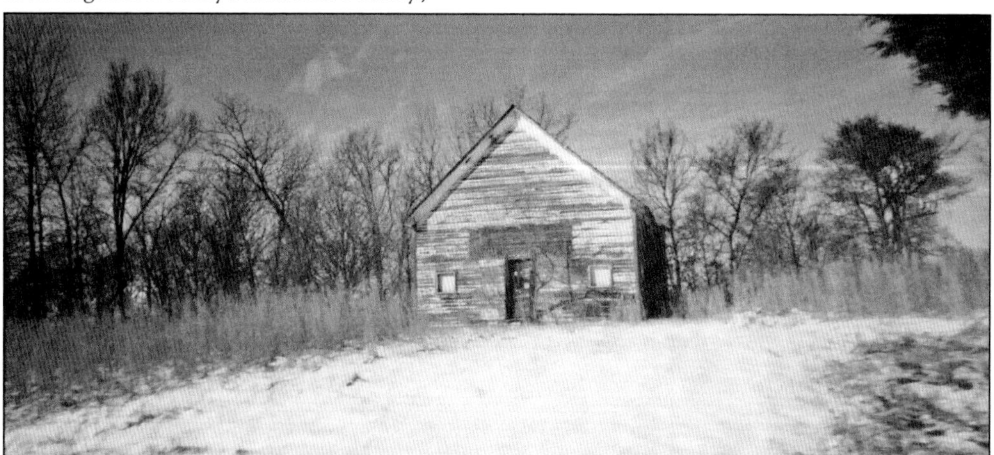

The old Threlkeld School is one of the last one-room schoolhouses still standing on what is now Mitchell Loop near Burna.

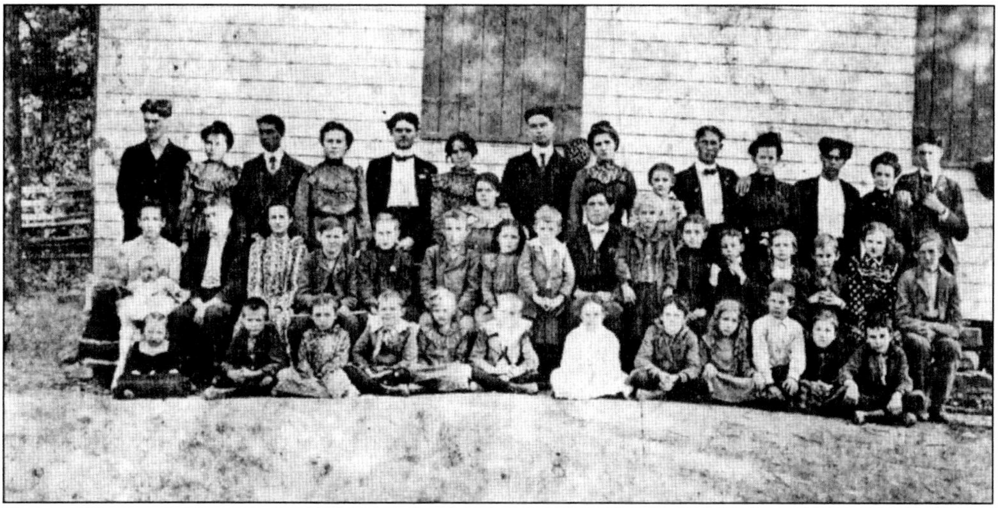

Keibler School students around 1902 are, from left to right, (first row) ? Roark, Billie Glass, Isabelle Curry Ellis, Fred Sisk, Lou Keibler, Allen Blankenship, Nora Lytton, Bob Lytton, Marie McCandless Davis, Henry Keibler, Emma Davis Earles, and Oda Burns; (second row) ? Roark and her two children, Lace McCandless, Dixie Glass Mitchell, Barney Smiley, Ada Blankenship, Carl McCandless, Kate Babb, Courtney Davis, Ben Vick (teacher), Roy Keibler, Bertha Teitloff, Si Baynes, Callie Baynes, Herman Smiley, Nonnie Burns, and Cecil Thompson; (third row) Russell McCandless, Pearl Teitloff, Frank Keibler, Carrie Blankenship, Bill Teitloff, Carrie Babb Thompson, Hazel Sisk, Lee Smiley, Myrtle Glass, Veda Keibler Sullivant, Everett Blankenship, Lillie Smiley, Walter Teitloff, Nettie Lytton Teitloff, and Tom Lytton. (Courtesy of Mary Lou Smith.)

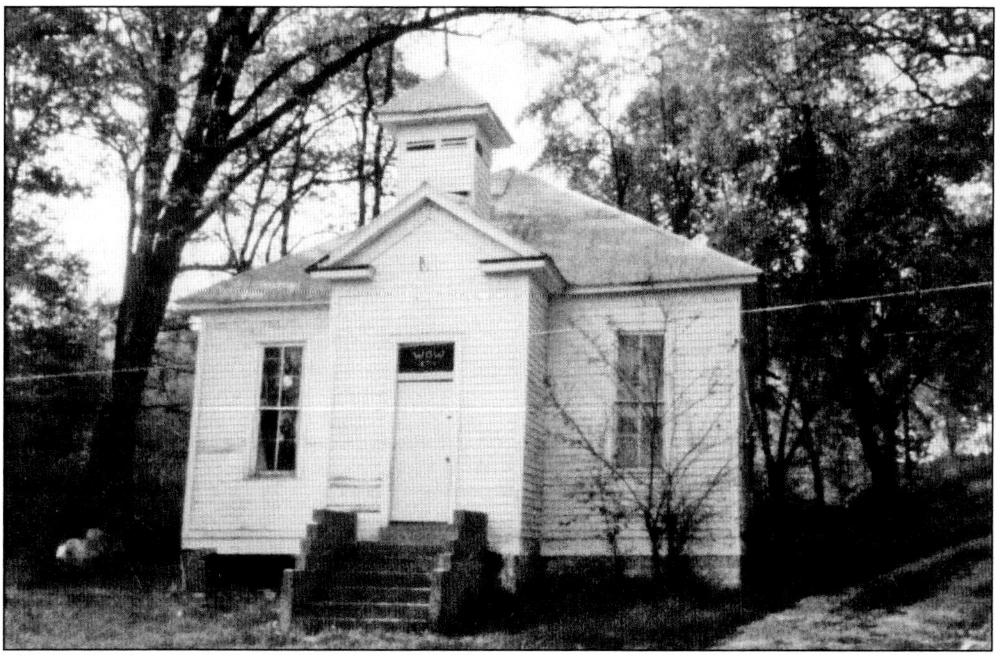

This 1985 photograph of the old Iuka School was taken before it was moved to a new location on Jake Dukes and Corinth Roads just a few miles from the original site. It is now being kept as a museum, and people are allowed to go inside and view the old furnishings that were there before the school closed.

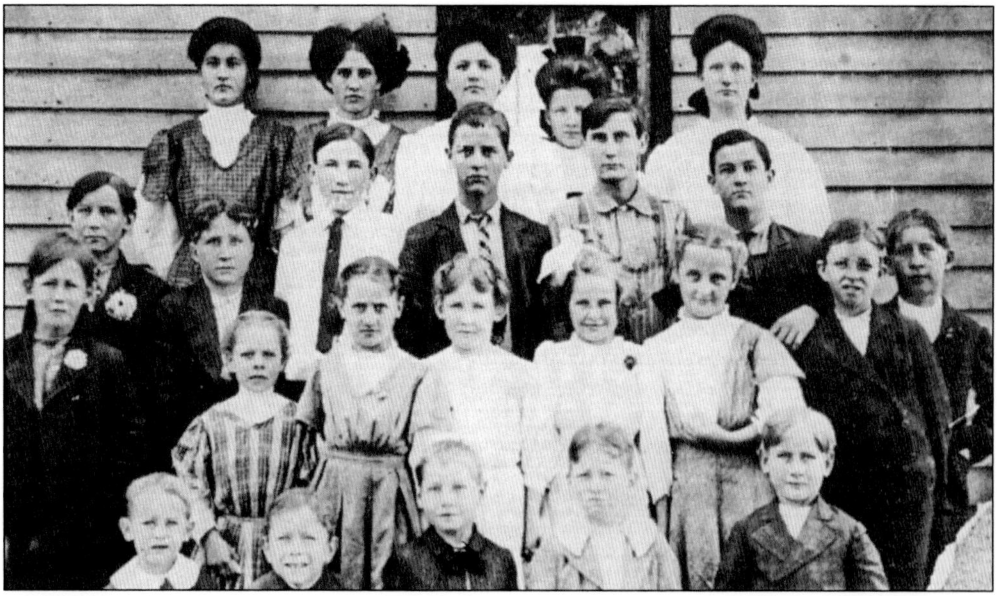

Brown School students in 1908 are, from left to right, (first row) Sidney Kirk, Allen Simpkins, Jim Pace, Ira Brasher, and Marvin Pace; (second row) Dowell Ring, Savannah Kirk, Virgie Howard, Drucie Howard, Jeannie Kirk, Irva Kirk, Bill Simpkins, and Ellet Pace; (third row) Ural Wring, Hobart Grimes, Leonard Kirk, Lawrence Simpkins, Claude Grimes, and Audrey Brown; (fourth row) Pearl Lockhart, Bertie Kirk, Elsie Riley, Mabel LaRue, and Eva Grimes. (Courtesy of Livingston County Historical Society.)

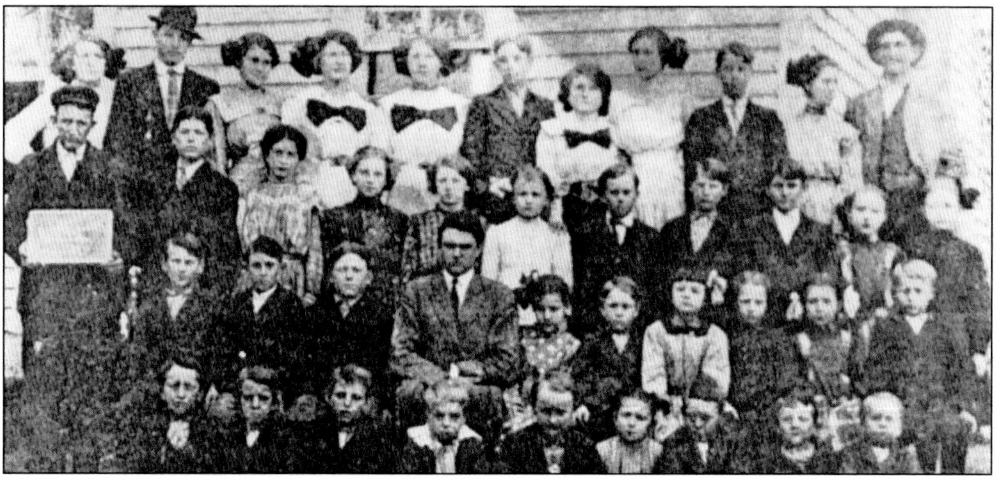

Gum Springs School students and visitors are shown in this photograph taken on December 7, 1911. From left to right are (first row) Everett Bennett, Willard Gainer, Lisha Bridges, Abbie Bridges, Fred Campbell, Roy Baker, Thomas Adkins, Lave Adkins, and Ernest Driskill; (second row) Clyde Jones, Bettie Compton, Altie Stringer, Violet Cooper, Allie Bennett, Nina Gainer, Cregg Dycus (teacher), Sid Jacobs, Marvin Cooper, and Lawrence Campbell; (third row) Maggie Compton, Lucy Compton, Riley Cooper, Ephrage Campbell, Henry Bennett, Gertrude Smith, Elcie Stringer, Wave Coffer, Ermal Champion, Lonnie Jacobs, and Jess Cooper (trustee); (fourth row) Lawrence Lucas, Marie Bennett, Thomas Bennett, Emma Campbell, Mae Cooper, unidentified, Flora Champion, Ora Champion, Vera Driskill, Harvey Stringer, and Lizzie Stringer. (Courtesy of Livingston County Historical Society.)

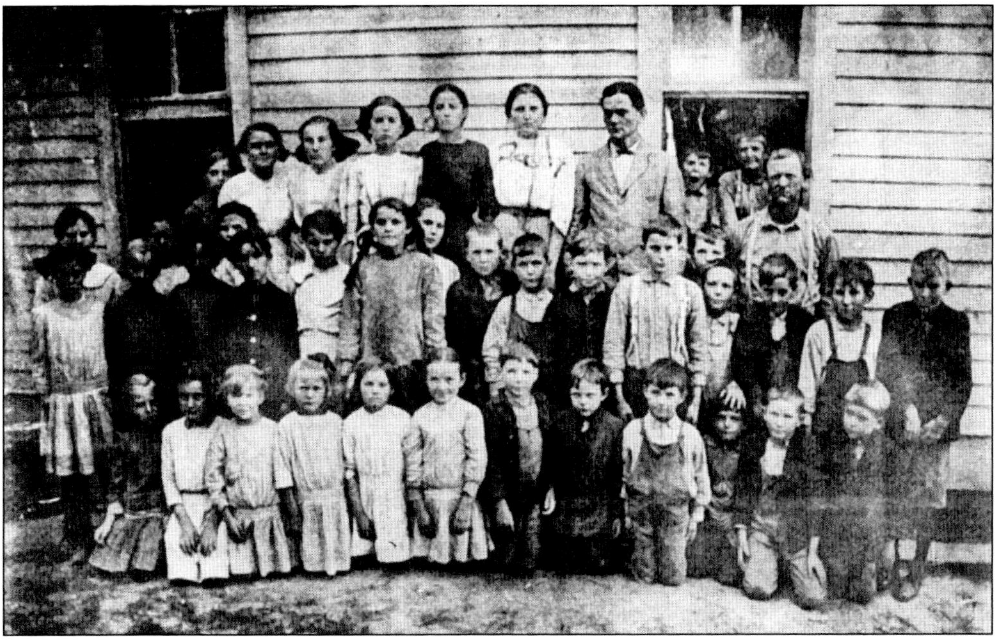

Cornith School students about 1913 are, from left to right, (first row) Melville Varnell, Iona Walker, Mary Lee Martin, Nonnie Walker, Carrie Mae Martin, Vesta Fuqua, Floyd Hale, Ford Pendergrast, Clifton Walker, Herman Martin, Charlie Evans, and Loyd Harris; (second row) Eula Varnell, Mona King, Madaline King, Fleety Mae Doom, Anna Sharp, Gracie Martin, Given Harris, Clifton Bennett, Otis Hale, Rollie Evans, Joe Fugate, Orville Dycus, Milton Hyde, and Dan Green; (third row) Allie Sharp, Ethel Harris, Kate Pendergrast, Della Schroder, and Wallace Rhodes; (fourth row) Eunice Fugate, Betty Fuller, Grace Evans, Anna Harris, Minnie Lindsey, Emily Harris, Eugene Tally (teacher), Willie Martin, unidentified, Leland Martin, and Harry Bennett (trustee). (Courtesy of Livingston County Historical Society.)

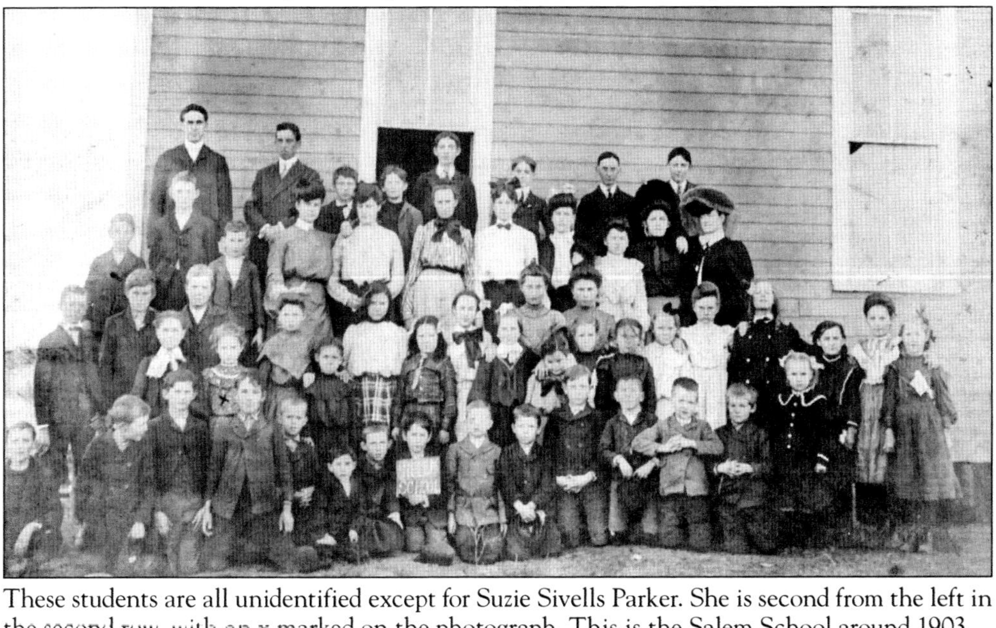

These students are all unidentified except for Suzie Sivells Parker. She is second from the left in the second row, with an x marked on the photograph. This is the Salem School around 1903.

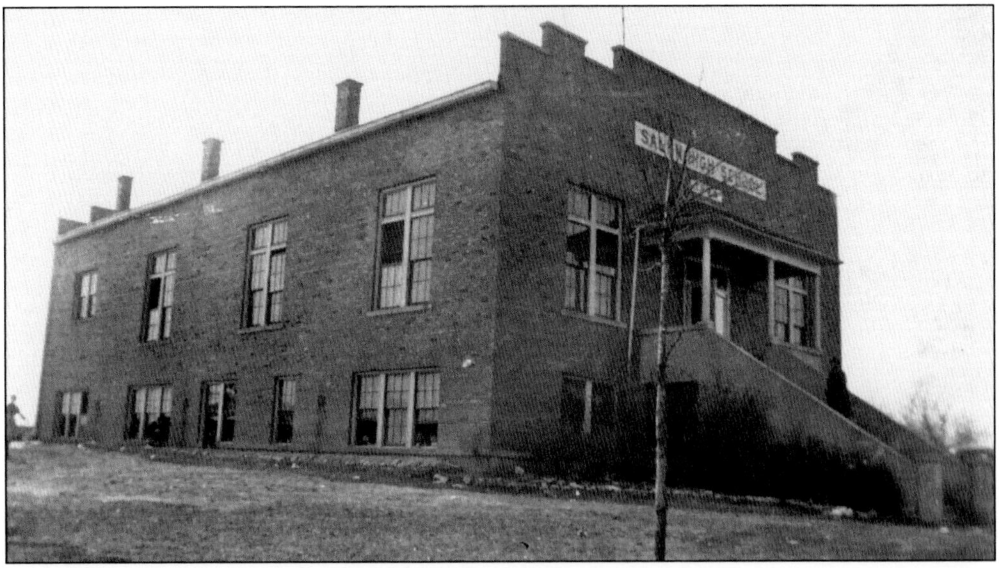

This red two-story brick high school was built in Salem in 1928, boasting a gym, a stage, and a small library. The building was used until a new high school was completed in 1940 by the Works Progress Administration (WPA). The WPA program was developed as part of U.S. president Franklin Roosevelt's New Deal during the days of the Great Depression. Grades one through eight remained in the old brick building until 1962, when it was torn down.

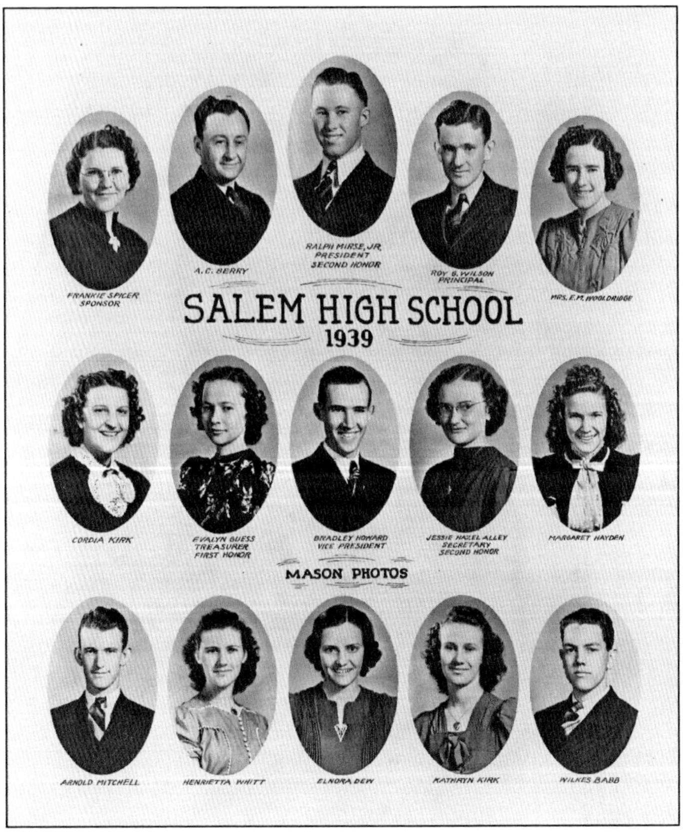

The 1939 class of Salem High School included, from left to right (first row) Arnold Mitchell, Henrietta Whitt, Elnora Dew, Kathryn Kirk, and Wilkes Babb; (second row) Cordia Kirk, treasurer Evalyn Guess (first honor), vice president Bradley Howard, secretary Hazel Alley (second honor), and Margaret Hayden; (third row) sponsor Frankie Spicer, A. C. Berry, president Ralph Mirse (second honor), principal Roy Wilson, and Mrs. E. M. Wooldridge.

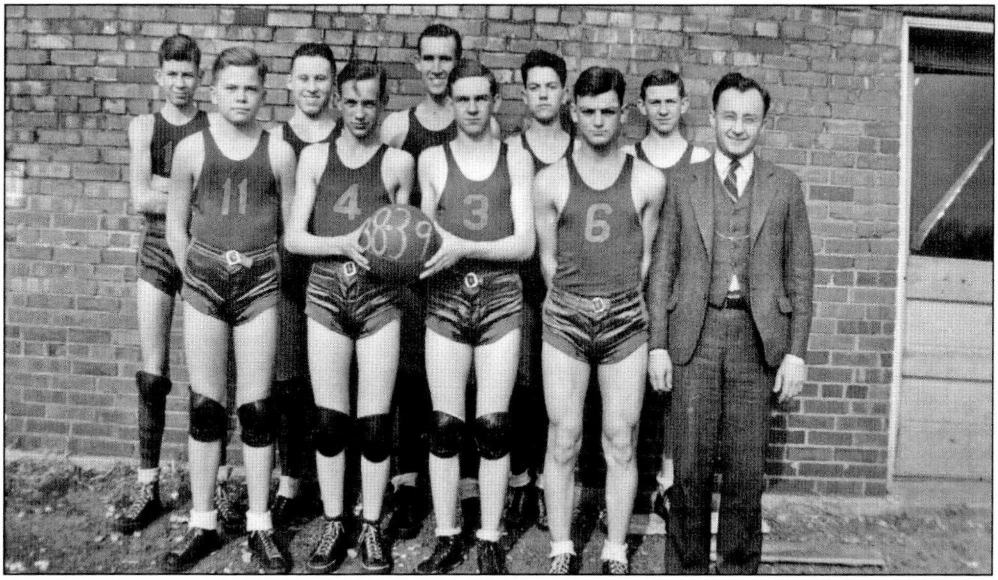

Armon Berry was the coach for the Salem High School basketball team during the 1938–1939 season. The team consisted of Gene Stevens, John Hayden, Ralph Mirse, M. H. Cloyd, Bradley Howard, Edwin Monroe, Wilkes Babb, Kelcy Driskill, and Charles Monroe.

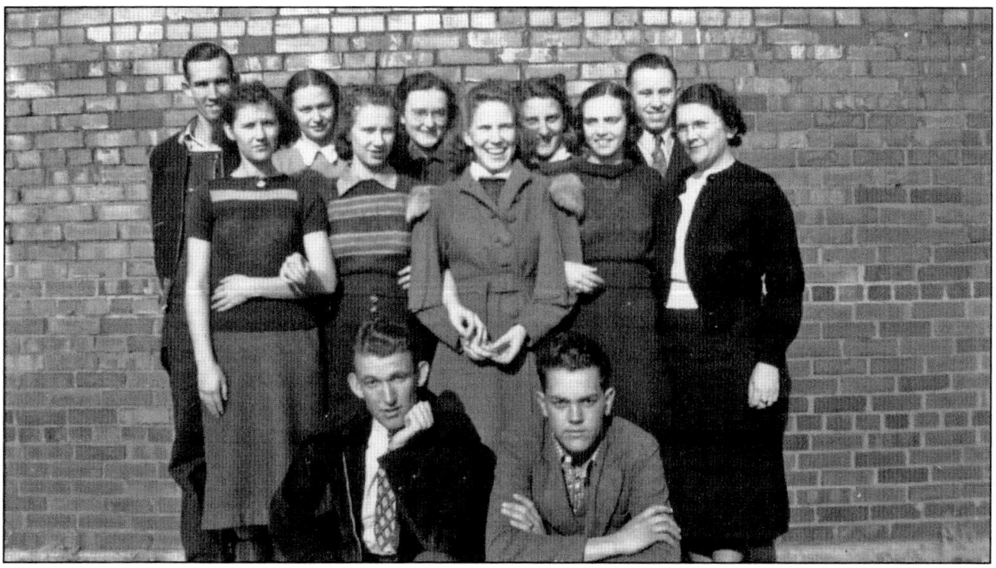

Written on the back of this picture is: Salem Senior Class of 1939; Bradley Howard, Henrietta Whitt, Evalyn Guess, Kathryn Kirk, Jessie Hazel Alley, Margaret Hayden, Cordie Kirk, Elnora Dew, Ralph Mirse, Frankie Spicer Davidson, and Arnold Mitchell.

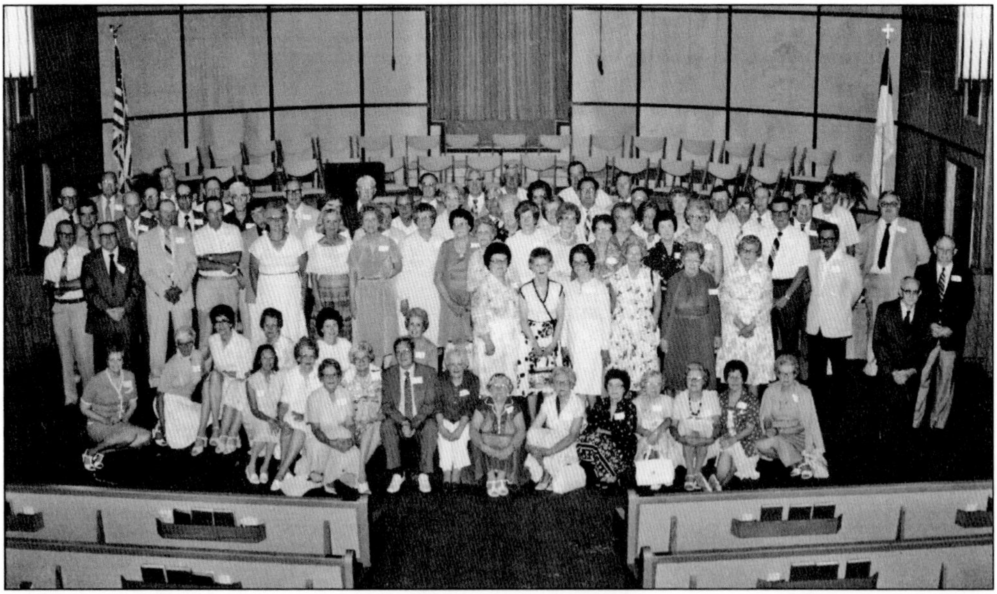

These Salem High School graduates of 1921 through 1940 are shown in 1981 at their grand reunion at a Salem church.

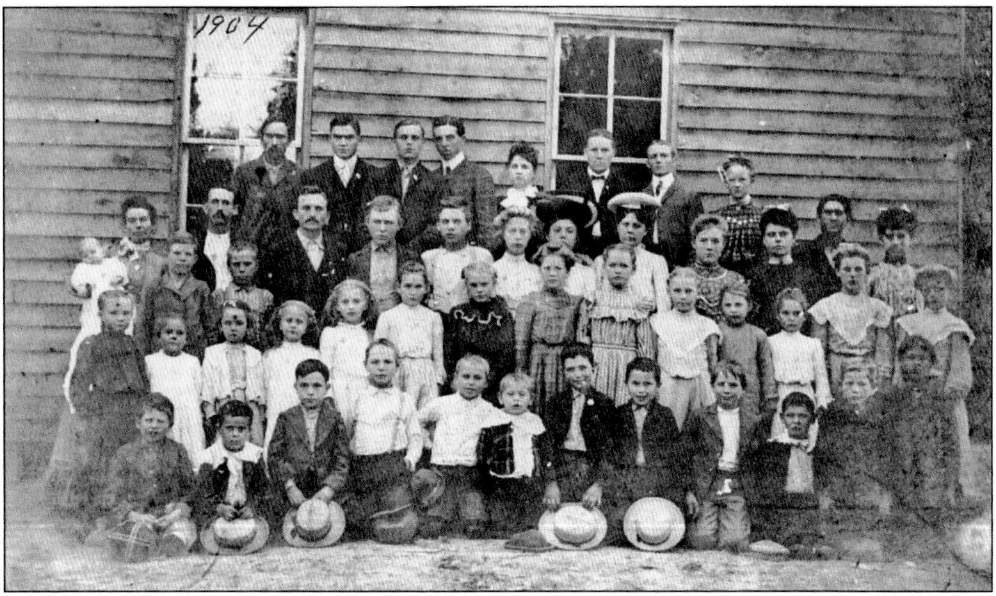

Shown at the Oak Ridge School in 1904 are, from left to right, (first row) Harry Champion, Berna Champion, Eulice Duckett, Will Crouch, Freeman Guess, Jim Crouch, Marion Scarbrough, Forest Scarbrough, Frank Vaughn, Dewey Vaughn, Lemon Heater, and Clarence Anglin; (second row) Vennie Doom, Mable Walker, Edith Story, Ruby Walker, Pearl Walker, Audrey Walker, Florence Anglin, Gertrude Hodge, Alva Vaughn, Elsie Heater, Euda Matthews, and Eva Walker; (third row) Everett Walker (baby), Zada Walker, Clyde Champion, Frank Walker, McGinnis Matthews, Lee Walker, Edd Heater, Harrison Matthews, Eliza Rednour, Myrtie Matthews, Effie Matthews, Lakie Heater, Florence Smith, Birchie Heater, and Vernie Heater; (fourth row) Tom Duckett, George Taylor, Clifton Matthews, Zed Bennett, teacher Laura Jones, Johnnie Sexton, George Devers, Ida Sexton, Claud Smith, and Alta Smith. (Courtesy of Livingston County Historical Society.)

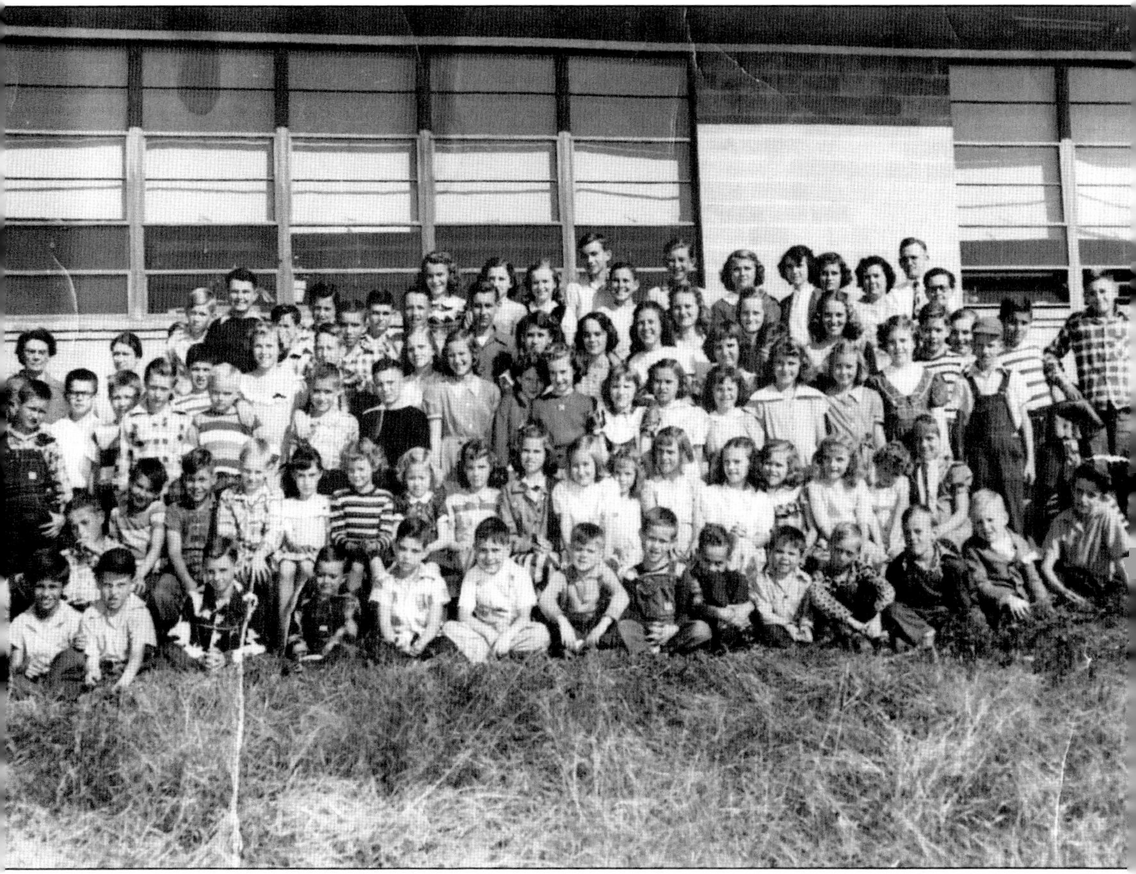

Pictured at Lola Elementary School in the 1950s are, from left to right, (first row) Carl Williams, Harold Tolley, Sunnie Ferrell, David Workman, Buddy Singleton, Lester May, Ronnie Watson, Harold Belt, Kenneth Belt, Butch Curnel, Leon Belt, Deon Belt, unidentified, and Carol Tolley; (second row) Paxton Crawford, Ronald Keith Singleton, unidentified, Dickie Quertermous, Robert Croft, Wanda Adams May, Linda Ferrell, unidentified, Charlotte Workman, Peggy Belt, unidentified, Linda Williams, Peggy Watson, Kay Williams, Joyce Williams, Annabelle Millikan, and Bonnie Watson; (third row) Sanford Franklin, Junior Tharp, Winkie Falls, Robert Arflack, Gene Damron, Mable Millikan, Sandra Watson, Floyd Ann Wright, Linda Sefret Padon, Janice Kennedy, Claudette Watson, unidentified, Shirley Crawford, and Richard Crawford; (fourth row) teacher Maude Steele, Donald Keith Franklin, Charles Black, Deon Williams, Shirley Williams, Kenneth Adams, Helen Rittenberry, Wanda Tharp, Geneva Damron, Genell Adams, Bonnie Wright, unidentified, Doris Croft, Michael Black, Dora Alice Campbell, Bobby Williams, and Don Perryman; (fifth row) teacher Alice Sunderland, Don Watson, Ralph May, Paul Kennedy, Robert Burton, Jimmie Barnes, Russel Quertermous, Carl Slayden, Nina Bebout, Donald Lee Tharp, unidentified, Mona Gay Wilson, Glendal Belt, Blanton Damron, Wayne Watson, Eva Jean Wilson, Melva Adams, Nellie Jean Tolley, Mona Fay Slayden, Geraldine Quertermous, cook Vera Slayden, principal Harley Sunderland, and cook Ruby Babb. (Courtesy of Livingston County Historical Society.)

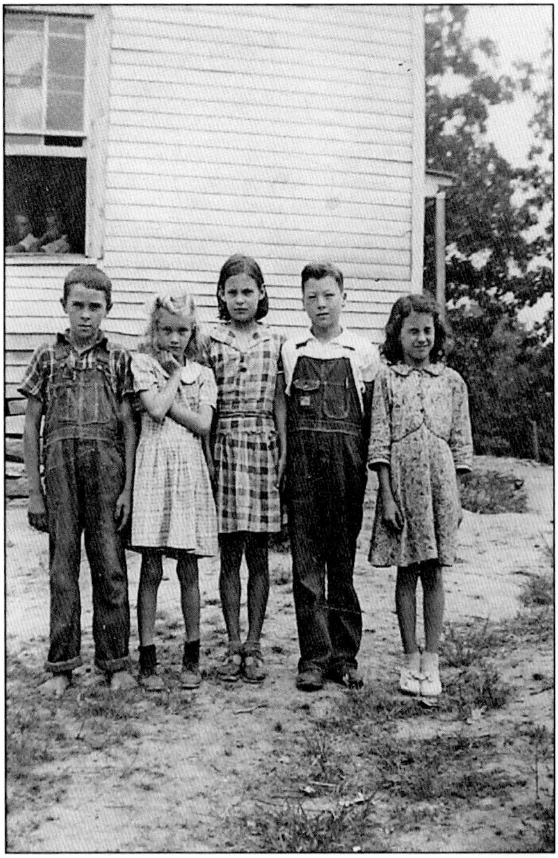

These students are standing by the Roe School, a little country school between Smithland and Burna. They are, from left to right, Jimmie Hall, Mary Jean Henry, Mary Alice Campbell, W. C. Edmonds, and Mary Esther Crotchett. (Courtesy of Esther Dubuque.)

The citizens of Smithland became the proud owners of a new high school situated on top of the hill at the conjunction of Court and Mill Streets in 1916. The first principal was Preston Dabney, and he stayed for 34 years. The last principals were Aurel Threlkeld and Kenneth Hardin. Before the completion of the school, classes were taught in the courthouse or in the old elementary school. A modern gymnasium was built in the early 1940s and was a source of great pride. The modern school was used until 1958, when Livingston Central High School was built near Burna and served as a high school for the whole county. The building was torn down to make way for the new Smithland Elementary School in 1961. In 1984, a new Livingston Central High School was built in Smithland, and the spacious building is used as the only high school for the county. (Courtesy of Livingston County Historical Society.)

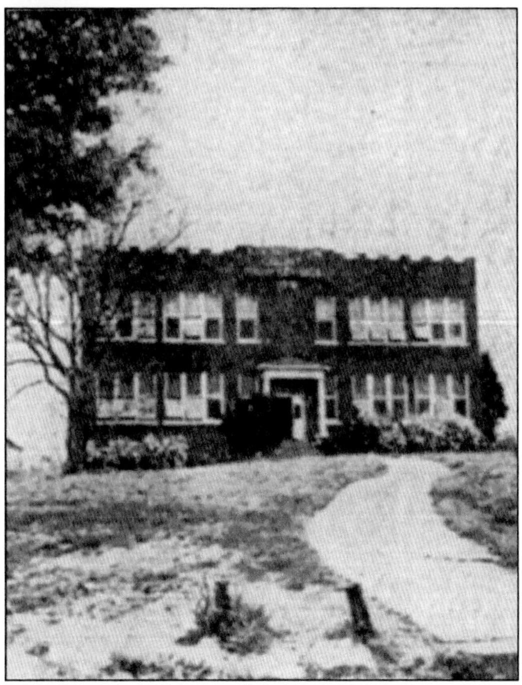

Six

PEOPLE

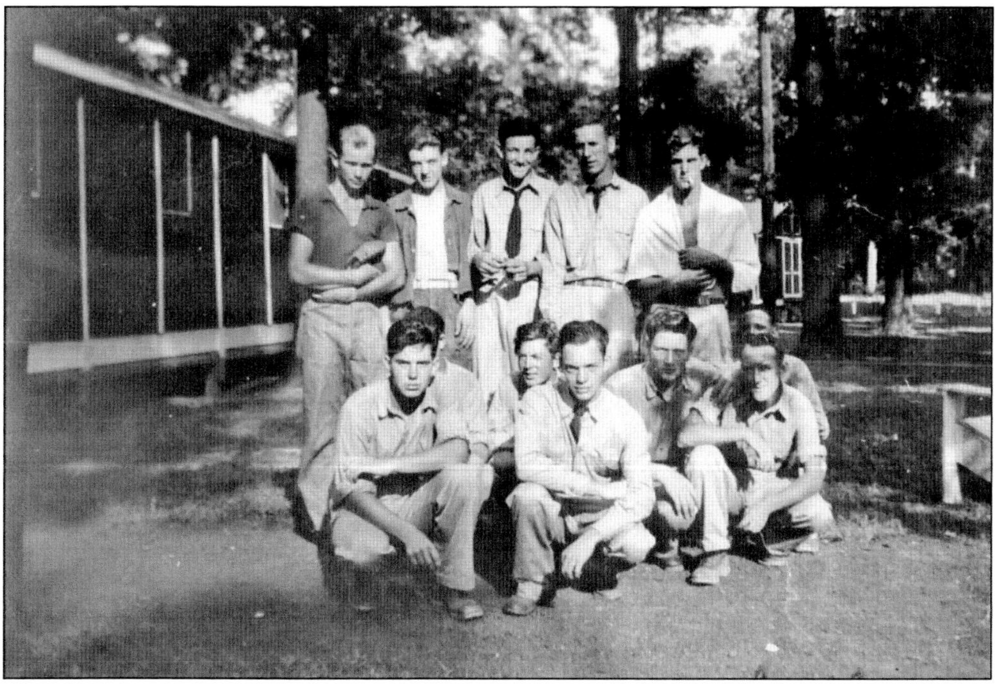

This photograph was taken of men in the Civilian Conservation Corps (CCC) located on Clay Street in Paducah, Kentucky. The only ones identified are Roy Stevens and James Normie Tramble, third and fourth from the left (respectively) in the second row. The men were paid $30 a month and were furnished uniforms and good meals. Many were from Livingston County. (Courtesy of Faye Teitloff.)

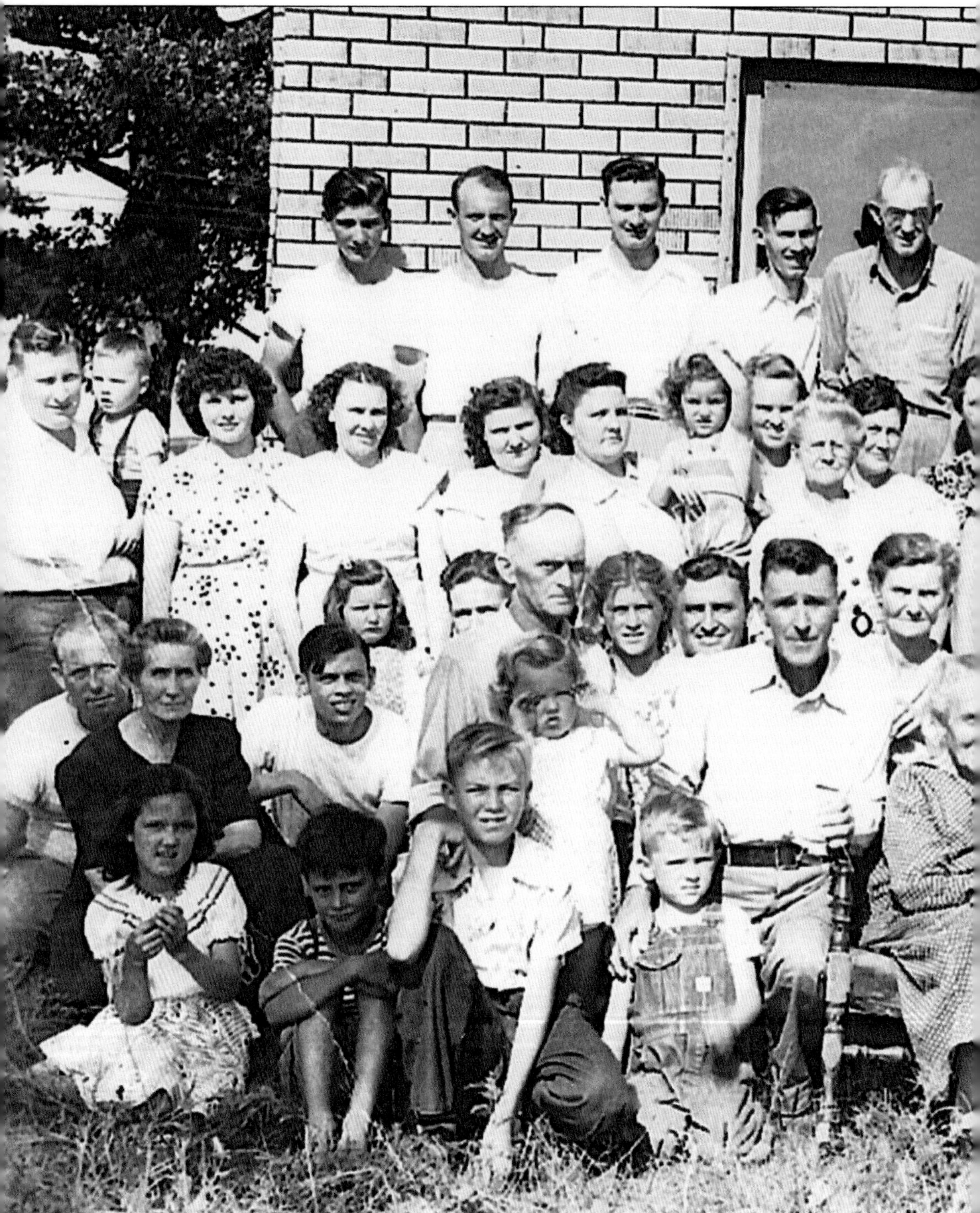

The Brooks family reunion was held about 1948 at the Andrews farm house near Joy. There are too many to identify. It is believed the Brooks family arrived in Massachusetts in 1632 and ventured southward, with different brothers settling in North and South Carolina, Maryland, and Virginia. James Benjamin Brooks married Alice Adams in 1875 and had seven girls and one

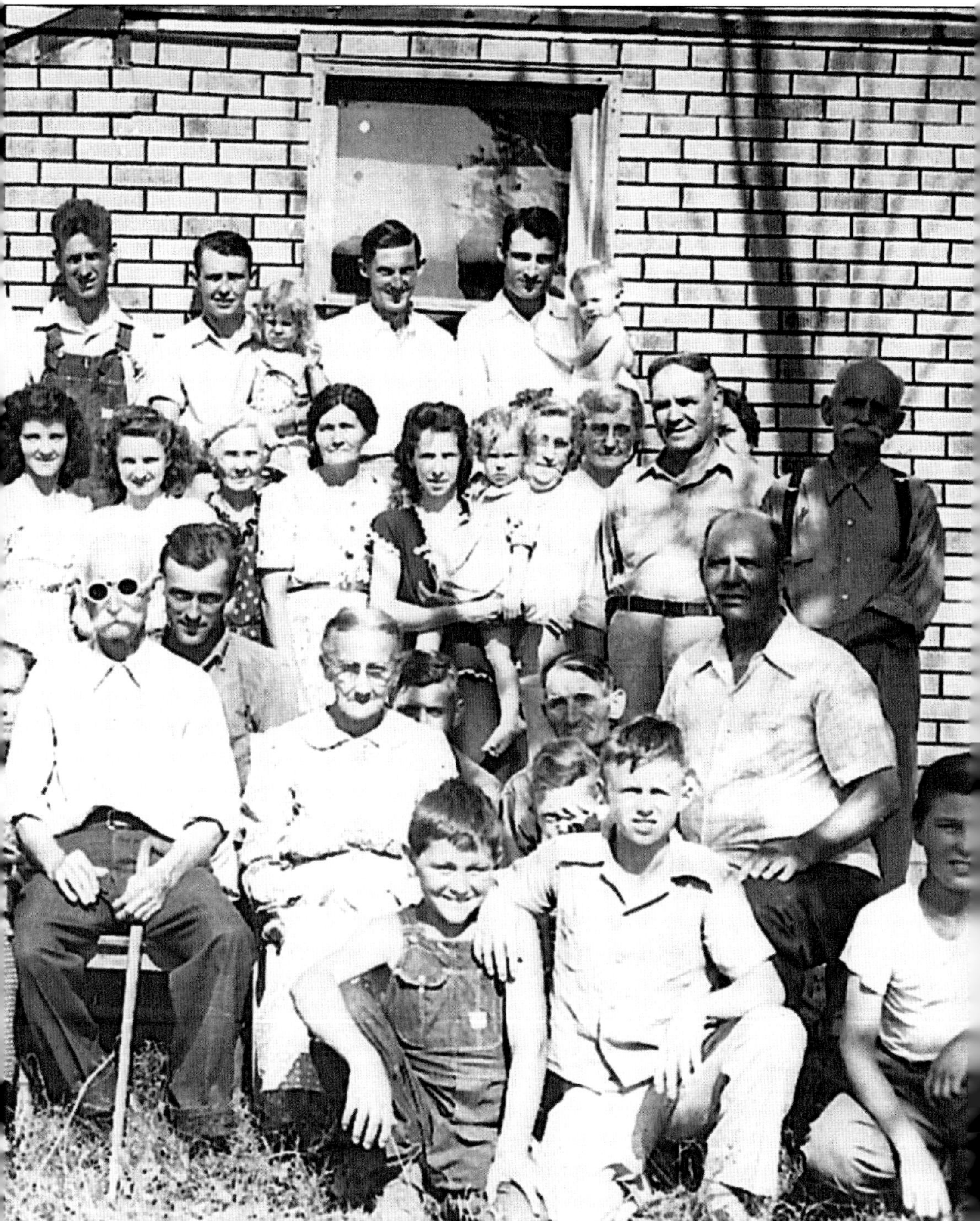

boy, and these families are mostly included in this photograph. The Brooks children with married names were Vadia Blankenship, Loretta Chappell, Cora Tramble, Reese Brooks, Evaline Lockett, Etta Alsobrook, Laura Ross, and Delia Andrews. The Andrews family had 12 children, and many of them attended the reunion. (Courtesy of Faye Teitloff.)

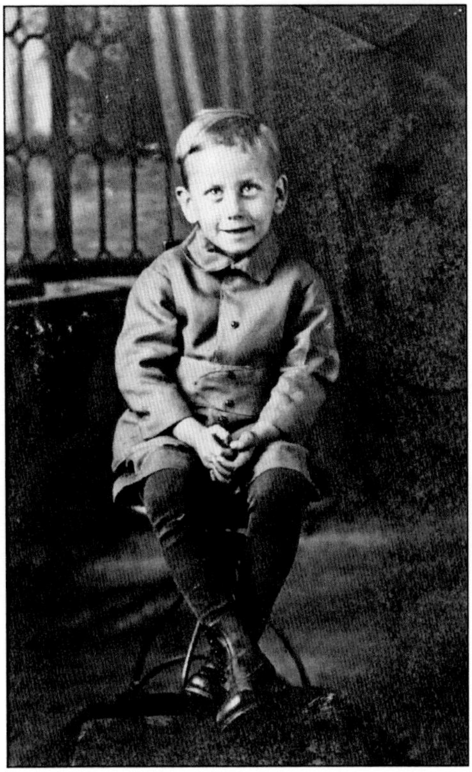

James Normie Tramble was born on June 14, 1916, to Cooper and Cora Brooks Tramble. He married Fannie Hosick on December 15, 1942, and had three children—Roy, Faye, and Tony—and 10 grandchildren. Normie grew up in the Tiline area and later bought a farm behind Three Rivers Rock Quarry. This postcard photograph was taken at Paschal Studios in Paducah, Kentucky, around 1918. He was dressed for the time period. (Courtesy of Faye Teitloff.)

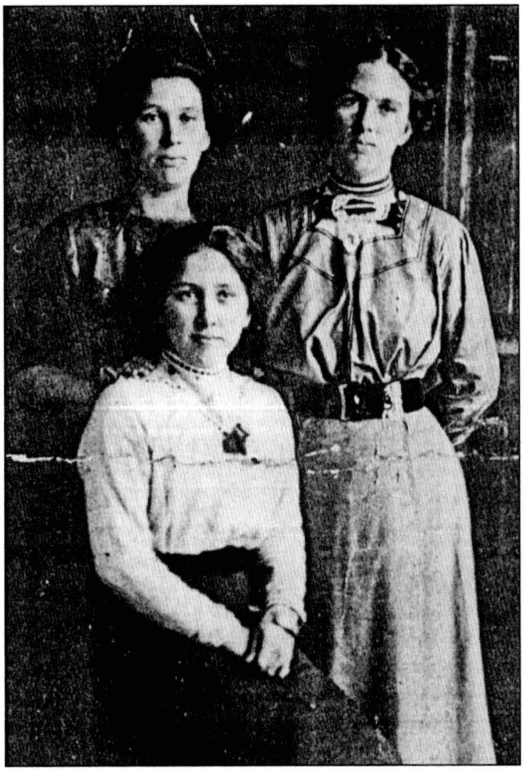

This photograph was taken on December 17, 1912, of Emma Mitchell (sitting), Della Dunning (standing, left) and Enna Hosick (standing, right). They were daughters of Thomas Richard and Minerva Hart Parks. Emma and Enna were twins, and their mother died when they were two years old. This left Della, who was 13, to help her father raise them. (Courtesy of Mary Lou Smith.)

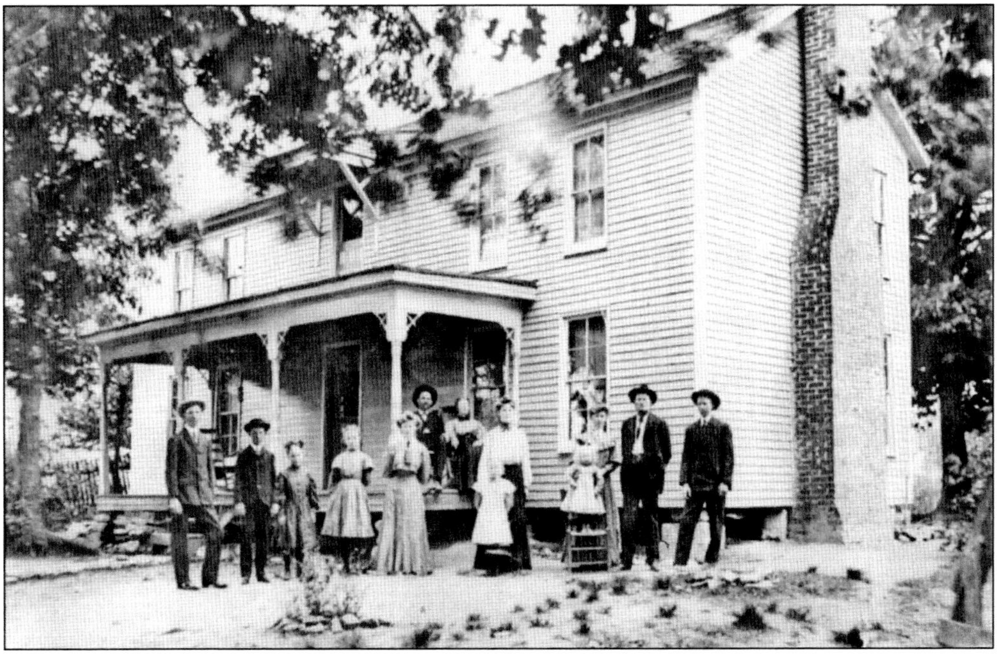

Seen in May 1911 near Pinckneyville, this house was built by Soloman Lee in 1906. Sitting on the porch are Soloman and Florence Lee. Standing are their children and grandchildren: (from left to right) John, Robert, Lyla Bell, Maggie, Nora, Essie Ilane, Carilla, and Florence Lee; Isabell Lee Daniel, her husband, Joe Daniel, and Roland Lee are on the far right of the photograph.

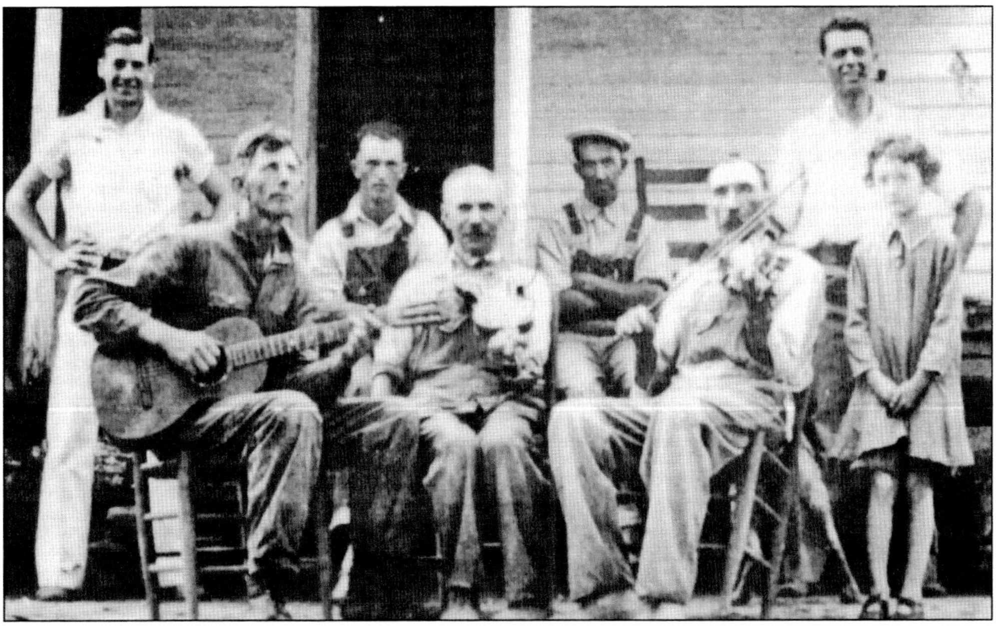

Two old bachelors, Bob and Daley Damron, lived near Salem in a log house with clean, white-washed walls. They loved to play country music, so the young people would go there on Saturday night, move furniture out, and have a dance. All are unidentified in the second row except for Coy Alley, who is second from the left. In the front row are unidentified, Daley Damron, Bob Damron, and Hazel Alley. This photograph was taken in 1925.

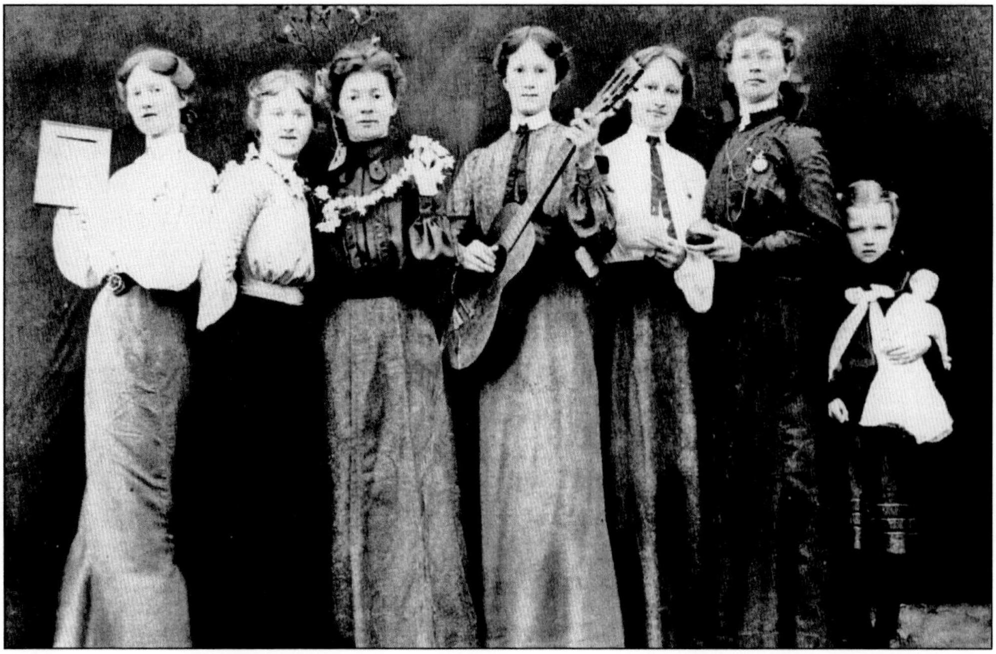

From left to right are Dorene Lee (Smith), Nora Lee, Mary Lee (Daniel), Essie Lee, Ruth Lee (Clark), Viola Lee (Mummy), and Maggie Lee. They are the daughters of Soloman and Florence Lee. The photograph was supposedly made in Pinckneyville about 1908 by George Martin, a local photographer and neighbor.

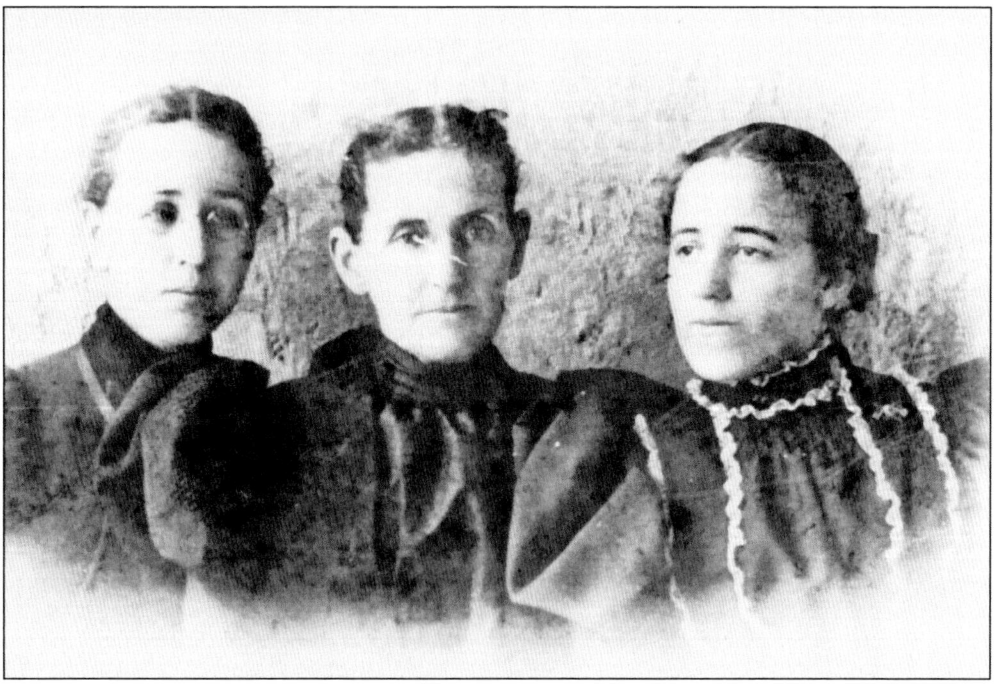

This photograph was taken in 1897 by Reed and Lindsay, Photographic. Electra Alvis (left), Mable Alley Alvis (mother), and Ophelia Alvis (right) are shown. Electra never married, but Ophelia married Lee Darroh. Mable was born in 1843 and died in 1925.

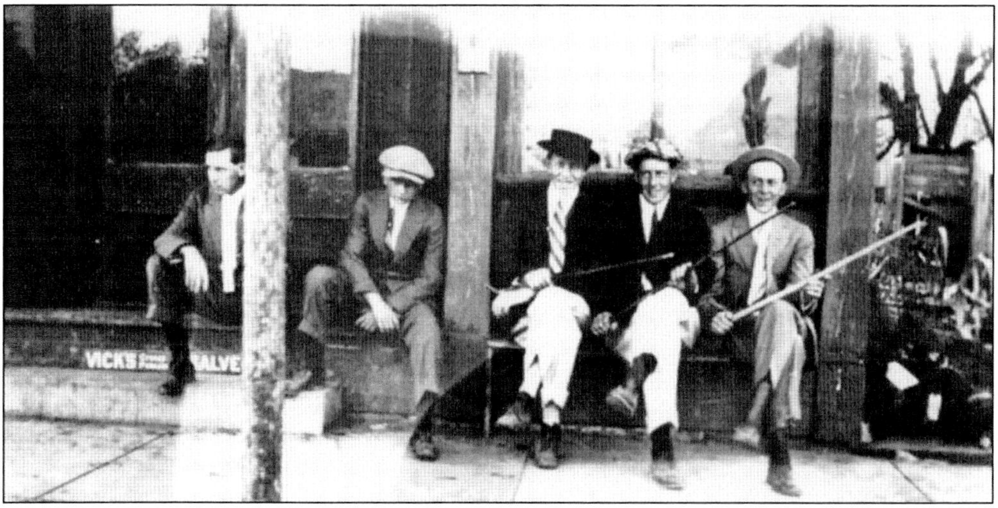

Sitting on the step are, from left to right, Pola Smock and Paul Threlkeld, and on the bench are Irvin Burke, Jesse Brewer, and Rurie Smock. They are pictured around 1920 in Carrsville. Note the canes; although not needed by these young men, they were deemed stylish in that time period.

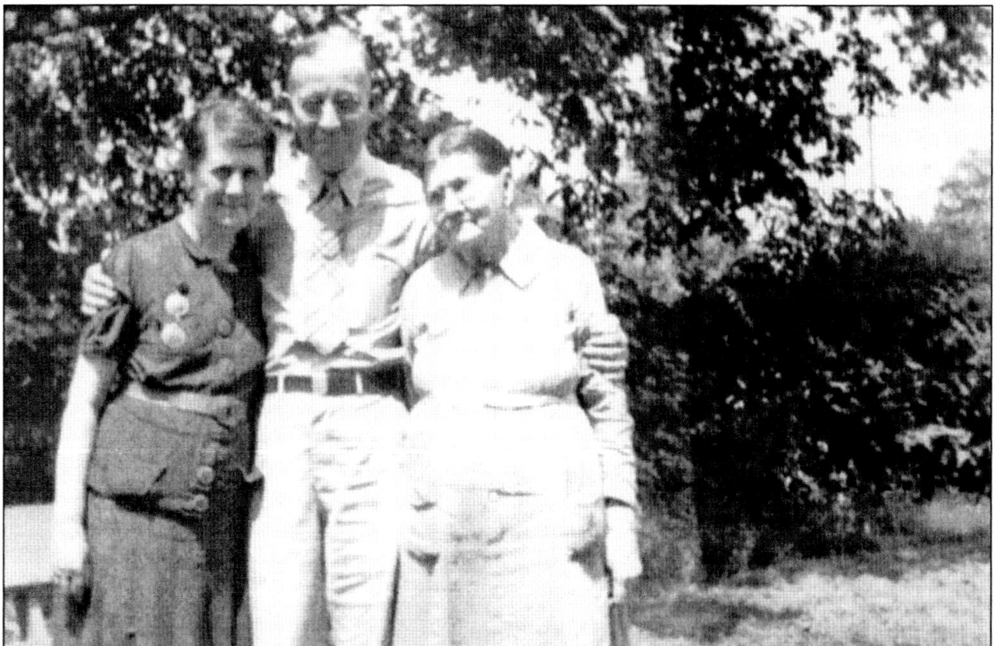

Seen here in the 1940s are Mamie Yates Ferguson, Jesse Brewer, and their mother, Mattie Brewer. Mamie Yates was born in Carrsville to T. H. and Mattie Yates in 1880. After her husband died, Mattie married W. C. Brewer and had Jesse. Jessie married Lucy Boyd Brewer and, in later years, lived on Wilson Avenue in Smithland.

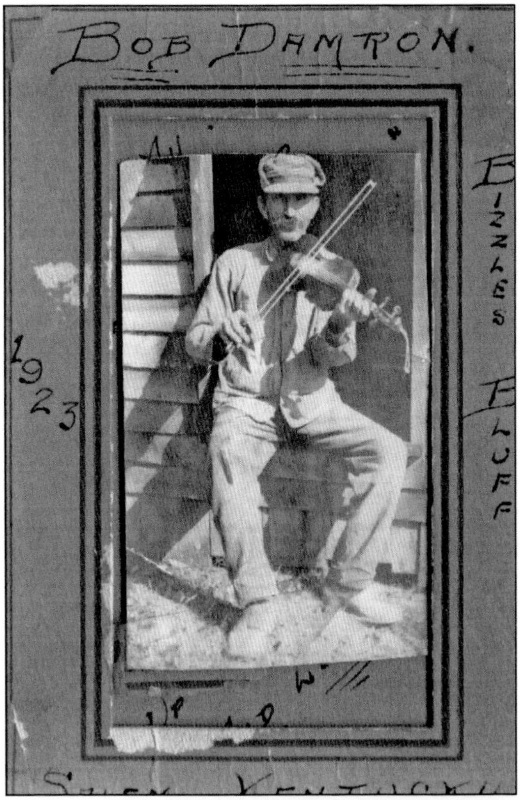

Robert (Bob) Damron of Salem played his violin quite well. He owned three of the good instruments, including a rare type of Stradivarius of which there were supposed to have been only six made. Pictured here in 1923, Bob was born in 1865 and died in 1969.

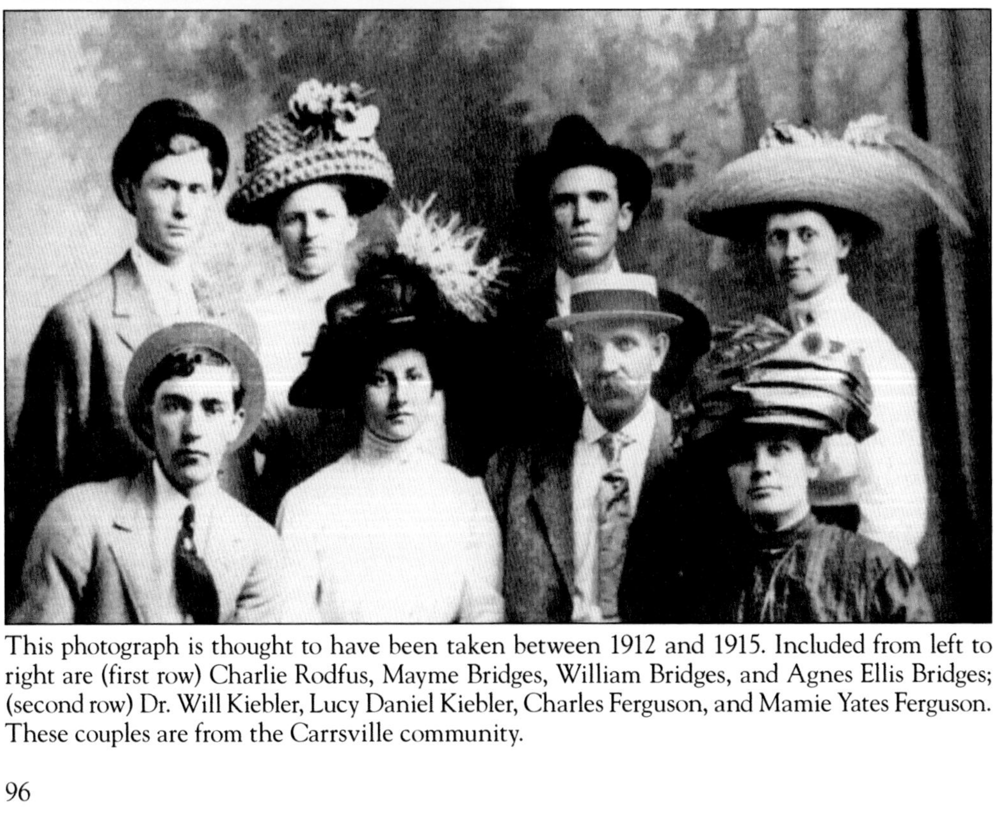

This photograph is thought to have been taken between 1912 and 1915. Included from left to right are (first row) Charlie Rodfus, Mayme Bridges, William Bridges, and Agnes Ellis Bridges; (second row) Dr. Will Kiebler, Lucy Daniel Kiebler, Charles Ferguson, and Mamie Yates Ferguson. These couples are from the Carrsville community.

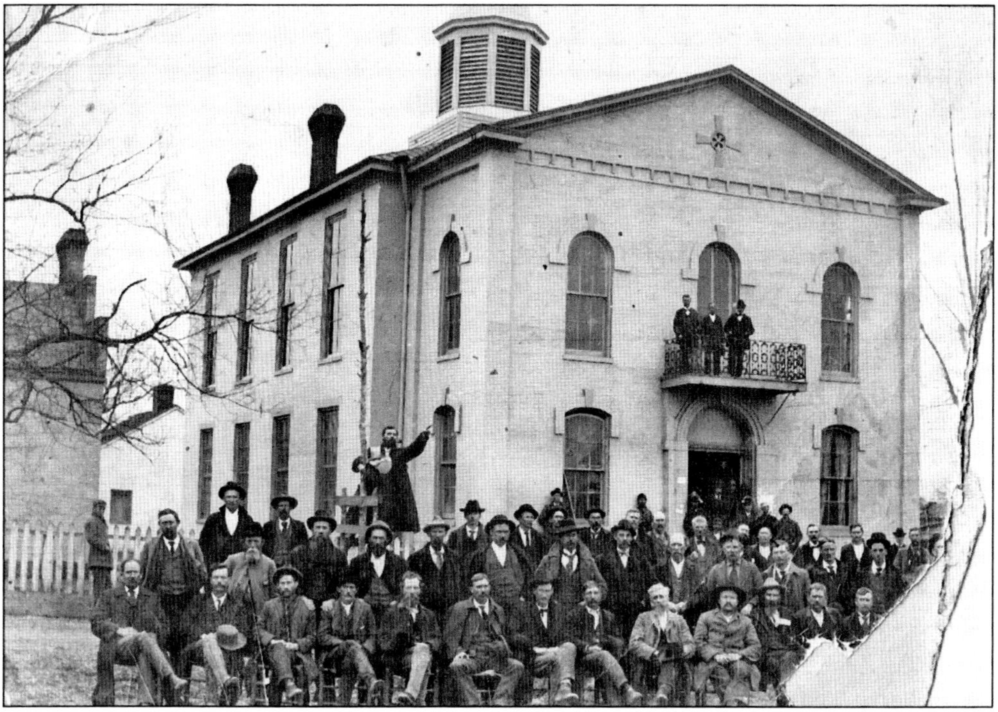

The courthouse in Smithland is the scene for this big political rally in 1901. Notice that these candidates for office are all men; women were not allowed to even vote until 1920. The courthouse has survived repeated flooding and has managed to protect the county's most important records dating back to 1798. (Courtesy of Livingston County Historical Society.)

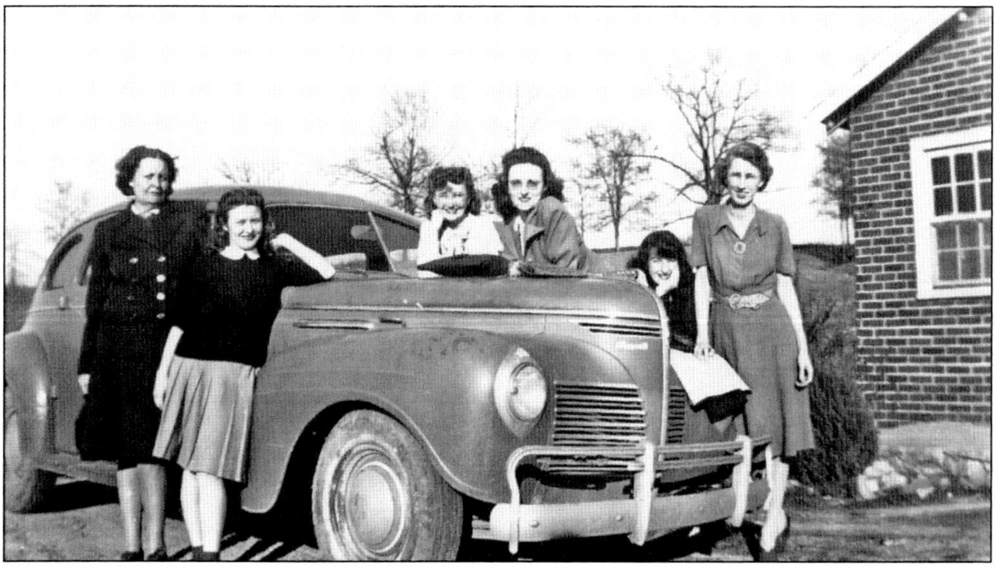

This photograph shows Smithland girls who ran around during the 1945 flood. From left to right are public health nurse Alice Owen, health department clerk Edith Rudd, deputy circuit clerk Geneva Woodson, health department clerk Hazel Alley, Pearl Ruth Travis, and circuit court clerk Reba Smith.

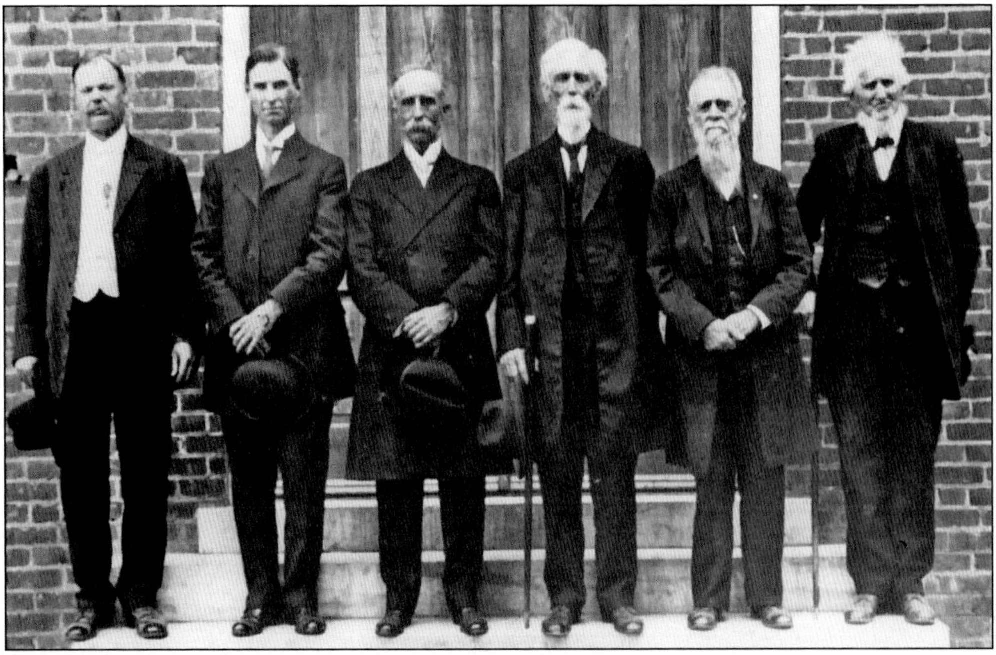

Seen here on May 29, 1910, for the dedication of Mount Zion Methodist Episcopal Church are, from left to right, Rev. C. C. Newbill, Rev. S. F. Wynn, Rev. C. D. Hilliard, Rev. J. T. McGill, Rev. W. H. Whitt, and Rev. Sim Weaver. Mount Zion was supposedly in the Tiline community. (Courtesy of Livingston County Historical Society.)

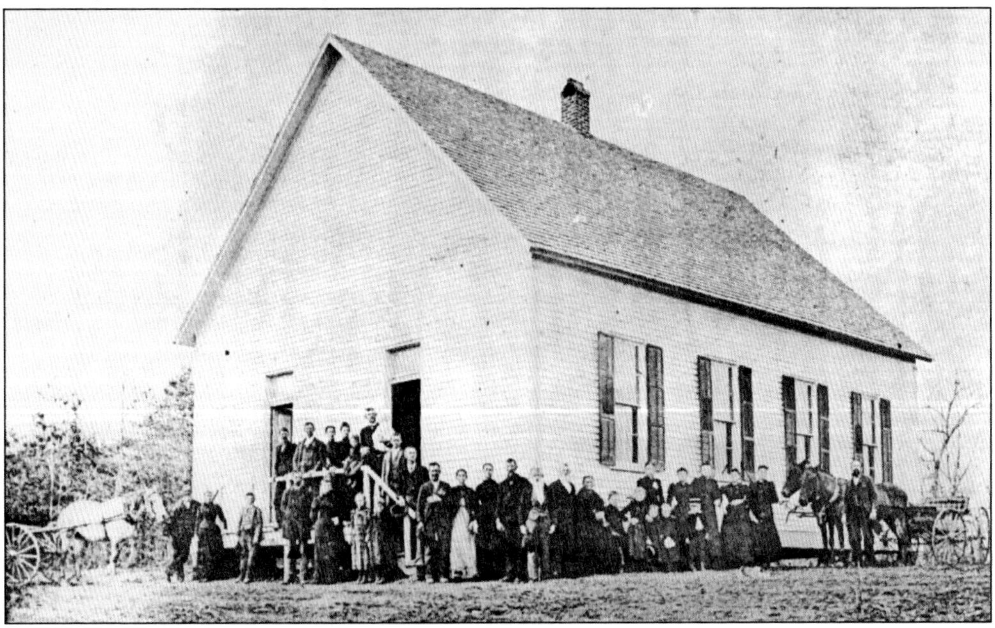

This photograph was taken at the dedication of Iuka Methodist Church in 1864. None of the people are identified. Iuka is a Native American name meaning "welcome". A common sight on Sunday afternoon was a large group of people gathered at the old ferry landing to see a preacher wading out into the river to baptize the awaiting candidates. (Courtesy of Livingston County Historical Society.)

In this photograph, taken about 1915, these children of Clementine and Lula Champion Davenport are Lovie Davenport (seated), Opal Davenport (standing, left), Norbin Davenport (standing, center), and Ray Davenport (standing, right). They are the grandchildren of John and Elizabeth Bray Davenport. Opal married Lonnie Singleton, who was a Pentecostal minister at a church near the old Barrett Rock Quarry for many years.

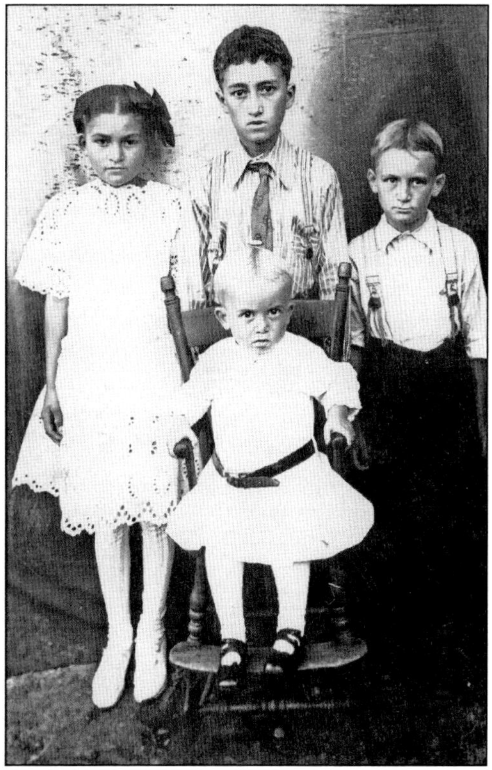

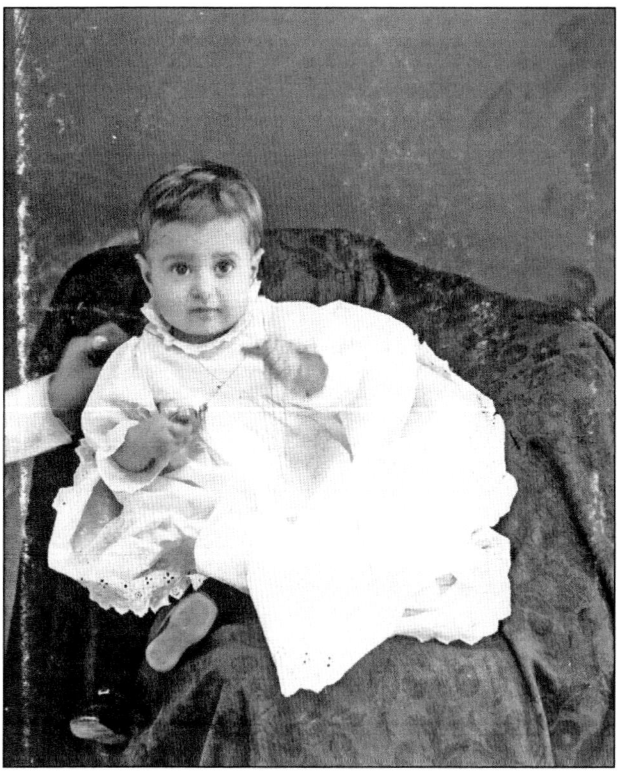

This old photograph, taken in 1896 by Griffin and Watkins in Princeton, Kentucky, is of Price Hollowell. He was the son of Robert and Mary Lou Hollowell, who were severely whipped by members of the Night Riders. They later sued the organization and won a settlement, with which they purchased a farm in the Pinckneyville community. Robert lost his life due to the beating.

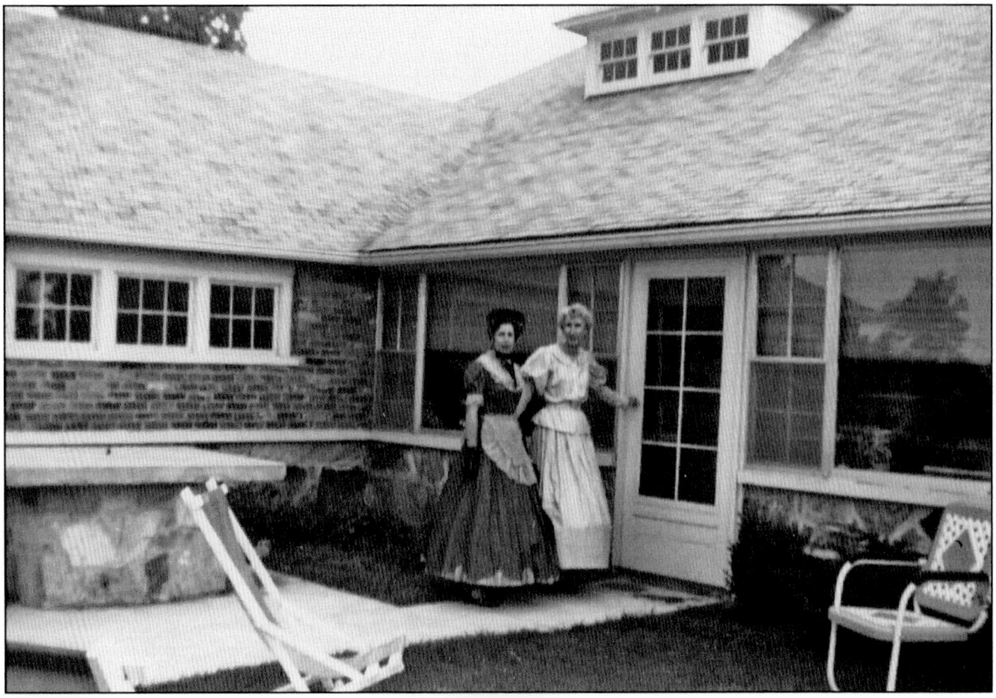

Pictured above are Grace McCandless (left) and Reba Smith in 1960 at the home of Kermit and Elizabeth McKinney in Smithland. They were attending a Woman's Club event. The McKinney home, which was built in 1838, was once known as the Conant house. The house seemed prone to fires, as it was partially burned in 1896 and 1919. After the McKinneys died in the 1990s, the home was destroyed by fire.

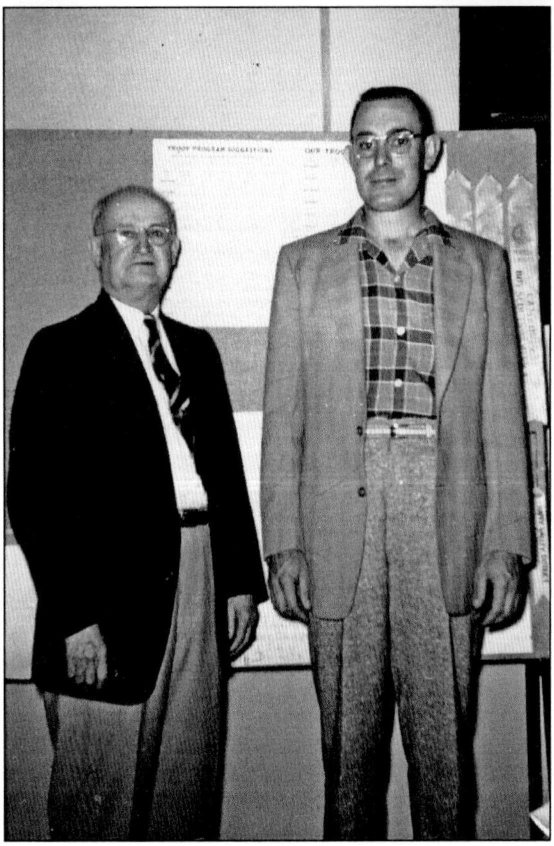

This photograph of Jefferson Davis Clopton (left) and Lee Barnes was probably taken in the 1950s in Smithland. They were both active members of the Smithland Methodist Church. Davis was a pharmacist and the owner of Clopton's Drugstore until his death in 1973. Lee retired in 1978 from Airco Alloys in Calvert City, where he worked as a mechanic on heavy-duty equipment.

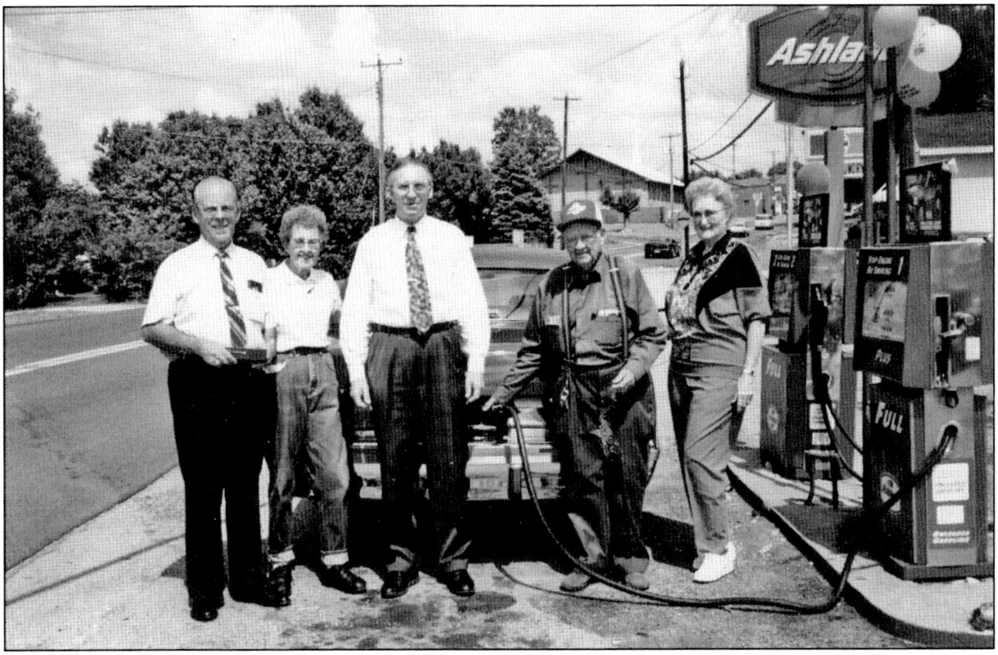

This photograph, taken outside the West End Service and Convenience Store on its 50th anniversary celebration in 1996, includes, from left to right, Farris Boyd, Loretta LaRue, Charles Fox, Douglas LaRue, and Hazel Robinson. The store was a campaign stop for all state and local candidates each time they passed through. The LaRues closed the store in 2001 after many years of great service. The store was known as the friendliest place around Salem.

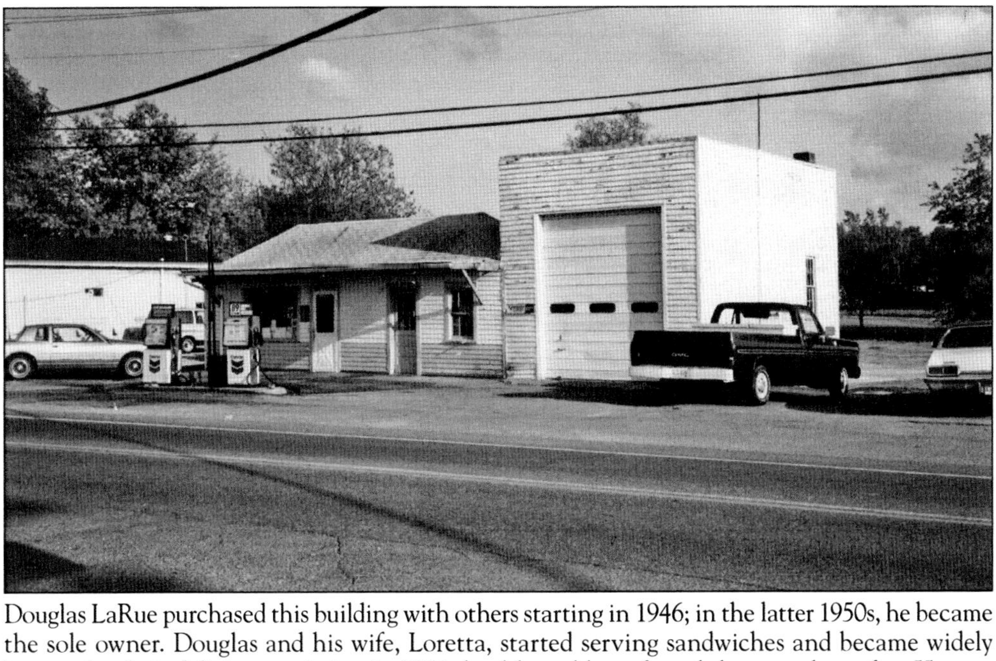

Douglas LaRue purchased this building with others starting in 1946; in the latter 1950s, he became the sole owner. Douglas and his wife, Loretta, started serving sandwiches and became widely known for their delicious varieties. In 2001, health problems forced them to close after 55 years of operating the West End Service Station and Convenience Store in Salem. The building was removed when the Farmers Bank was built in 2003.

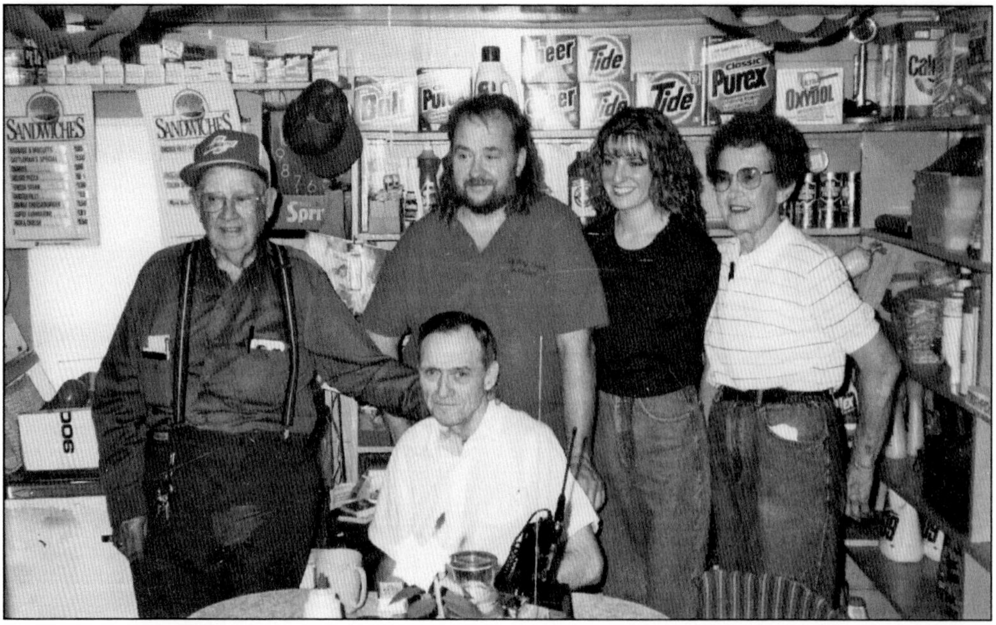

Celebrating the 50th anniversary of the West End Service Station and Convenience Store in 1996 are, from left to right, (standing) Douglas, Eric, Mary Beth, Loretta, and Pete Larue (sitting) in the Salem business. Pete is Douglas and Loretta's son and is a retired Kentucky state highway engineer. Their youngest son, Eric, is a retired schoolteacher, and Douglas and Loretta are both deceased.

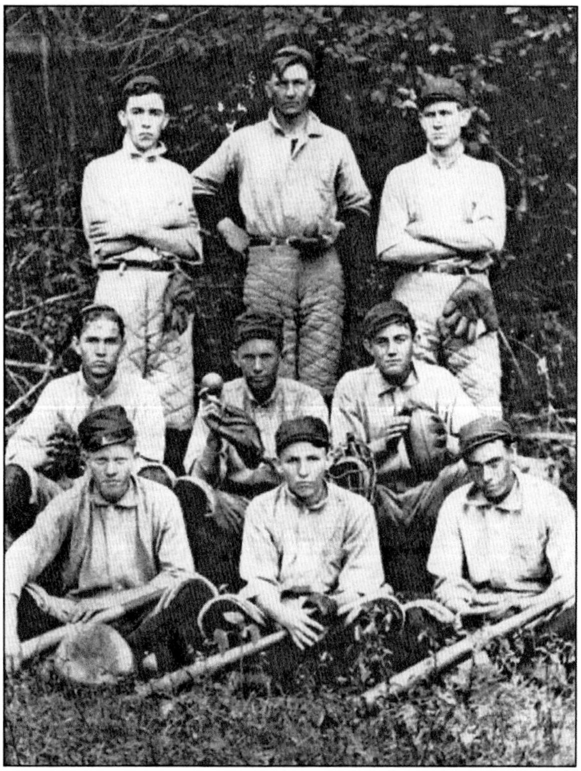

The Carrsville baseball team, pictured about 1910, included, from left to right, (first row) Charlie Rodfus, Jess Barnes, and Harry Ellis; (second row) Owen Spees, Bob Fowler, and Tom Fowler; (third row) Harry Brewer, Barney Rodfus, and John Glass. Carrsville was named for Billy Carr (or Karr), who owned the land and divided it into lots for sale. The original plan can be seen at the courthouse as drawn in 1868.

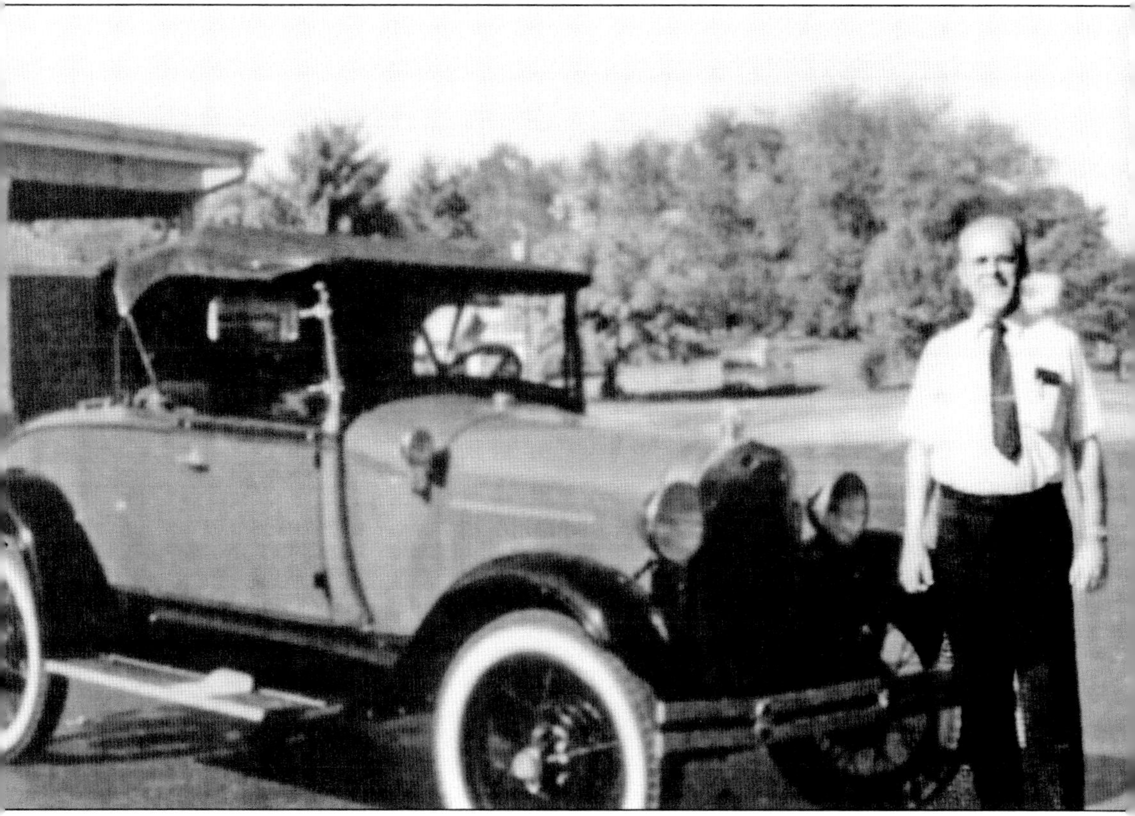

Taken about 1986, this photograph shows Farris Boyd with one of his many antique automobiles. He was a familiar site in Salem-area parades and shows. Farris was born to Lewis and Laverne Farris Boyd on December 7, 1932. Farris entered into partnership with his father at Boyd Funeral Directors when he came out of the service in 1957. Boyd Funeral Directors was founded in 1902 by F. M. Boyd. It sold hardware and caskets in Carrsville. In 1926, the business was moved to Salem. F. M.'s son, Lewis, became a licensed mortician and joined his father in 1927. The business moved into several locations in Salem until it built a new facility in 1950 on Main Street. Up until this time, local funerals were held in churches and homes. There have been several additions to the facility through the years. Lewis and Farris Boyd have since died. Charles Fox and his son, Andrew, are in partnership with the business under the same name of Boyd Funeral Directors.

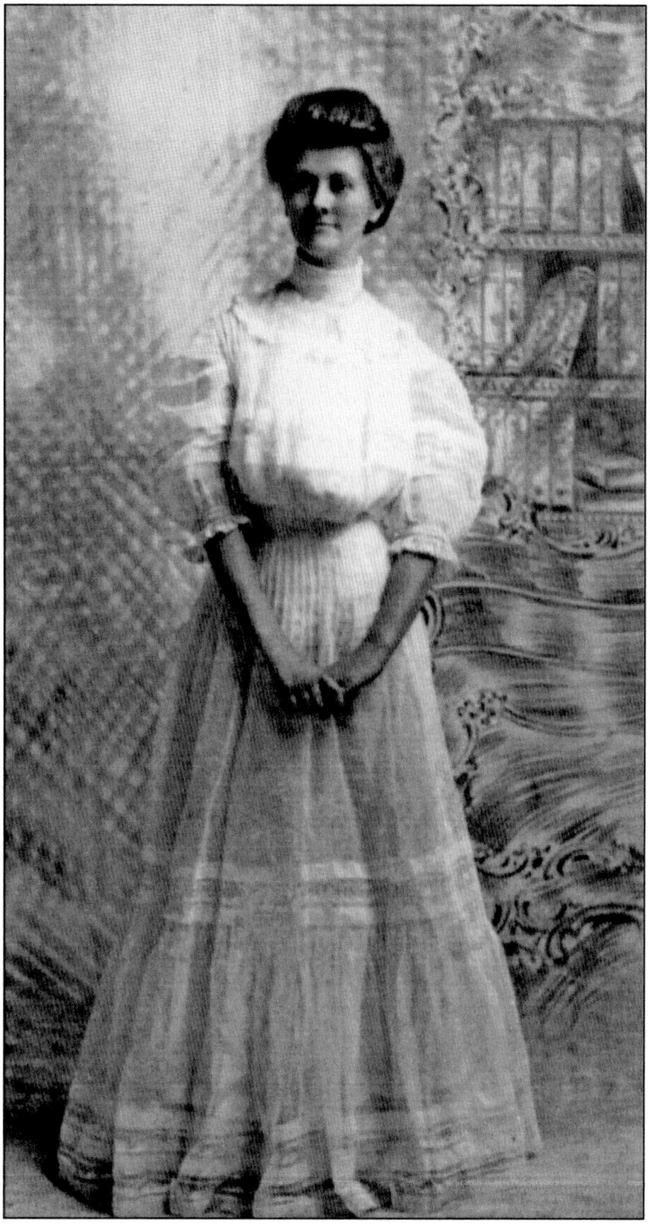

Mamie Yates Ferguson was born on December 20, 1880, to T. H. and Mattie Yates in Carrsville. She was educated as a teacher and began teaching at the Carrsville School in 1904. She married a promising young attorney, Charles Ferguson, in 1911 at the Palmer Hotel in Paducah. In 1920, Mamie was asked to become the Livingston County school superintendent, serving until 1938, when a new board was elected. During those 18 years, she regularly visited the schools, driving dirt roads in her Ford Model T. The county had 48 one-room schools, with larger schools in towns. In 1941, the board asked Mamie to resume her duties as superintendent. In 1947, tragedy struck when Charles Ferguson was murdered by his mentally ill sister, who also took her own life. Mamie retired in 1951 after seeing the one-room schools disappear and buses running throughout the county. She had worked in a time period when it was unheard of for a woman to hold such a position, but she accomplished her goals and oversaw many improvements in the county schools.

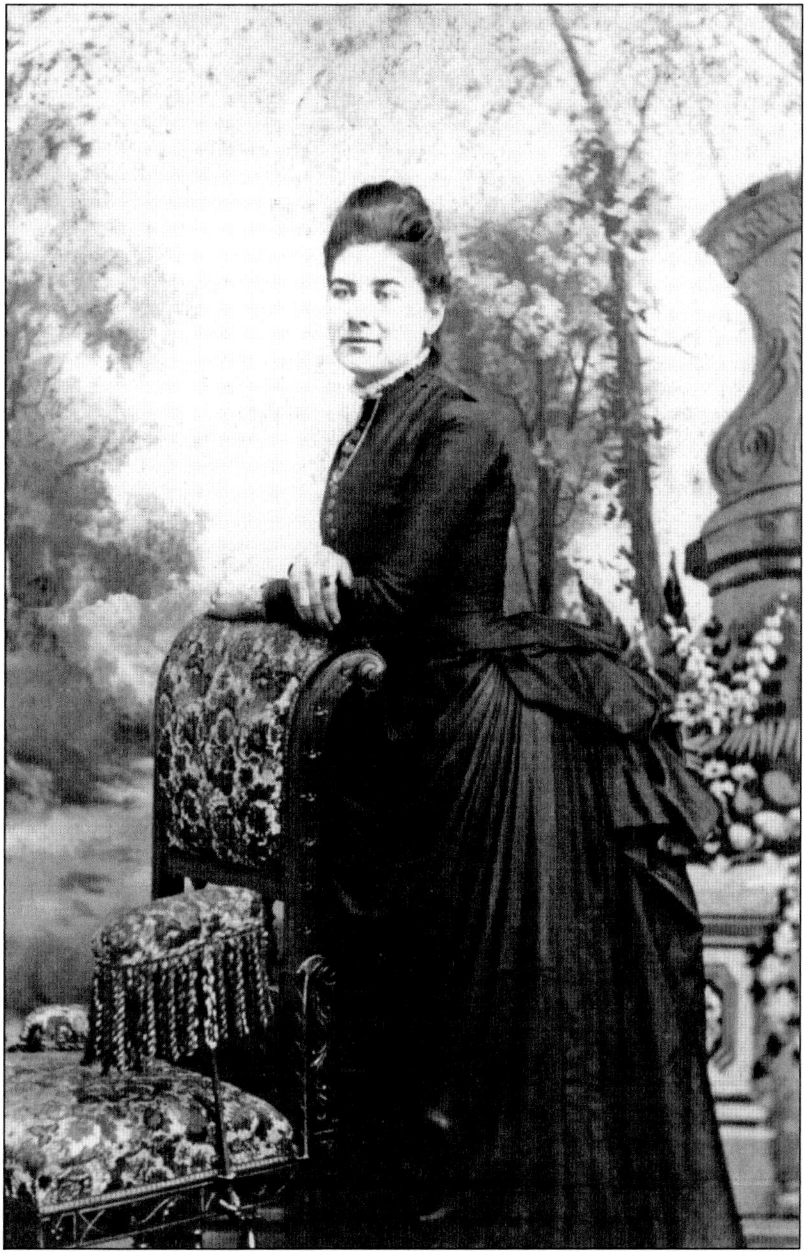

Mary Lou Eastman married Robert Hollowell. They resided in Caldwell County in 1907, when the Black Patch Tobacco War was brewing. Mary Lou operated a boardinghouse where county officials and others ate. This put her in a perfect position to gather information about the Night Riders. Mary Lou was outspoken about her opposition to the association and appeared in court to testify about the raids with names of the people involved. Robert and Mary Lou were severely whipped by members of the Night Riders, which allegedly included some of the Hollowell relatives. Robert, Mary Lou, and their son, Price, established an out-of-state residence and sued members of the organization. They won a settlement, with which they purchased a farm in the Pinckneyville area. Robert lived only a few years, eventually losing his life as a result of the beating. Mary Lou (1869–1965) and Price lived on the farm or in Salem for the remainder of their lives.

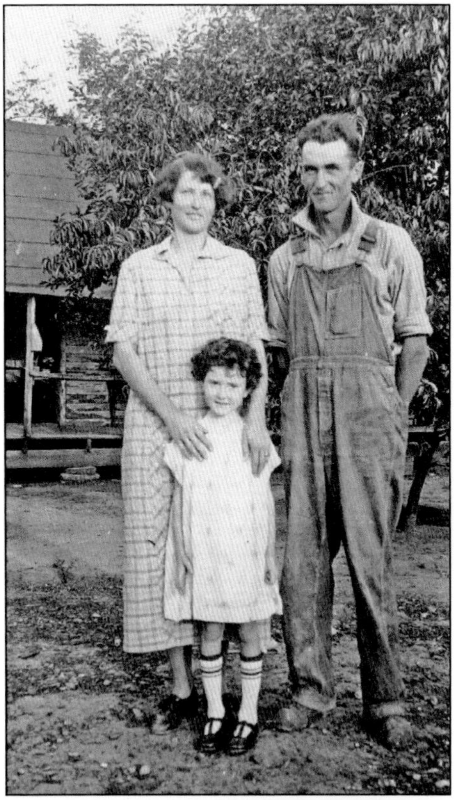

This photograph was taken in 1925 of Susie, Coy, and Jessie Hazel Alley on their farm near Salem. Coy was the son of Absolum Lafayette (Fate) Alley and Mary Jane (Mollie) Davidson. Coy Alley married Susie Sivells, who was reared by Joseph and Amanda McCollum Parker due to her mother's death. Their daughter, Hazel Robertson, is a retired social worker living on the family farm.

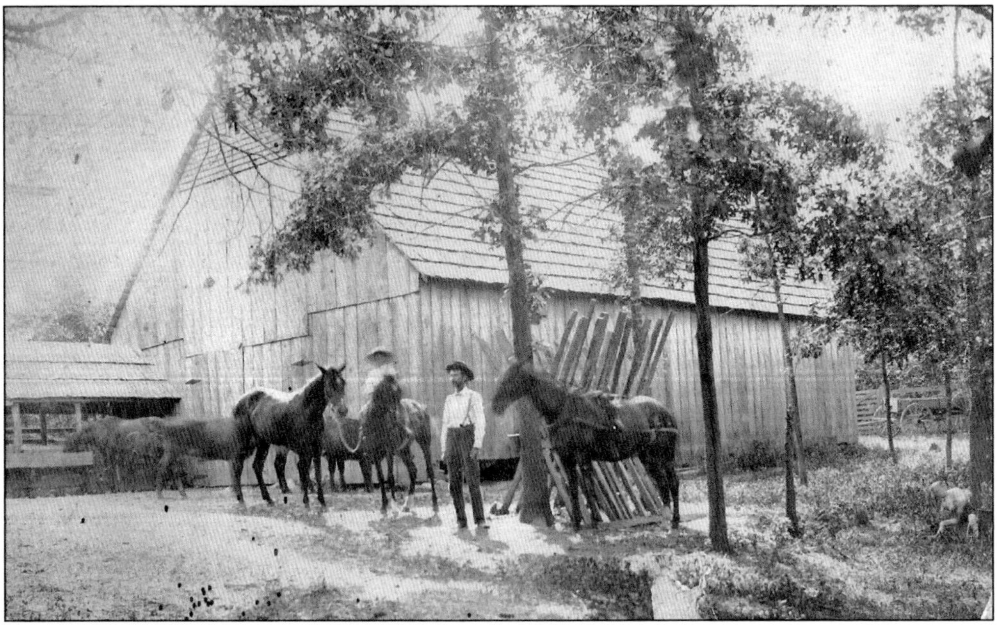

This photograph has James Huey and Amanda Robertson written on the back. The Robertson family history shows that James Huey was born in 1861 and died in 1931. He married Amanda Durham, and their children were Anna Lillian, Herman, Glenn, Duley, Ocie, and Maude. The family owned a farm near Tiline. (Courtesy of Livingston County Historical Society.)

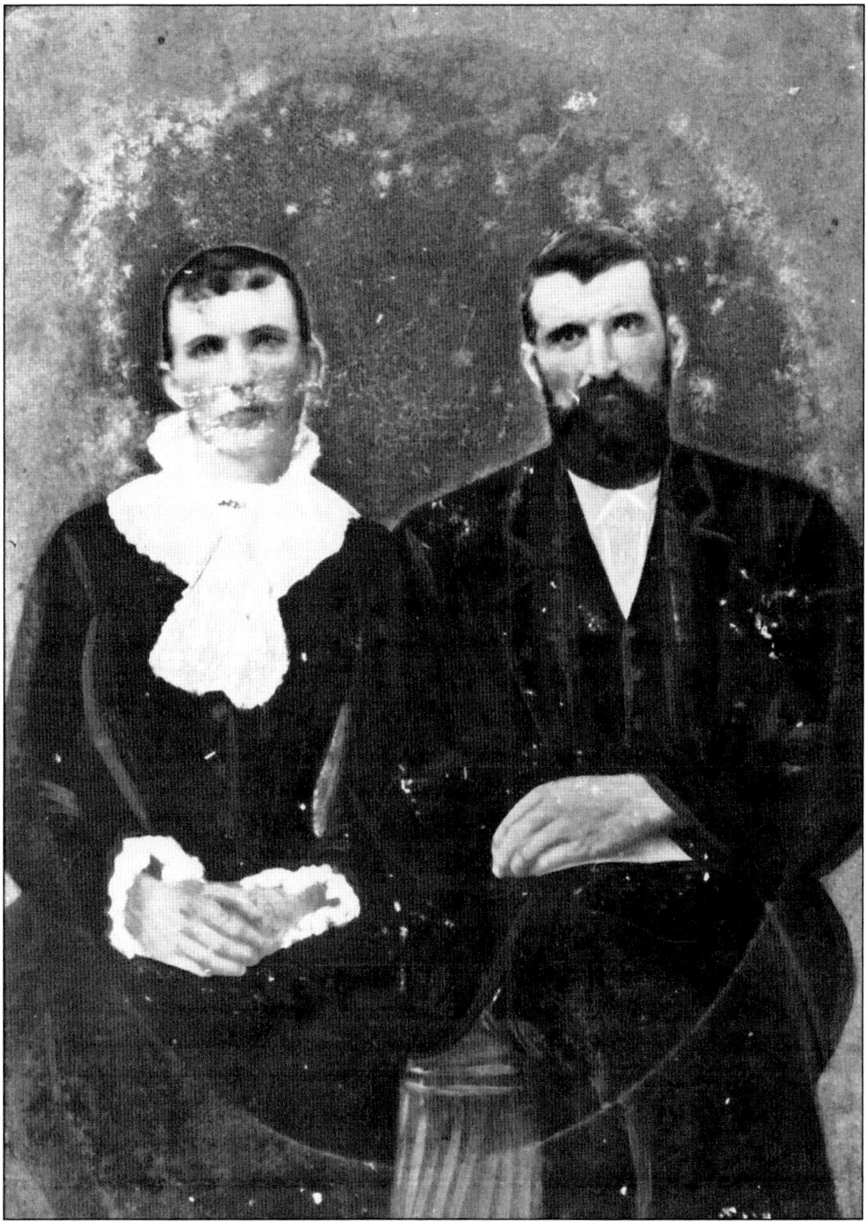

The date of this photograph of Absolum Lafayette (Fate) Alley and his second wife, Mary Alvis, daughter of Asa and Blanch Alvis, is unknown. Fate's parents were Augustus and Mary Adeline Sherill Alley. They moved to a farm near Salem in 1852 from North Carolina. Augustus became a constable. On March 1, 1860, Augustus went to Pinckneyville to levy a tax on some property of James Washington Shelby. Trouble arose between the two, and some shots were exchanged. Shelby threw a chopping ax, striking a deathblow to Alley's neck, and stabbed him repeatedly with a large hand-made knife. The knife had been used in Indian fighting by Mose Shelby, brother of the first governor, Isaac Shelby. Fate, who was 12 years old at the time of his father's death, remembers the not-guilty verdict rendered by reason of insanity. Fate was a livestock dealer who rode his horse around the area, buying livestock and driving them to Carrsville and Marion to ship by boat or train to Louisville.

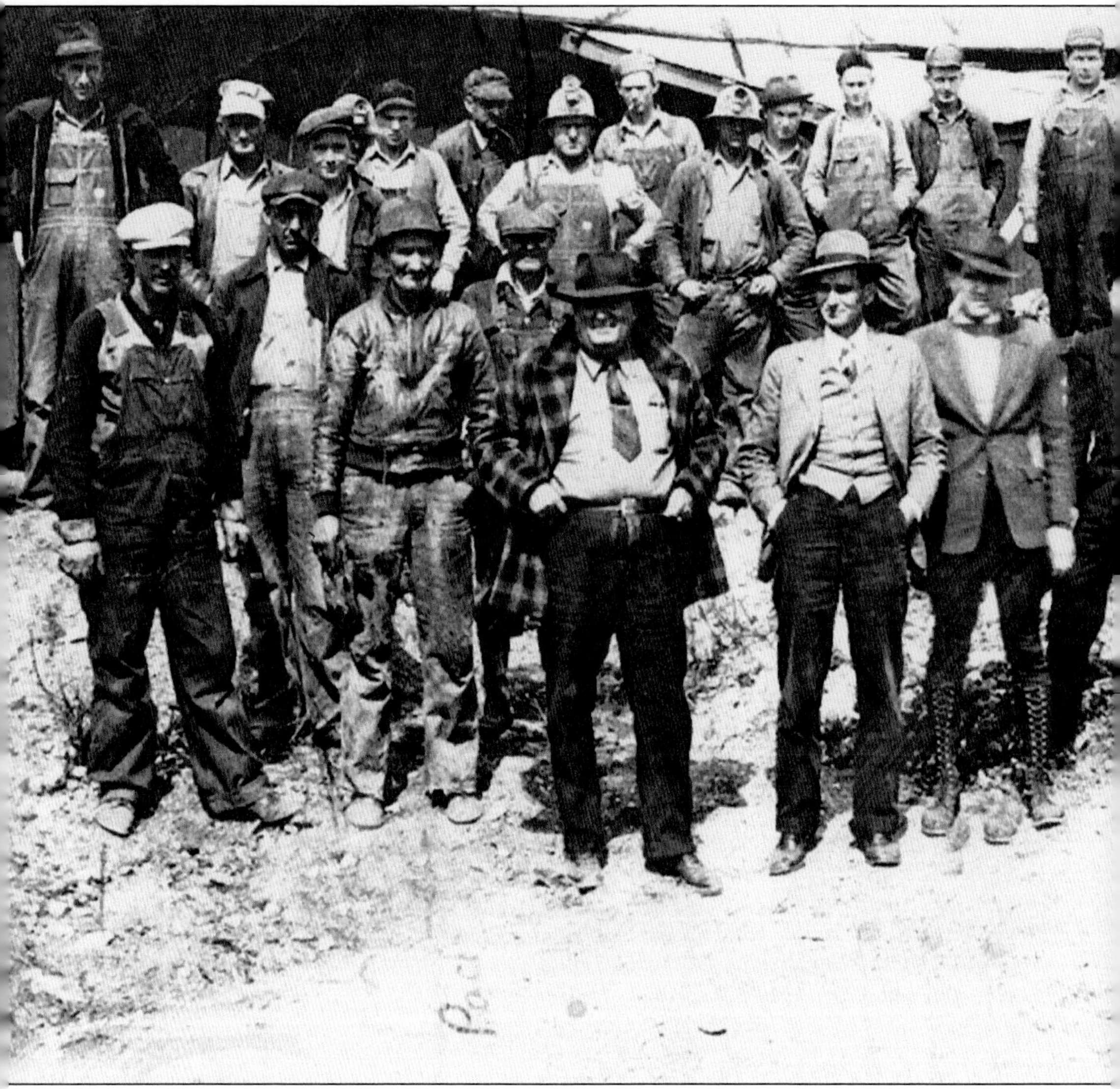

In 1940, attorney Charles Grassham of Paducah, owner of the Livingston County Mineral Ridge Mine near Salem, was selling the mine. This photograph was made when he had called employees and officials together to inform them of his decision. Their names are, from left to right, (first row) Sylvan Simpkins, ? Hunter, Etha Tharp, ? Doom, Paducah attorney Tom Garrett, unidentified Paducah *Sun Democrat* reporter, three unidentified, and the Charles Grassham family—his wife, daughter, two grandsons, and Charles Grassham; (second row) unidentified, Burnett Hardin, two

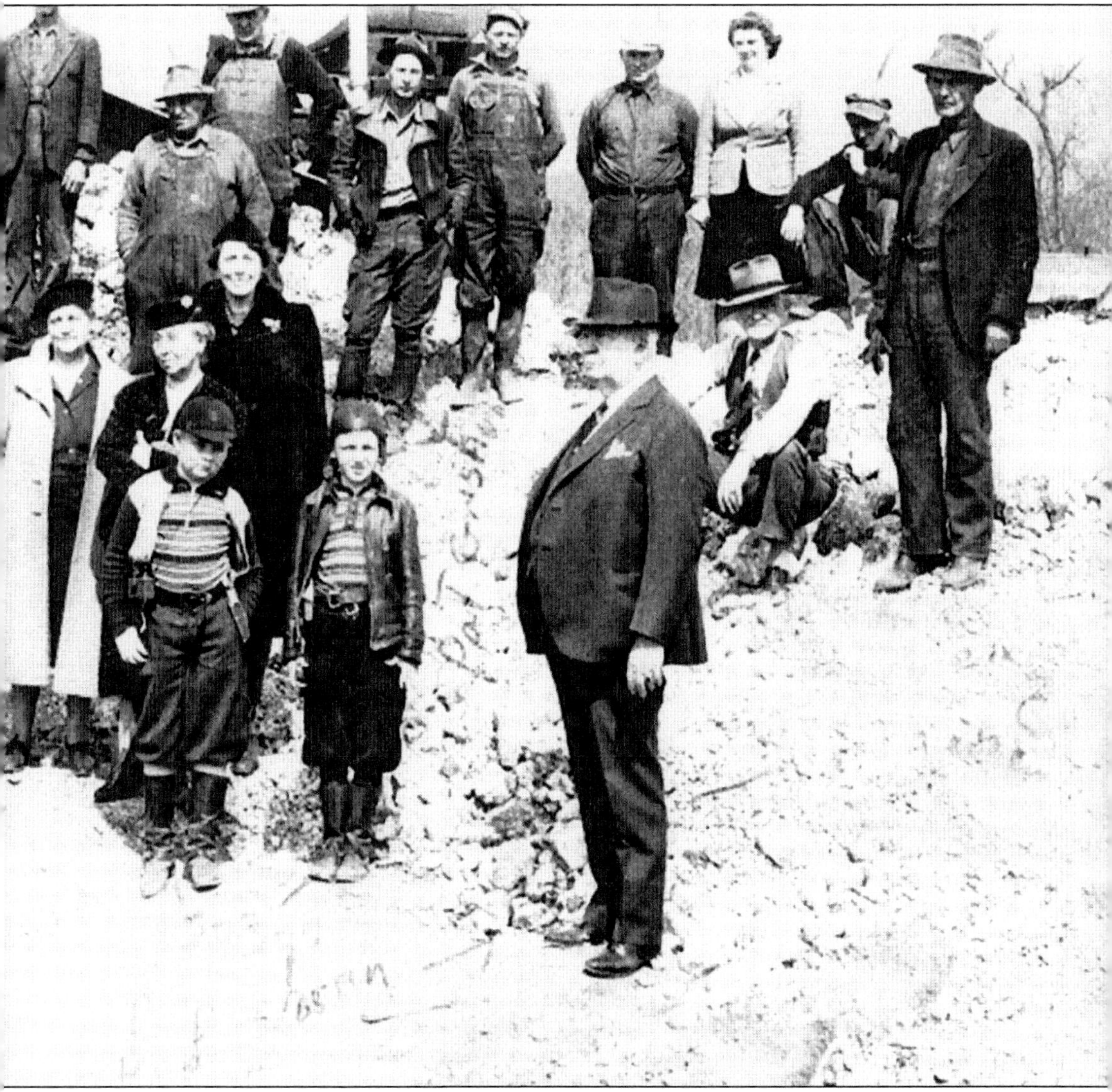

unidentified, George Doom, Herman Travis, two unidentified, Freeman Travis, Hershel Tabor, Eulen Guess, Elvis Guess, Luther Pace, Walter Hunter, Ira Driskill, O. T. Pace, J. S. Pace, Earl Hale, Everett Tabor, Nannie Bell Tabor, Crawford Tharp (sitting), John Pace, and Hendrix Mitchell (sitting). There were many mines in Livingston County, with fluorspar being the most productive. Men employed in mining were exempt from the draft for World War II because fluorspar was so important to national defense.

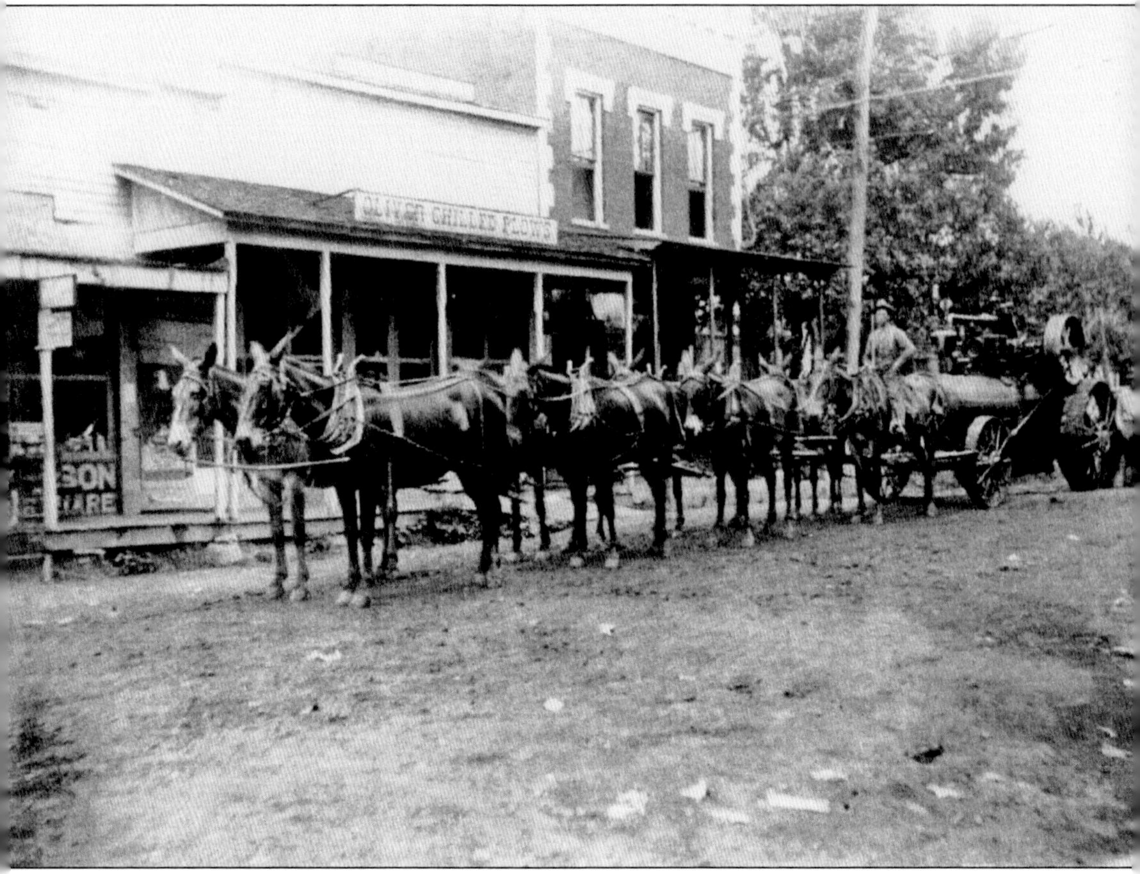

The man pictured at the extreme right is thought to be Henry Moore, and the others are unidentified. This is an eight-mule hitch belonging to Henry Moore of Crittenden County, Kentucky, that pulled a steam boiler and other machinery used for wheat thrashing. The photograph was made in Salem around 1911 in front of the first Salem Bank, which opened in 1903. The telephone office was housed on the second floor and opened in 1911. The telephone line to the upper floor is evident in the picture. Felix G. Cox and his son operated the hardware store next door to the bank. Henry Moore and his brother-in-law Thomas H. Carter, both morticians, purchased the hardware store from Cox and operated an undertaking business and hardware store there for a short period of time. Henry and Lelia Carter Moore were the grandparents of Salem resident John Weaver.

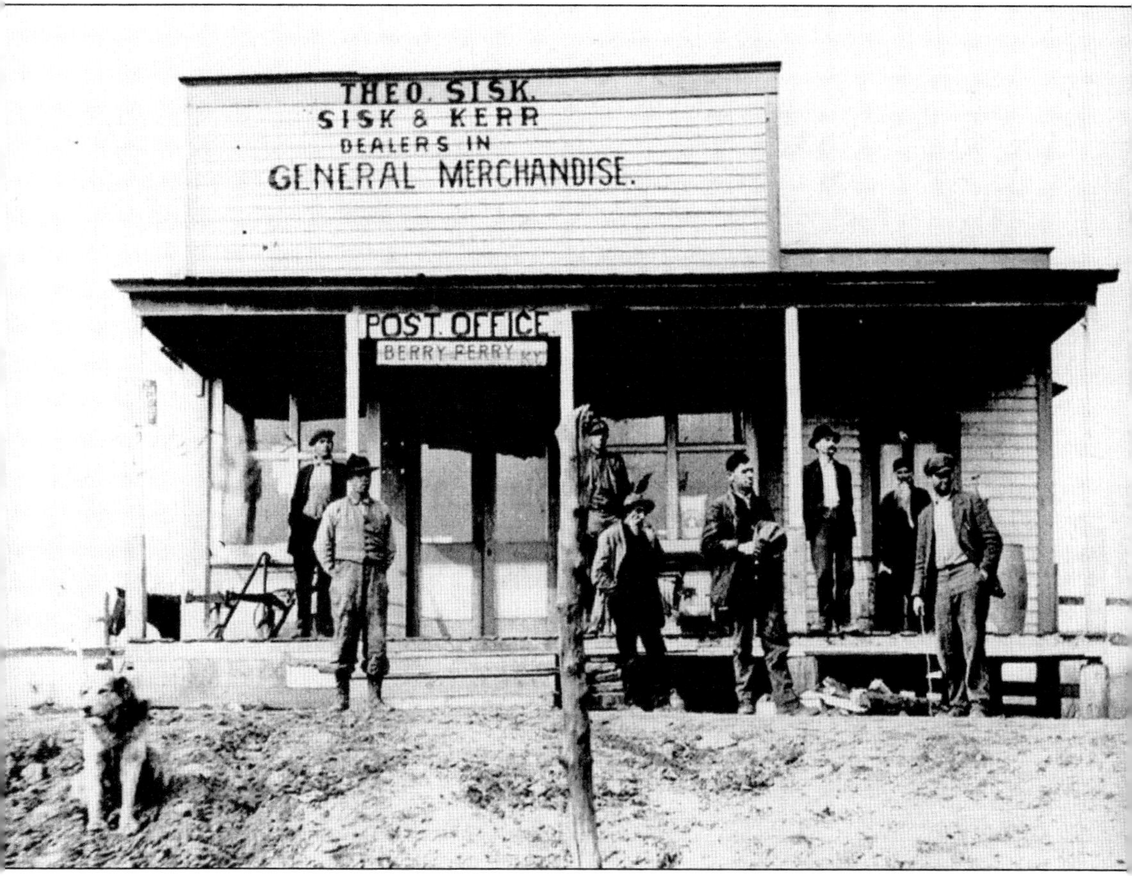

The Berry Ferry Post Office was at one time located near Mantel Rock in the northern part of the county. It was by the Ohio River, and a ferryman named Berry operated it. He was the man hired by the government to ferry the Cherokees across the river during the famous Trail of Tears in 1838. The date of this photograph is unknown, but it was taken some time between 1912 and 1920. The men in foreground are, from left to right, Will Hughes, Edd Grissom, Holland Capron, and Norval Louis; the ones on the porch are, from left to right, Erick Metcalf, Walter Stroud, Grant Stokes, and Dick Stroud.

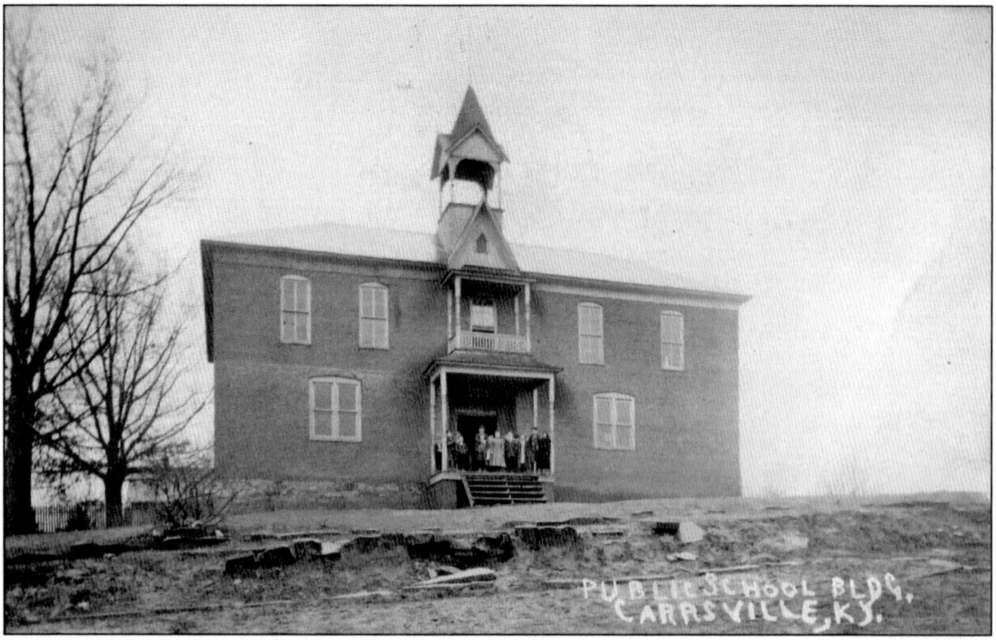

The Carrsville Public School Building was used by children of all 12 classes. Prof. M. C. Wright conducted a "normal school," or teachers college, in this building at one time. He was reared in Carrsville and was known as one of the area's finest teachers. Students came from many miles away and boarded with local families to go to this school. (Courtesy of Don Foster.)

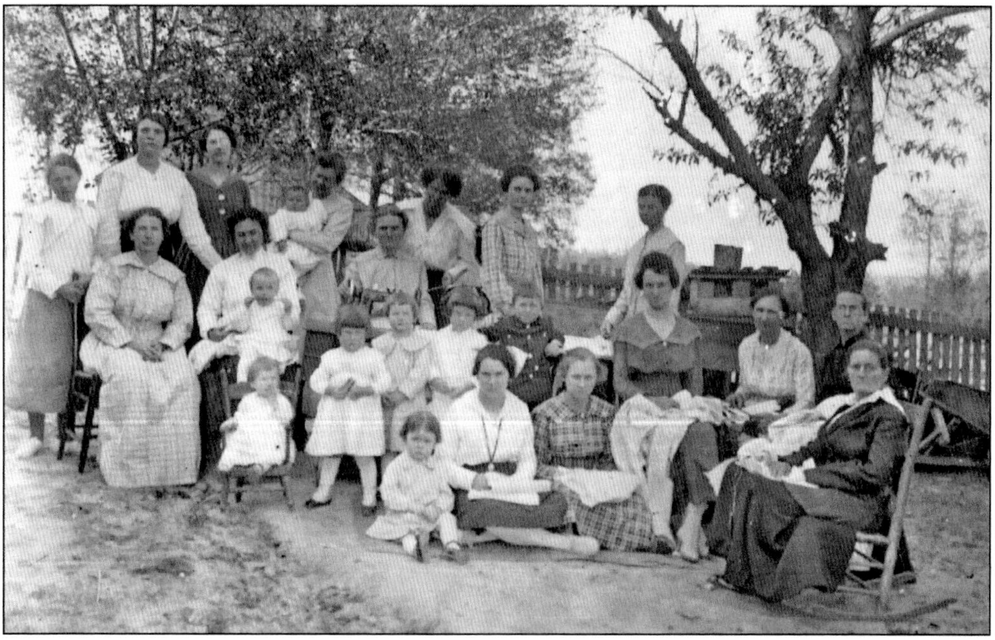

This photograph shows women making quilts to contribute to the war effort around 1918. It was taken outside the Perce and Meacy Duvall residence in the Mullikin and Cedar Grove communities between Burna and Salem. Most are unidentified, but some are said to be Ruth Carter, Betty Foster, Emma Bridwell, Nelle Nunn Foster, Katie Parker, the wives of Quince Ramage and Tobe Coker, Ruth Foster, Imogene Martin, and the mother of Ed Riley. (Courtesy of Don Foster.)

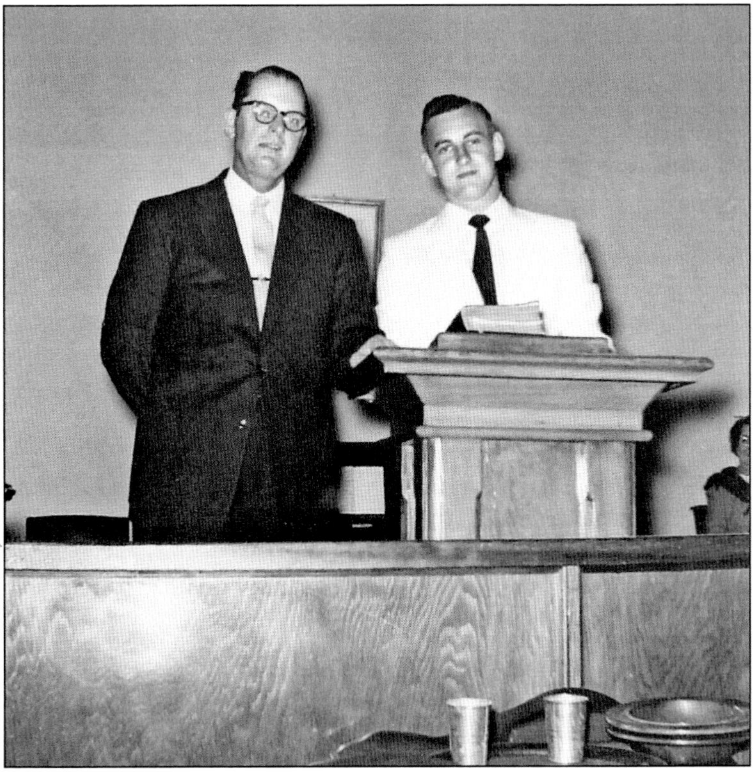

This photograph shows Brother J. W. Hansen and his son, Brother Max Hansen, on April 8, 1956. This was at Brother Max's ordination service at the Ohio Valley Baptist Church in Ledbetter, where his father was pastor. This father-and-son duo were pastors to many area churches. (Courtesy of Todd Hansen.)

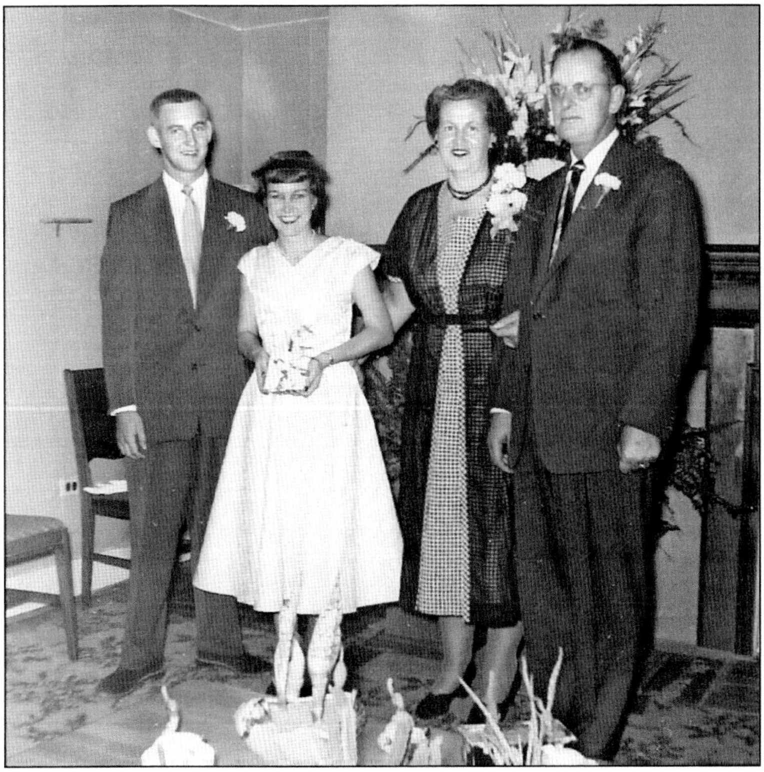

This photograph was taken on September 4, 1953, following the wedding ceremony of M. H. Hansen and Juanita Kirk. Shown from left are M. H. and Juanita Hansen with his parents, Mary Lou and J. W. Hansen. Brother J. W. Hansen, the father of the groom, performed the ceremony. (Courtesy of Todd Hansen.)

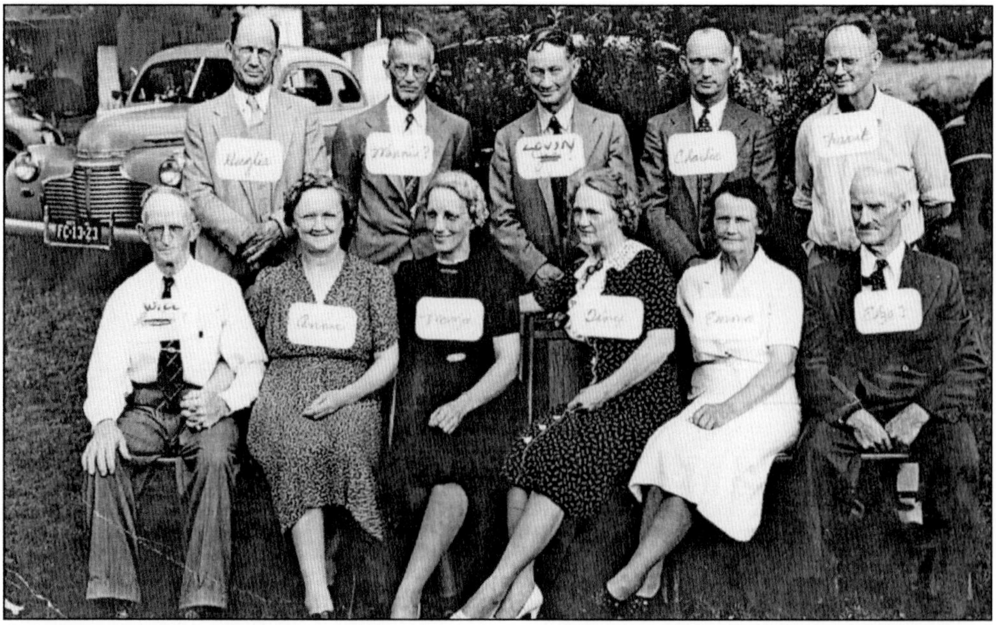

This image is of the Dunlap family reunion in 1942. From left to right are (first row) Will Dunlap, Annie Sullivant, Maggie Meacham, Tiny Jarrett, Emma Driskill, and Elza Dunlap; (second row) Hughie Dunlap, Minnis Dunlap, Lovin Dunlap, Charlie Dunlap, and Frank Dunlap. These are the children of John M. and Elizabeth Ann Ross Dunlap, and all were raised in Livingston County. (Courtesy of Bobbie Ross Hill.)

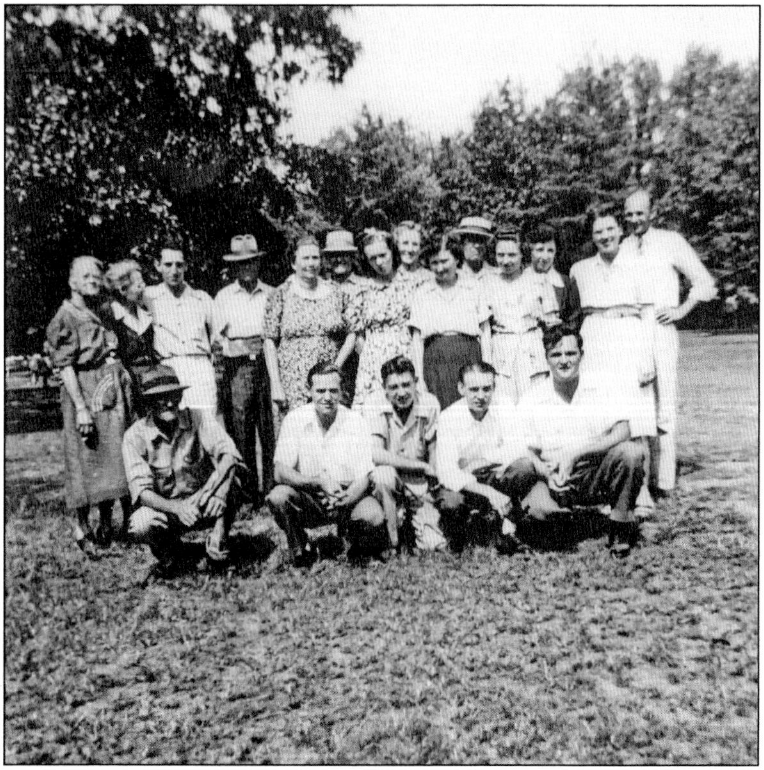

No date or location is given for this group of relatives and friends enjoying the day. From left to right are (first row) Will Tracy, unidentified, Russell Taylor, Everett Taylor, and Neil Sharpe; (second row) Maggie Durham, Virgie Tracy, Gracial Jewell, unidentified, Lois Mitchell Tracy, Lee Ruth Sharpe, and eight unidentified. (Courtesy of Bobbie Ross Hill.)

These handsome boys, Clarence (left) and Howard, are the sons of Emory and Ada Crotchett. They grew up in the Barrett Quarry community, where the men all worked until the Depression caused them to seek other employment. During the 1930s, more than 200 people were employed at the quarry, with wages averaging from 25¢ to 40¢ an hour. (Courtesy of Esther Dubuque.)

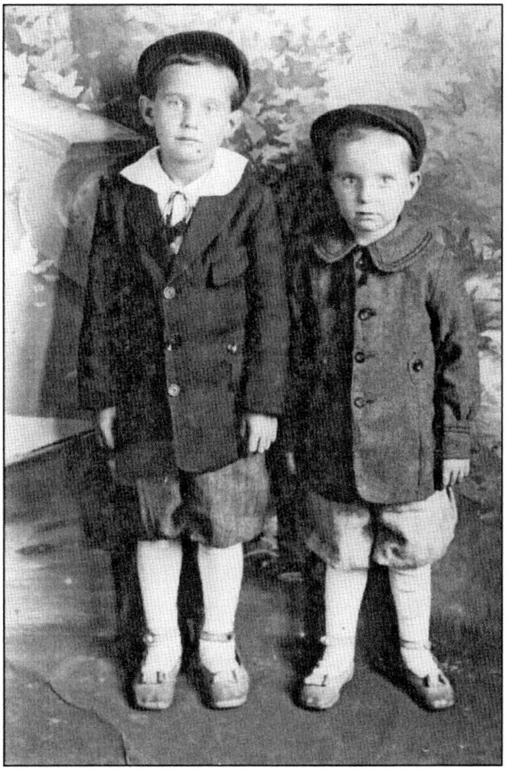

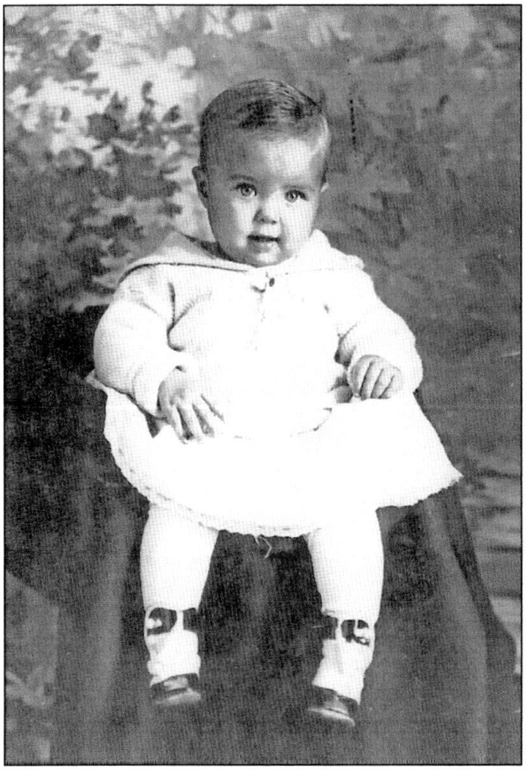

Edna Mae Crotchett is the daughter of Emory and Ada Hall Crotchett. She grew up in the Barrett Quarry community, where all the Crotchett men were employed. Edna Mae married Paul Molnor, and they had one son, P. H. (Courtesy of Esther Dubuque.)

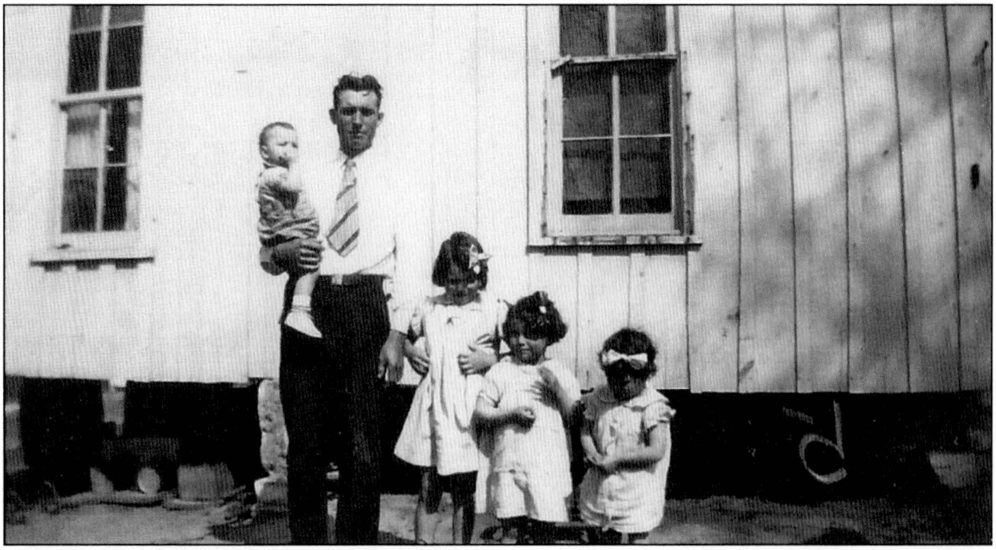

This photograph, taken in 1937, shows Clarence Crotchett holding his son, Allen and his three daughters (from left to right) Melba, Becky and Esther. The Crotchett family lived at the Barrett Quarry in the Bizzel Bluff community, near Burna. Clarence died in a mining accident about a year after this was taken. (Courtesy of Esther Dubuque.)

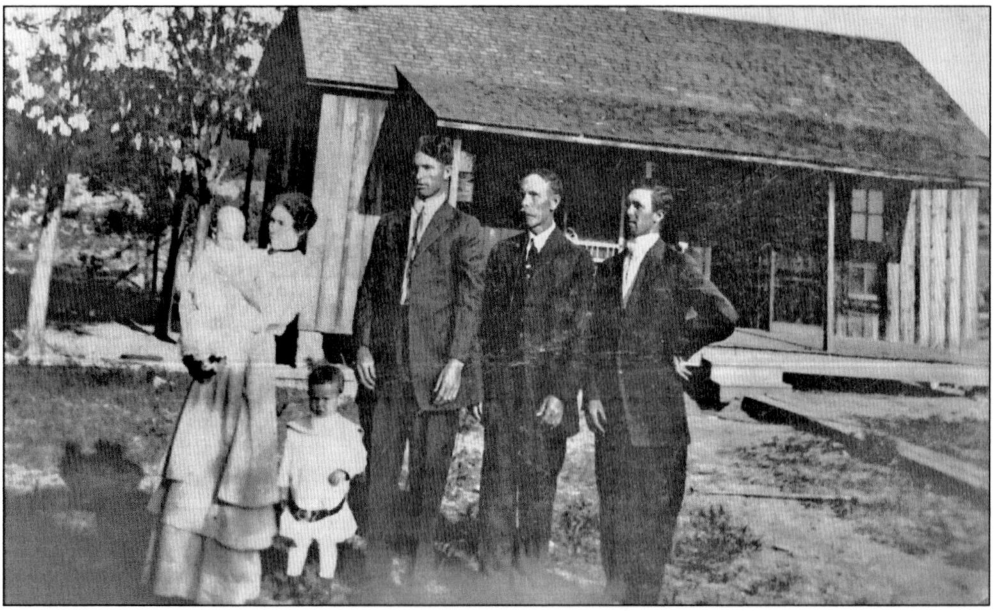

This photograph shows the Crotchett family: (from left to right) Ada holding Howard, Clarence, Emory, Jim, and Dudley Crotchett. Jim was the father of Emory and Dudley. Dudley married Janie, and they had six children: Cecil, Bulah, Kathryn, Pauline, Dudley Hershal, and Willard. (Courtesy of Esther Dubuque.)

Clarence and Bonnie Crotchett are pictured on their wedding day, January 1, 1930. They are standing on a barge at the old Barrett Quarry. Clarence worked at the quarry for several years. He was killed in an accident while working at the Klondike Mine, located between Burna and Salem. Bonnie then married Lewis Wadley and had a daughter, Wanda, who married Jim Lockett. (Courtesy of Esther Dubuque.)

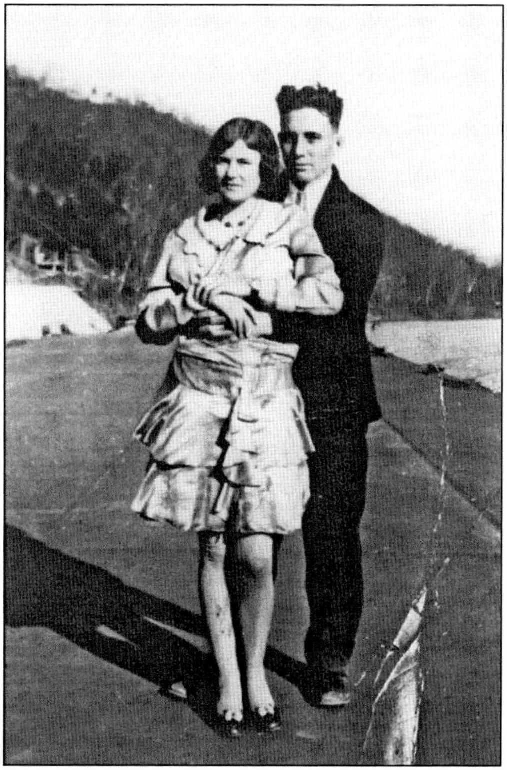

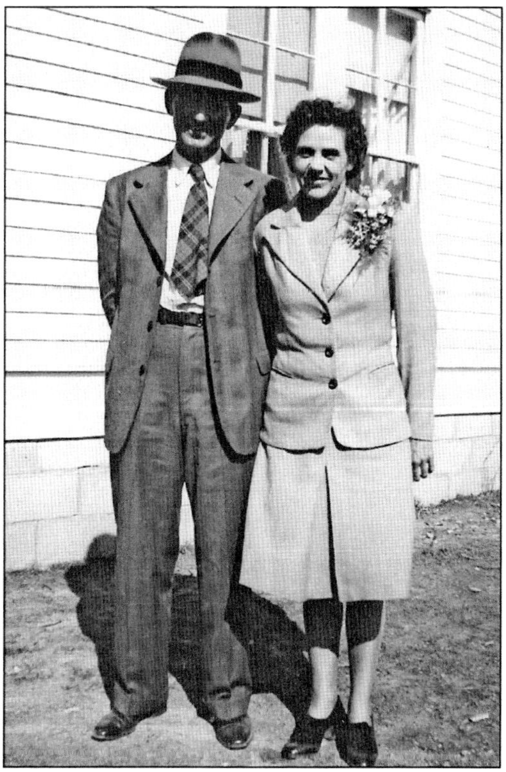

On Easter Sunday in 1945 this photograph of John and Cora Parker Dubuque was taken at their home in Ledbetter. They had one son, Charles, who married Esther Crotchett. The town of Ledbetter was first called Panhandle, because it is a 5-mile-long peninsula shaped like a handle between the Ohio and Tennessee Rivers. (Courtesy of Esther Dubuque.)

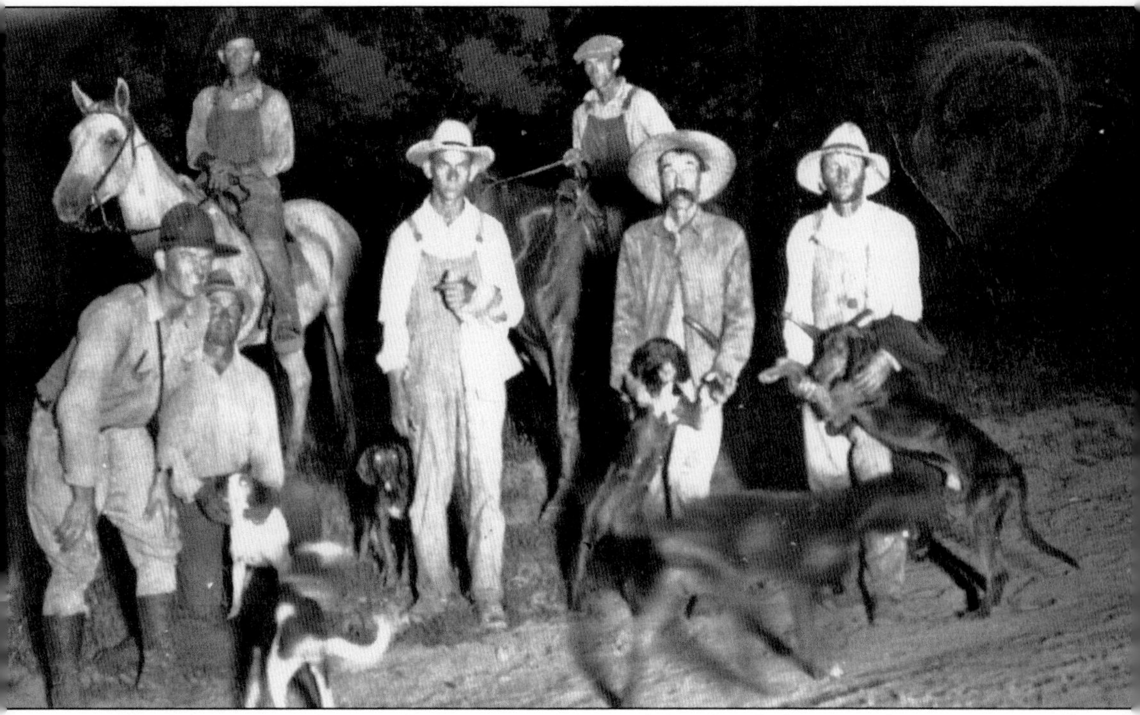

This July 23, 1925, photograph shows (from left to right) Salem foxhunters Ed Damron, Coy Alley, Walter Berry, Charlie Lockhart, Floyd Guill, Bob Damron, and Arthur Wilson. Several decades ago, foxhunting was a sport enjoyed by many men in the county who owned foxhounds. Foxes were not hunted to kill but for the pleasure of hearing the hounds baying in the chase. Every man knew the voice of his dog, and it was a beautiful chorus when there were several dogs in the group. If the dogs manage to pick up the scent of a fox, they will track it for as long as they are able. Scenting can be affected by temperature, humidity, and other factors. Foxhunting originated in the United Kingdom in the 16th century but is now practiced all over the world.

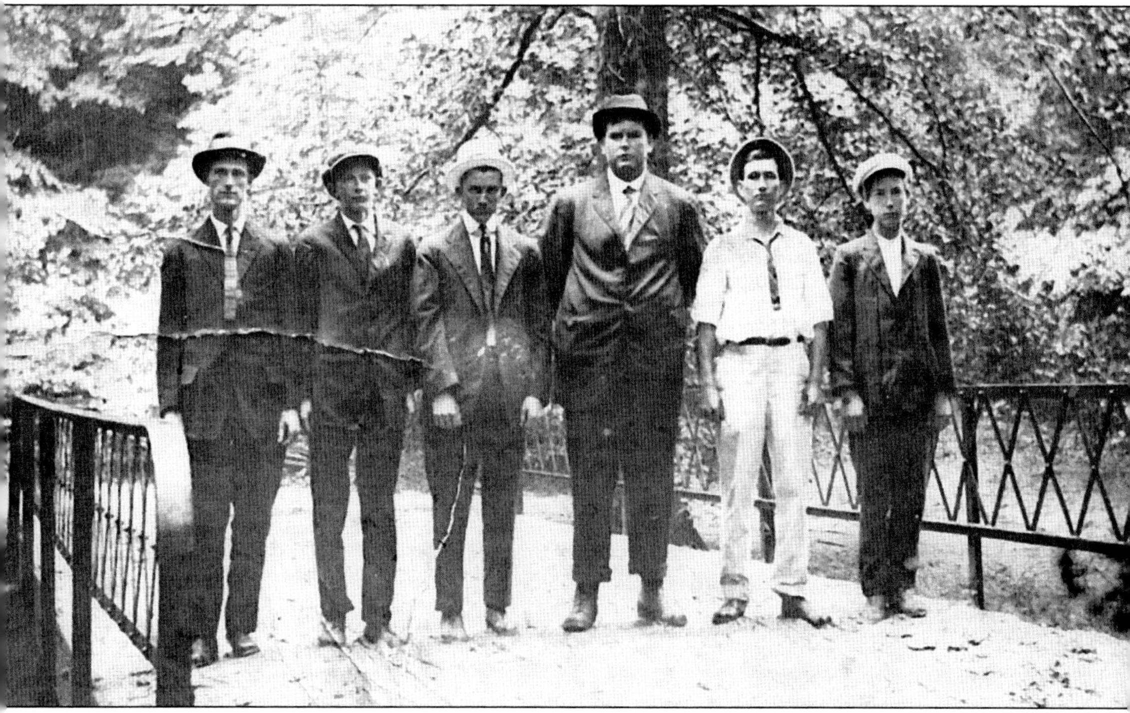

All these men are unidentified except the tall one near the center, who is Oscar Hosick. An article written in the *Courier Journal* reads, "The biggest soldier in the American army was headed for his home in Salem today. Young Hosick weighs 315 and is six feet five and a half inches tall. Since he has been in the army, he was given a free trip to Washington so the President might see the biggest man in Uncle Sam's uniform. The young giant was stationed at Camp Sherman before he was sent overseas. He was discharged January 23, 1919." Hosick was a corporal in World War I and was the largest man in the American Expeditionary Forces. His parents were Henry Lee Hosick and Maude Ladd Eaton Hosick of the Ledbetter area. Hosick married Ellen, and they had no children. He died at Outwood Home, a veteran's home, near Dawson Springs, Kentucky. (Courtesy of Faye Teitloff.)

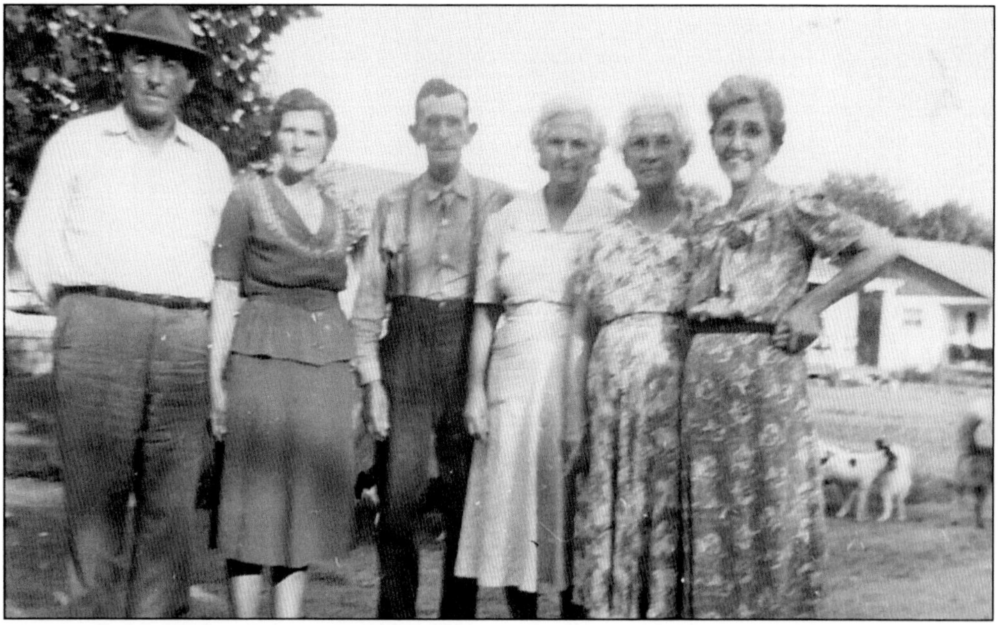

This image shows (from left to right) Hosea Parks, Mary Deneal Parks, Calvin Hosick, Enna Parks Hosick, Della Parks Dunning, and Emma Parks Mitchell. Hosea, Enna, Della, and Emma were the children of Thomas Richard and Minerva Hart Parks. Enna and Emma were twins. Emma married Elit Mitchell, and they had four children who grew up in Livingston County: Beulah Waters, Lois Tracy, W. E. Mitchell, and Flossie Oldham. (Courtesy of Faye Teitloff.)

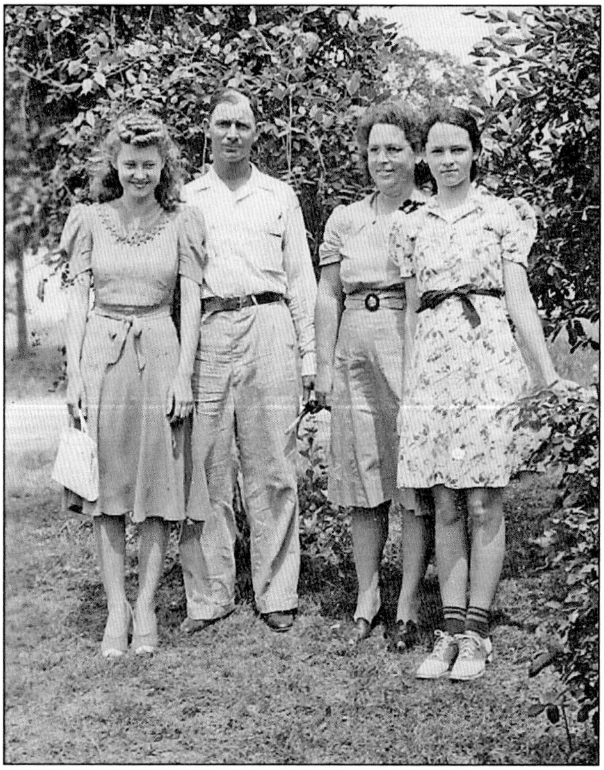

This photograph of the Audie Jones family, (from left to right) Helen Thomason, Audie, Bertha, and Mildred (Mittie) Fletcher, was taken in the 1940s. Bertha's parents were Tom and Della Dunning, and they had seven children: Charlie, Elva Baker, Clarence, Mae Lytton, Bertha Jones, Ralph, Thomas Roy, and James Albert, who died young. (Courtesy of Yolanda Thomason.)

An image taken in 1920 shows Fannie Hosick Fiers and her namesake and niece, Fannie Hosick, daughter of Calvin and Enna Parks Hosick. They had three other daughters: Marie, Mary McDonald, and Callie Jones. Fannie Fiers married Edward Fiers, and their children were Vernon, Clifton, Elvis (Bo), and Delmar (Noke). (Courtesy of Faye Teitloff.)

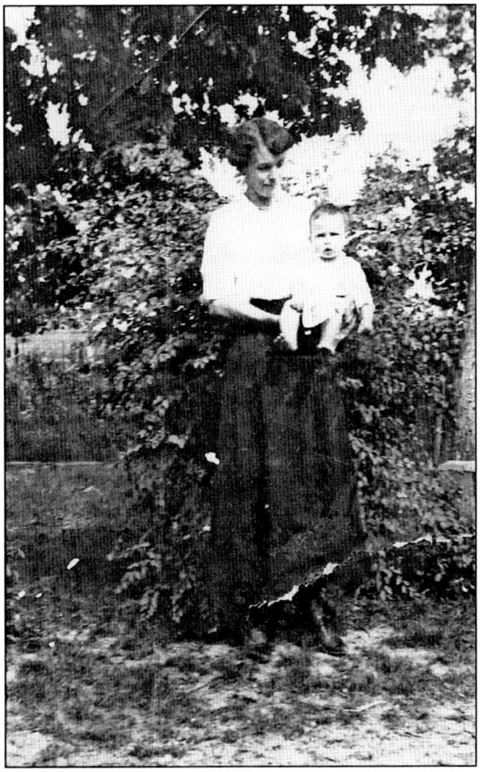

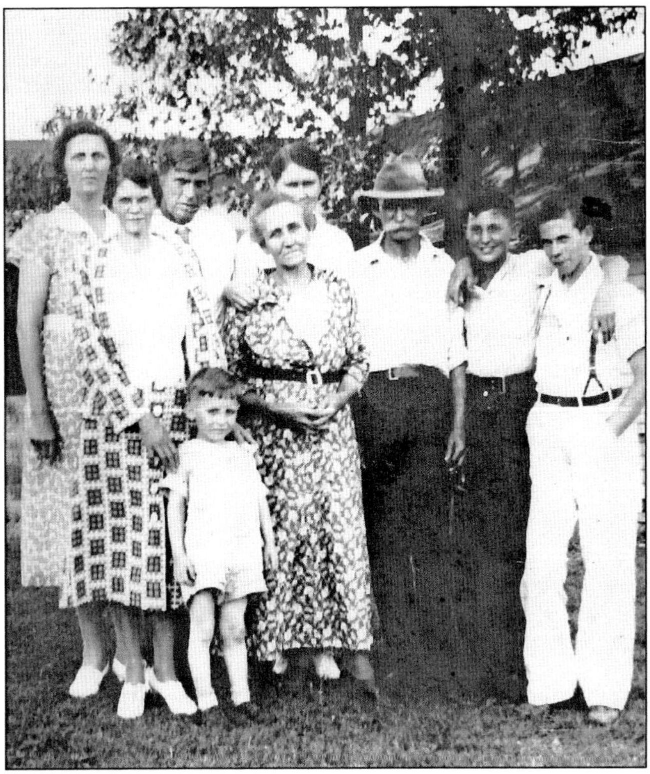

Taken in the late 1930s, this image shows, from left to right, (first row) ? Knight, unidentified boy, Cora Brooks Tramble, Cooper Tramble, J. E. Reynolds, and Frank Knight; (second row) Elsie Brooks Reynolds, Frank Reynolds, and unidentified. They all lived in the Smithland or Tiline communities. (Courtesy of Faye Teitloff.)

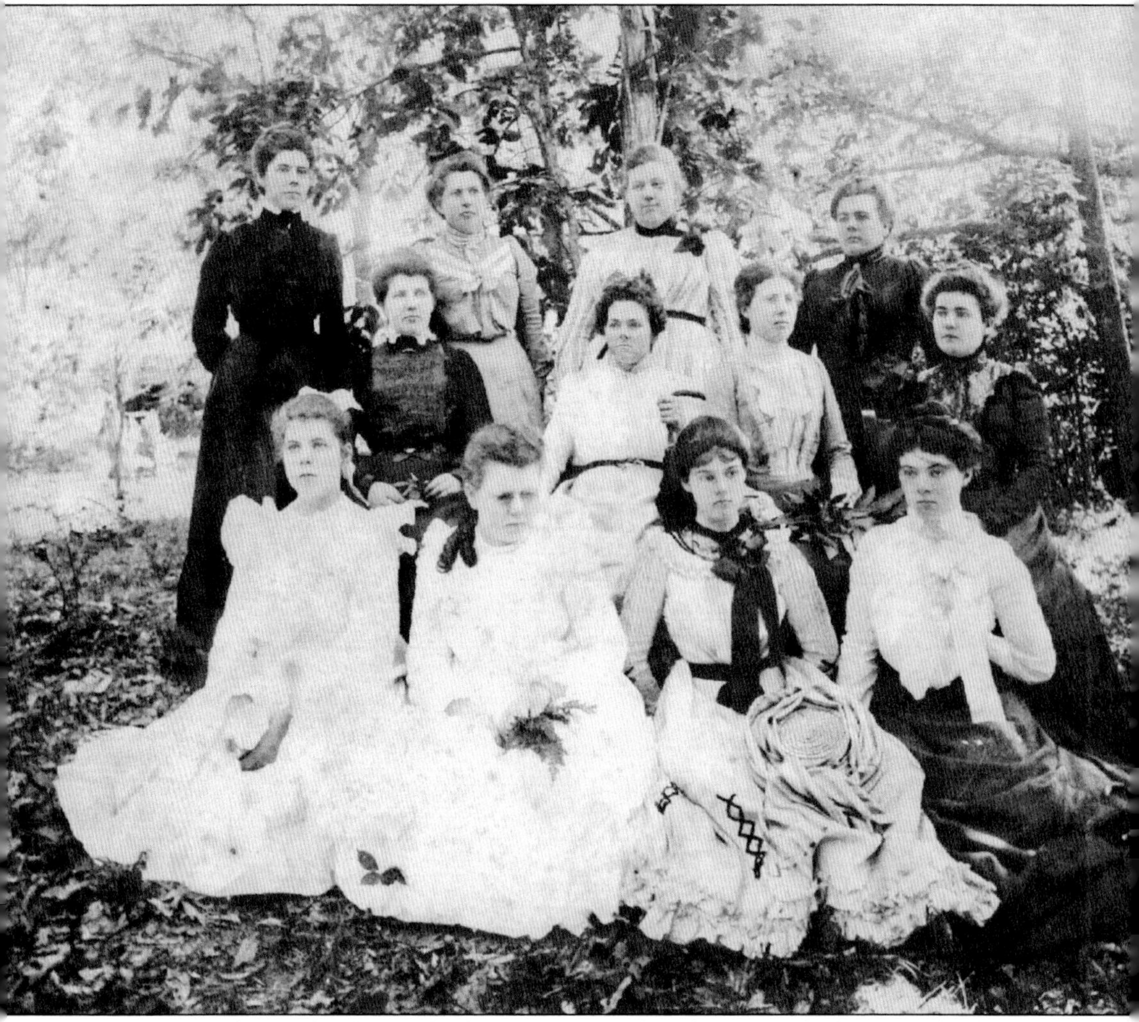

These are the 12 daughters of John R. Farris and Evaline Crawford Farris of Salem. In this photograph are, from left to right, (first row) Linnie Bryant, Addie Farris, Lucy Pierce, and Eva Cochram; (second row) Lake Doom, Lillie Phillips, Maggie Threlkeld, and Rosa Pierce; (third row) Cora Sexton, Ada Carlton, Georgia Pierce, and Hattie Moxley. Their dresses were all handmade by the girls themselves, except for Addie, who was blind. They had one brother who lived to be an adult, John A. Farris, and two brothers who died in infancy. The Farris children were born from 1867 to 1899 and were taught to work on the farm. The large two-story house built in 1820, which was the scene of family reunions, weddings, and funerals, was destroyed by fire in 1957. The family cemetery is on a high hill above where the barn once stood. The farm was sold out of the family in 1984.

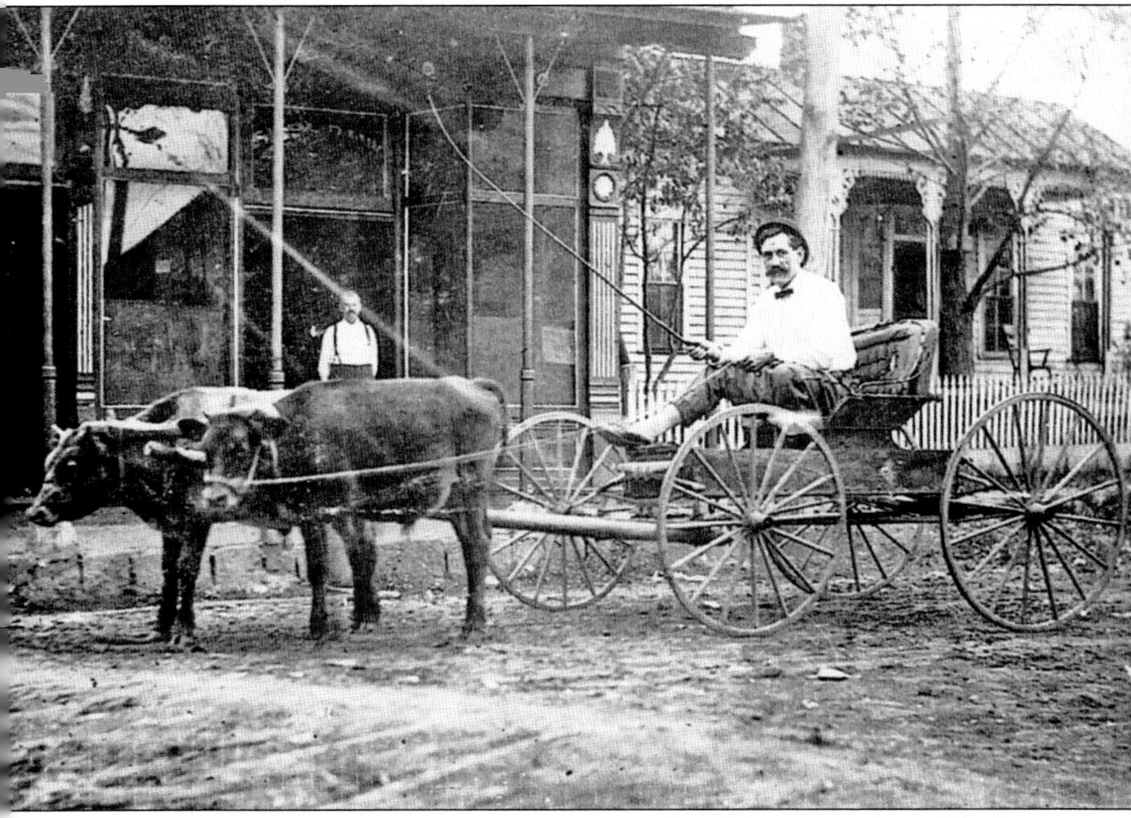

Dr. Herbert B. Wolfe is shown in this early-1900s photograph with his oxen in front of the first Salem Bank. He was born in 1871 in Ohio to George and Ruth Wolfe. He became a dentist first in Carrsville and then in Salem, where he worked for most of his life. Dr. Wolfe married Mayme Boyd Bauer in 1920, and they had two sons: William B. and Charles Edward Wolfe. Dr. Wolfe had two grown children by a previous marriage: Russell Wolfe and Mina Wolfe Bebout. Mayme had been married before to Ed Baer, uncle of prizefighter Max Baer. The Wolfes divorced when their boys were still young. Dr. Wolfe married Josie Ramage just prior to his death in 1944.

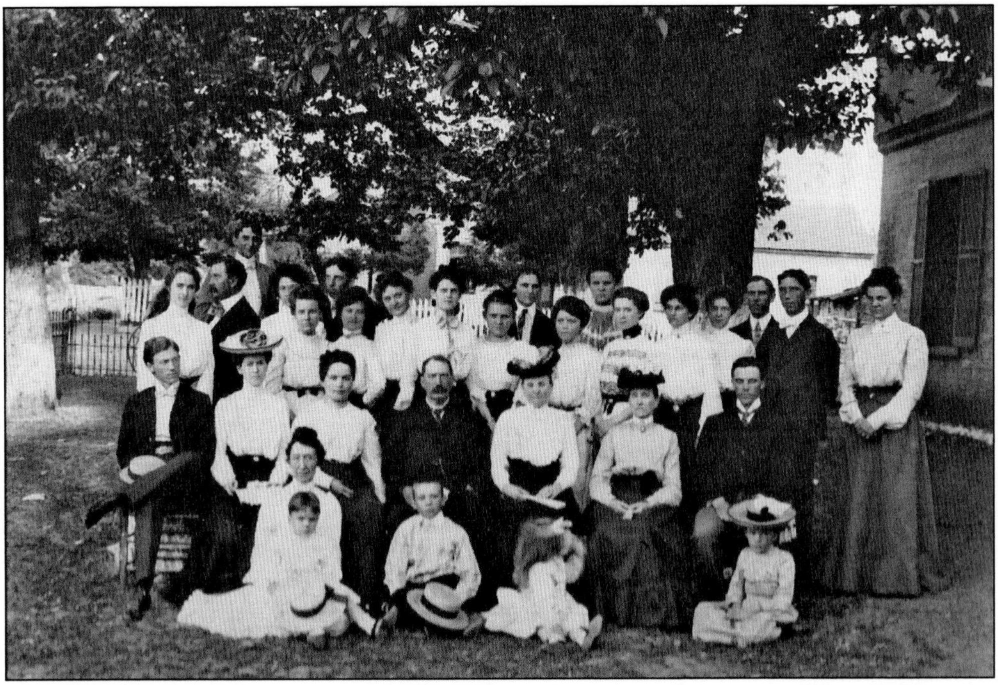

This photograph and the next two were brought to the historical society by Diana Kohler, who was living in the Vickers house on Court Street in Smithland. She found them in a wood box by the fireplace, and the papers mention the family names Dean, Vickers, Robertson, and Sanders (or Saunders). No one is identified. (Courtesy of Livingston County Historical Society.)

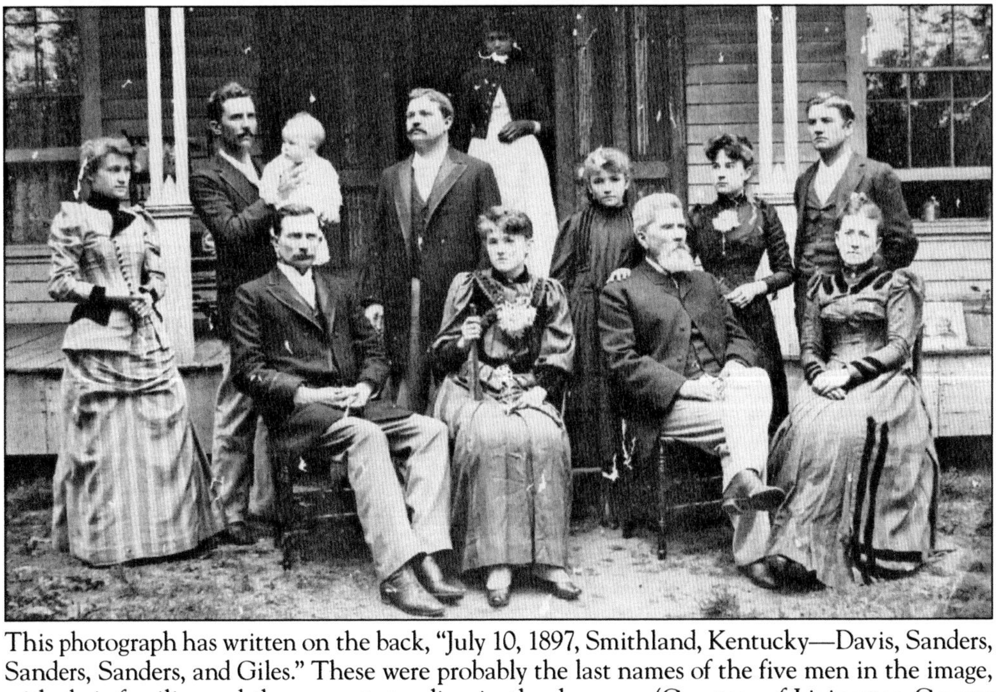

This photograph has written on the back, "July 10, 1897, Smithland, Kentucky—Davis, Sanders, Sanders, Sanders, and Giles." These were probably the last names of the five men in the image, with their families and the servant standing in the doorway. (Courtesy of Livingston County Historical Society.)

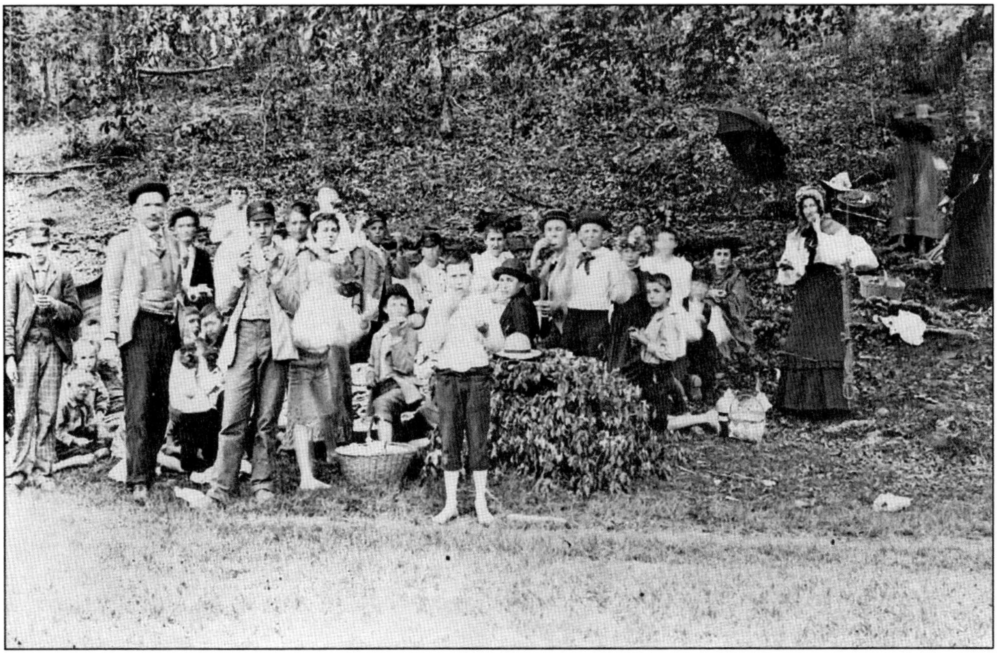

A vintage photograph like this is worth a million words. The only thing written on the back is, "Our May party on May 3, 1894—raining, raining!" This was probably written by a Vickers lady because there was a church record book in the box that was kept by her. (Courtesy of Livingston County Historical Society.)

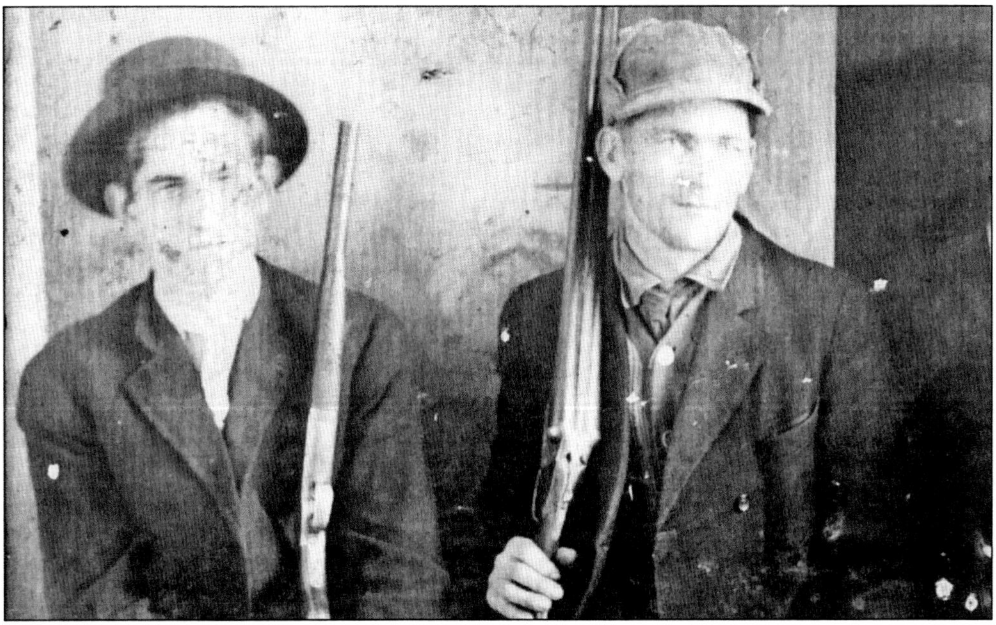

This image shows Joe Vick (left) and Matthew Clyde Tracy. Vick was the son of John L. and Martha May Vick. John was a Livingston County clerk from 1866 to 1882, and the community of Vicksburg was named for him. Tracy wrote a book on his ancestors in 1911. He was a toll collector on the Cumberland River Bridge. He married Mary Ellen Durham, and they had one son, James Clyde, who married Lucille Massey. (Courtesy of Lucille Tracy.)

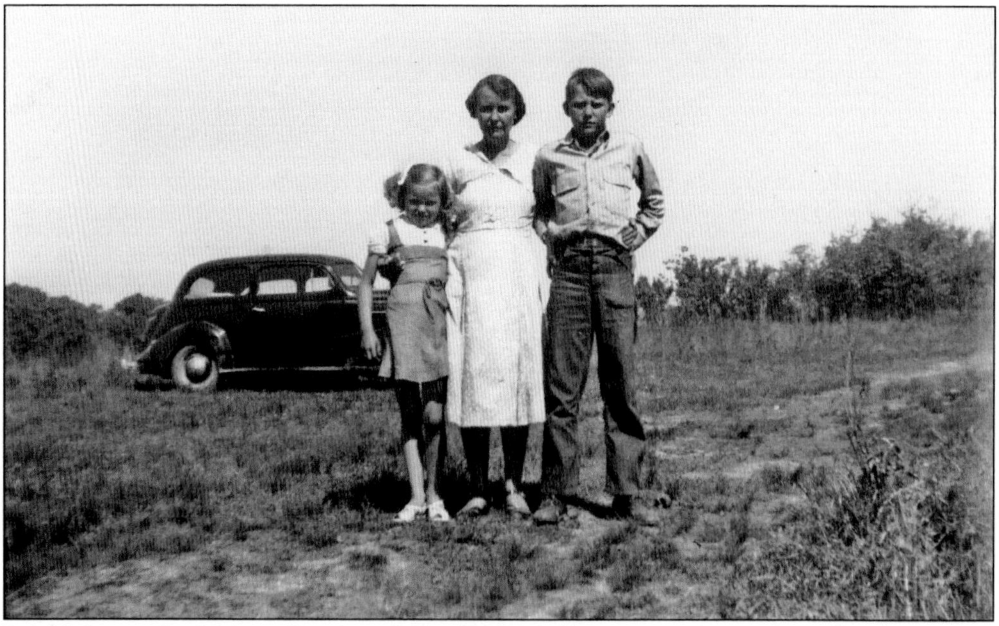

From left to right, Halene, Hazel, and Charles Teitloff are pictured in 1951 at their home near Joy. Hazel Wood Teitloff married William Teitloff on May 1, 1924, and they had five children: J. D., L. C., Odetta (Hughes), Charles, and Halene (Manhart). William died in 1944 when Halene was 18 months old, but Hazel managed to finish raising her family. Charles started working at a young age on farms to help support the family. (Courtesy of Faye Teitloff.)

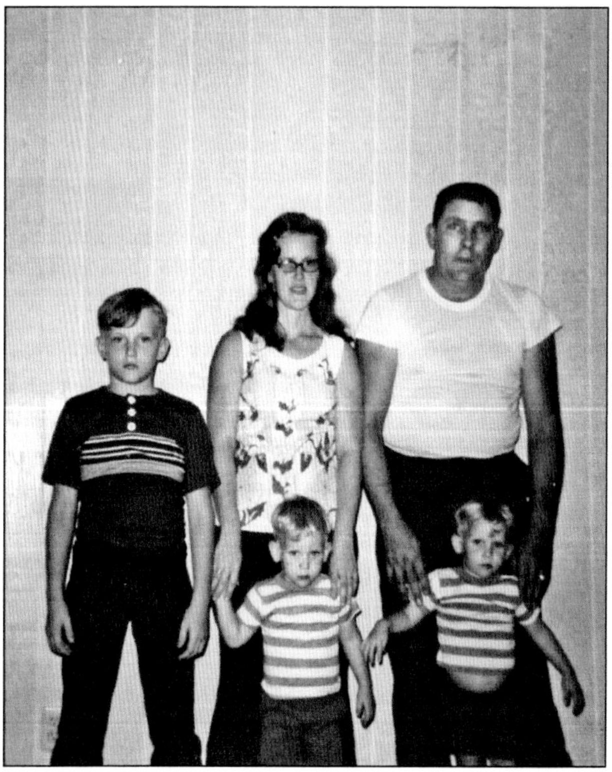

This photograph was taken in White Bluff, Tennessee, while the photographer was visiting the L. C. Teitloff family in 1973. They were celebrating the 66th birthday of Hazel Teitloff, the mother of Charles and L. C. Shown from left to right are Timothy, Faye, Charles, and twins Kevin and Kendall Teitloff. The twins are easy to tell apart, because Kendall fell down some stairs and had a knot on his head. (Courtesy of Faye Teitloff.)

Author Faye Tramble Teitloff is pictured in 1962 at Smith's Studio in Paducah. She was married to Charles Teitloff on February 16, 1963, at Southland Baptist Temple by Rev. Harold Council. Faye worked at the Smithland office of the Cabinet for Families and Children until her retirement in 2004. (Courtesy of Faye Teitloff.)

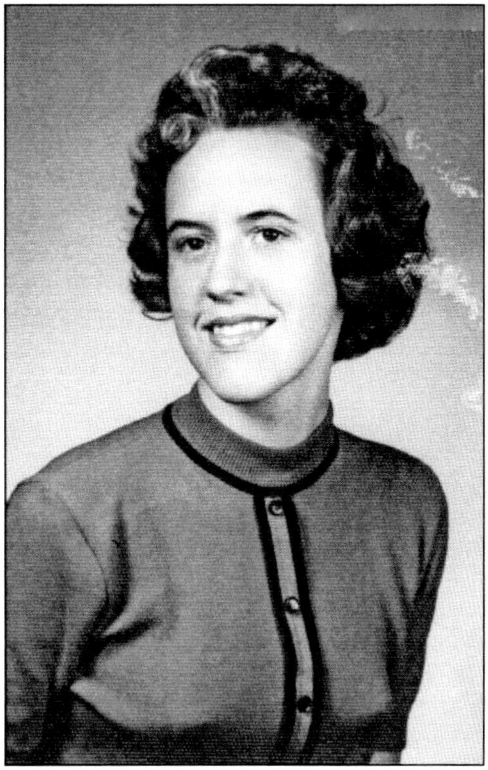

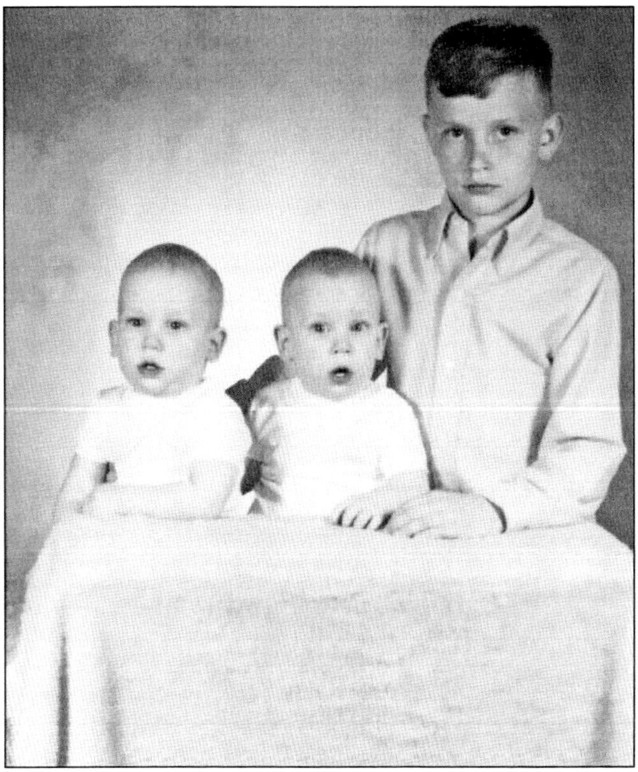

From left to right, the author's three sons, twins Kendall Lynn and Kevin Glen and Timothy Charles Teitloff, are shown in this 1972 photograph. Kendall is a correctional officer at the Kentucky State Penitentiary in Eddyville. Kendall and Kevin both live near Smithland and have never married. Timothy is a professor at Clemson University and resides in Anderson, South Carolina, with his wife, Jana, and their three children, Jonathan, Eric, and Laura. (Courtesy of Faye Teitloff.)

ACROSS AMERICA, PEOPLE ARE DISCOVERING SOMETHING WONDERFUL. *THEIR HERITAGE.*

Arcadia Publishing is the leading local history publisher in the United States. With more than 4,000 titles in print and hundreds of new titles released every year, Arcadia has extensive specialized experience chronicling the history of communities and celebrating America's hidden stories, bringing to life the people, places, and events from the past. To discover the history of other communities across the nation, please visit:

www.arcadiapublishing.com

Customized search tools allow you to find regional history books about the town where you grew up, the cities where your friends and family live, the town where your parents met, or even that retirement spot you've been dreaming about.

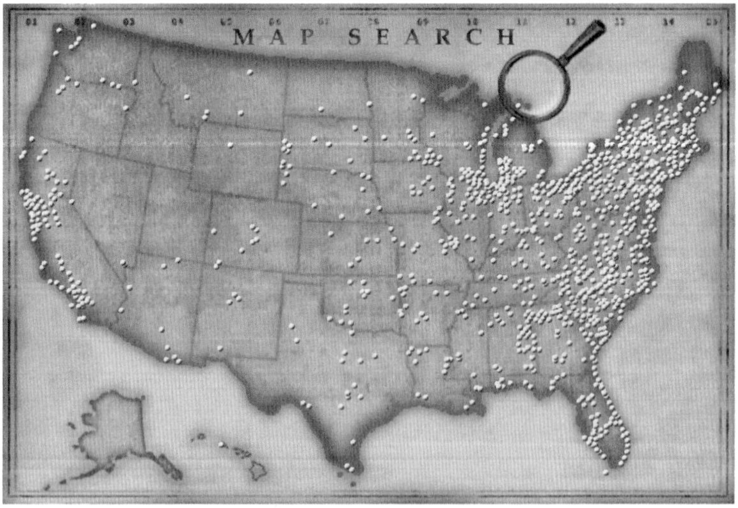